Marriages in Trouble

Marriages in Trouble

The process of seeking help

Julia Brannen
and
Jean Collard

Tavistock Publications
London and New York

First published in 1982 by
Tavistock Publications Ltd
11 New Fetter Lane, London EC4P 4EE

Published in the USA by
Tavistock Publications
in association with Methuen, Inc.
733 Third Avenue, New York, NY 10017

© *1982 Julia Brannen and Jean Collard*

Typeset in Great Britain by
Scarborough Typesetting Services
and printed at the
University Press, Cambridge

British Library Cataloguing in Publication Data
Brannen, Julia
Marriages in trouble.
1. Marriage counseling
I. Title   II. Collard, Jean
`362.8'286   HQ10

ISBN 0 422 78100 2

Library of Congress Cataloging in Publication Data
Brannen, Julia.
Marriages in trouble.

Bibliography: p.
Includes indexes.
1. Married people—England—London.   2. Marriage
counseling—England—London.   3. Help seeking
behavior—England—London.   I. Collard, Jean.
II. Title.
HQ616.B7   1982   362.8'286   82–12561
ISBN 0 422 78100 2

Contents

Acknowledgements

We wish first of all to thank Jack Dominian, Director of the Marriage Research Centre; without him this research project would not have taken place. Our gratitude is also owed to the Trustees of the Centre, who have uncomplainingly funded our study, and to the charitable trusts and individuals who have generously given money to the Centre. We would also like to record our appreciation of the continuing practical support which the Centre receives from the Central Middlesex Hospital.

Many people have given us help in various ways. Our particular thanks are due to Alan Tait, a member of the research team during the first year of the project, who helped to shape its design and also shared in the field-work. Barbara Thornes contributed to the study by examining our face-sheet data, and other colleagues at the Centre, particularly Penny Mansfield and Margaret Stoneman, provided us with a ready forum for the discussion of our ideas.

For academic appraisal, we wish first and foremost to thank Bob Chester for his constant advice and encouragement. We are also grateful to Noel Timms for his detailed and useful comment on an early draft of this book. In the course of doing the project we have talked to many people, amongst whom we wish to thank David Robinson, and members of the Institute of Marital Studies, the Institute of Family and Environmental Research, and the Study Commission on the Family.

In order to carry out this research we were dependent on the co-operation of the agencies. We owe a strong debt of gratitude to Marriage Guidance: at the national level, Nick Tyndall and Jill Heisler who have always shown interest and support and, at the local level, the officers and counsellors from the two Marriage Guidance Councils who cooperated with us. We also wish to thank those general practitioners in the Brent and Harrow Health District who gave time to us, especially the practice which allowed one of us to observe it in action.

We have been well-served by the librarians at the Post-graduate Medical Centre (Central Middlesex Hospital): Nicky Whitsed, Brigid Farrant, and Sheila Cook have taken endless trouble. Secretarial help (transcribing taped interviews and drafts of the manuscript) has been ably provided by: Louise Derry, Janet Pelaez, Cecily Morgan, and Ruth Russell.

It is no trite acknowledgement to say that, without the considerable forbearance, imagination, and support from our families and friends, this book would not have been possible, particularly since one of us (Julia) left the Marriage Research Centre in 1980 to start a new job involving continuous and stressful field-work and, although the other (Jean) continued to work from the Centre, her home base is in South Wales. Our special thanks to Peter Brannen and Chris Collard. We value the encouragement and practical support given to us and we recognize how essential it has been in reconciling the diverse and competing responsibilities of our public and private lives.

Finally, and of course most of all, we wish to thank our respondents. They made us welcome in their homes, and they entrusted us with their experiences: we are most grateful to them, we valued meeting them, and we hope we have treated their disclosures with care and confidentiality.

Julia Brannen
Jean Collard

London, January 1982

Introduction

It is fashionable to suggest that marriage as an institution is in trouble, but there are widely differing views as to whether or not this is really so. Marriage is increasingly popular in that around 90 per cent of people in Britain marry at least once in their lives.[1] Marriage rates of those marrying for the first time rose to a peak in the late 1960s and early 1970s but they have since fallen to levels current twenty years ago (Leete 1979). One explanation for this could be that people are deferring marriage and another that some people are choosing co-habitation in preference to marriage; it is too early to estimate the significance (if any) of the apparent fall and there are indications that this trend is being reversed.[2] At the same time, the rate at which marriages are breaking up has accelerated and there can be little doubt as to the scale and magnitude of divorce. On current projections there is approximately a one-in-four chance that each person in the population will have been divorced by the age of forty-five (Leete 1979); the rate of divorce is even higher than this for divorces which take place in the first four years of marriage.[3] However, the majority of people who divorce remarry and, in 1979, one in three new marriages involved remarriage for one or both partners (Central Statistical Office 1981) though it seems that second marriages may be at even greater risk of divorce than first marriages.[4] Such trends have led some commentators to the view that divorce, rather than being the antithesis of marriage, is simply a transformation (Delphy 1976), with serial monogamy replacing marriage for life.

To some extent marriage has always been both popular and problematic and, as Dr Samuel Johnson suggested, it represents 'the triumph of hope over experience'. However, the apparent growth in marital breakdown needs to be viewed in a broader context than simply the proliferation of unique marital difficulties. Some twenty years or so ago Wright Mills (1959) wrote about making sociological connections between private troubles and public issues and Rex (1974) later re-emphasized the importance for sociology of engaging in this imaginative activity. Both writers see divorce as more than a mere private trouble and suggest that the divorce statistics are a reflection of structural issues 'having to do with the institutions of marriage and the family' (Wright Mills 1959: 9). A number of commentators have argued that marriage is undergoing structural change. According to one popular view marriage is said to be in transition from an institutional form 'with family behaviour controlled by the mores, public opinion, and law' towards a 'companionship' or 'companionate' form 'with behaviour arising from the mutual affection, equality and consensus of its members' (Burgess, Locke, and Thomes 1963: 3). There are two ways of analysing marriage: one is to examine what people say and believe about it, and the other is to explore the lived experience. A great deal has been written about the former, though rather less about the latter. This has happened partly because of the considerable strength of the ideologies surrounding marriage, but also as a consequence of the privatization and lack of visibility in which people conduct their married lives.

It has been suggested that the trend towards companionate marriage has been effected partly by an increase in equality between men and women within marriage. The few pieces of research which have explored how far marital equality has *in practice* been achieved in the different areas of family life have produced rather different findings (Pahl and Pahl 1972; Oakley 1974; Robertson 1975; Edgell 1980). Edgell (1980) has concluded that the emphasis on those aspects of marriage where some measure of companionship has come to exist conceals the existing power divisions between men and women, husbands and wives.

It therefore seems more likely that the trend towards companionate marriage represents an *ideological* change in terms of people's expectations of marriage rather than any material change in the power divisions within it. For example, Gorer (1970) claims to have found that, compared with twenty years previously, couples *aspired* in marriage to an egalitarian partnership and placed less emphasis on material resources and security and sexual compatibility. Moreover, the extent to which people define their marriages as having problems is likely to be related to their ideological beliefs and expectations of marriage. It is significant that some of the *dissatisfaction* with marriage described in the literature is attributed to those aspects of marriage which are salient for the construction of the ideology of the companionate marriage: that is, the extent to which couples *feel* they have a sharing relationship, make joint decisions, exchange love, affection, and private confidences — experience a feeling of intimacy and togetherness. Conversely, such people appear to have expressed but little dissatisfaction with the existing division of labour in which there is still an imbalance of real power (see for example Heisler and Whitehouse (1976) and Walker and Chester (1977)).

Sociologists of the family have discovered a substantial amount of dissatisfaction with marriage. All major studies have shown a decline in marital satisfaction during the early stages of the family life cycle (Rollins and Cannon 1974) with the greater part of this dissatisfaction being expressed by wives and not husbands (Thornes and Collard 1979). This gender difference is unlikely to be simply a reflection of sociologists' use of women as rapporteurs of family life since, paradoxically, the research evidence based on women's accounts (at least until the beginning of the 1970s) has, as Oakley (1974) suggested, rendered them largely invisible. Moreover, there is a body of research which has concluded that women rather than men have had to make the greater adjustment at marriage (see Thornes and Collard (1979) for a discussion of some of this literature). Furthermore, studies of the mental health of the married have suggested that marriage is more stressful for women than for men (Gove 1972; Gove and Tudor 1973).

Marriage provides one of the principal sources of purpose and meaning in life for the vast majority of people at some time in their lives. However, its very exclusivity and predictability tend to inhibit people whose marriages end (whether because of breakdown or the death of their partner) from easily creating alternative relationships and patterns of living. It is perhaps not surprising that individuals in such circumstances may display considerable concern about being different from the stereotypical 'normal' nuclear family. (For a discussion of the problems of the divorced see Hart (1976).) Undoubtedly, the increase in divorce and remarriage generates greater diversity in family patterns but the long-term implications of reconstituted families for patterns of social relationships have not as yet fully emerged (Burgoyne and Clark 1980).

It is significant that the exclusive and very considerable emotional commitment demanded by modern marriage has arisen in an industrialized rational-bureaucratic society. In such a society marriage and the family have been made to bear and to compensate for the strain generated by the dehumanized activity performed in the public world of outside employment. It is also significant that women, as carers and servicers within the family, have borne much of that strain. Given the nature of the market place and its strict segregation from family life, it is thus not surprising that the 'normal' family has come to be seen, at least in one extreme view, as a weapon for destroying human personalities and as one of the most common sources of private troubles (Cooper 1972).

In spite of the pervasiveness and the seeming inevitability of marriage, it is a peculiarly opaque area for social enquiry. The location of samples of the married and the collection of good data both pose problems for those attempting to conduct empirical investigations into marriage. Moreover, the study of troubled marriages poses special problems, not the least of which is definitional, that is how to decide which marriages can be said to have problems. Equally problematic for research are the seeming obviousness of marriage and the 'taken for granted' assumptions which underpin it, together with the lack of 'fit' between its ideology and practice. Marriage as a substantive area of enquiry has characteristics which, for many researchers, make it almost 'too close for comfort'. Few marriages are trouble free and most of those who are married encounter periods of difficulty at some time or another.

The public discussion concerning the current state of marriage in our society constituted the general context in which the idea for this study of marriages in trouble arose, and this will be fully discussed in our concluding chapter. The specific context generating the present study was work being conducted at the Marriage Research Centre at the Central Middlesex Hospital in London. This Centre was established with two principal aims: on the one hand to undertake research relating to contemporary marriage and, on the other, to provide a clinical service for marital therapy and courses for practitioners with an interest in marital work. The instigator and Director of the Centre is Dr Jack Dominian, whose involvement in the topic of marriage reflects both a moral concern about the consequences of marital breakdown, and a practitioner concern which derives from his work as a consultant psychiatrist and marital therapist. The Director had for some time wished to set up research of a 'clinical' nature, in which clients receiving marital help could be studied. A sociologist, Julia Brannen, was therefore appointed in 1978 to carry out such a project and was given the major responsibility for its design. She was joined by two other researchers (both in a part-time capacity). Alan Tait, a psychiatrist, contributed to the early stages of the project and to the interviewing; he then left the Centre to take up an appointment else-where. Jean Collard, a sociologist (and one of the present authors) joined the project six months after its inception, took part in the field-work, and has remained throughout.

It had originally been envisaged that the project would explore the 'psychological and social factors' related to marital breakdown. Julia Brannen had an interest in treatment in medical settings and, having been given a brief to research clients with marital problems, was also interested in investigating, at least initially, the problem of how people came to seek help from agencies for marital difficulties. During the first phase of the project, in which Julia Brannen was 'getting to know the area', she spent a period observing clients in therapy. It soon became evident to her that clients (at least those seen by the marital service attached to the Centre) did not necessarily regard their marriages as being on the point of breaking up, and it was unclear how far they themselves had been instigators of their search for help. Furthermore, given at that time the apparent lack of published research concerning help-seeking and marital problems, it seemed reasonable, at least in the first instance, to conduct a small-scale exploratory study of clients with marital problems. The main focus of the project was reformulated and the new point of departure hinged on the process of becoming a client. One obviously important source of clients with marital problems consisted of people who approached Marriage Guidance Councils, and we eventually gained access to a number of these clients. In addition, both for the purposes of making comparisons and also because of their accessibility, we included in our research a group of couples who had been referred for marital problems to the marital service at the Centre. This marital service which, together with the research staff, constitutes the Marriage Research Centre, is located in a general hospital where its Director is also a senior consultant psychiatrist in the adjacent Department of Psychological Medicine. The couples who became clients of the hospital marital service had been referred to it through their general practitioners, all of whom practised in the area serviced by the general hospital.

Since it was our view that any existing notions of how people with marital problems become clients tended to be somewhat narrow and simplistic, we considered it necessary to develop and articulate a broad theoretical framework on which to test the analysis of our data. (For an exegesis of our initial ideas see Brannen (1980).) The field of illness behaviour within medical sociology offered a number of interesting ideas and constructs; these, together with a number of structural concepts adopted in sociological analysis, suggested a framework for the study. This conceptual framework is outlined in Chapter 1.

The research design thus provided for two groups of clients with marital problems: those being given help within a medical setting, and those who sought help in a non-medical setting. We decided to investigate our research respondents by means of detailed in-depth interviews, to be conducted separately with husbands and wives. We eventually interviewed forty-eight husbands and wives from twenty-eight marriages (in eight marriages we were able to interview only one partner), and we did so shortly after they had approached, or had been offered marital help, by the two types of agency mentioned above (the hospital marital service and Marriage Guidance). An account of the project design, the research methods we employed, and the characteristics of our group of respondents, is given in Chapter 2.

In this study we have sought to emphasize the processual elements of becoming a client rather than to consider the approaches to agencies as single decisions and actions. In this endeavour we have developed the notion of a help-seeking career, composed of a number of stages. In a somewhat flexible way, these stages can be seen to constitute the overall structure of this book with Chapters 1 and 2 describing the concepts and methodology and Chapters 3 to 11 being concerned with the presentation of our data analysis.

In Chapter 3 we describe our respondents' basic orientations towards the disclosure of personal and marital problems. In Chapter 4 we go on to look at the ways in which the husbands and wives perceived and interpreted their marital situations, at the time when they were approaching agencies. In this chapter we also endeavour to consider the evidence from their accounts which suggests that these interpretations and definitions had changed over the course of their marriages, and in relation to specific events and contexts. In Chapter 5 we examine the range of critical events and problems which constituted the contexts of seeking help, and the development of the marital difficulties. We focus on the critical events and problems that had occurred in the eighteen months preceding the approaches to the agencies. Interestingly, the substance of these events and problems appears not to have been limited to what was happening in respondents' marriages at the time, and suggests that respondents were under considerable stress emanating from a variety of different sources.

The next part of our data presentation (and the next stage of the help-seeking careers of our respondents) concerns the influence of their significant social contacts, which we have termed social networks. In Chapters 6, 7, and 8 we discuss some of the ways in which social networks influence both formal and informal help-seeking. Social networks constitute the structures and contexts within which people view and conduct their marital relationships, and in which beliefs and actions about turning to others − family, relatives, and friends as well as agencies − are shaped. In Chapter 6 we develop a typology of the structures of our respondents' social networks, and we analyse the relationship between these network types and the characteristics of the marriages. In Chapter 7 we examine the patterns of respondents' consulting and confiding in network members in relation to the critical events and problems, including the marital ones, they had experienced. In Chapter 8 we analyse the structure of respondents' networks in relation to their approaches to agencies.

The final part of our data presentation concerns our respondents' perceptions, expectations, and experiences of the agencies themselves. In Chapter 8 we trace the different pathways to and through the agencies, the key persons and agencies encountered in the search for formal help, and the part they played in defining clients' marriages as having problems. In Chapter 9 we describe respondents' expectations and experiences of all the agencies they encountered in the course of their help-seeking careers. In Chapter 10 we consider respondents' assumptions about the goals of counselling, especially in relation to the idea and practice of marriages being preserved. We also analyse respondents' prescriptions and preferences concerning counselling and its various approaches. We examine the extent to which counselling approaches match clients' preferences, and we suggest that counselling can have quite different meanings for different client groups. In Chapter 11, the final chapter of the data analysis, we return to the subject of disclosure and we consider respondents' perceptions of the ideal situation for the disclosure of marital and personal problems in general.

In the postscript (Chapter 12) initially we move away from an analysis of our data to take a broad view of marital problems as a product of knowledge. We discuss some of the ways and means by which marriage has come to be seen as problematic in our society and has become part of wider public discourse. We identify what we consider to be some of the main interest groups who have contributed substantially to the debates on marriage. We finally return to the theme of this book concerning clients and the help-seeking process, and we conclude with a consideration of some of the implications of agency intervention in this, a most sensitive area of our personal lives.

Notes

1 Nearly everybody gets married; 95 per cent of women and 91 per cent of men have done so by the age of forty. The source of these figures is the Office of Population Censuses and Surveys 1966–1977. These figures are given in a publication by Central Policy Review Staff and Central Statistical Office (1980).

2 In 1978 there was a 3 per cent increase in the number of marriages and this increase was sustained in 1979 and in 1980 (Central Statistical Office 1982).

3 *Social Trends* (Central Statistical Office 1982) notes that the proportion of divorces occurring within the first four years of marriage rose from 13 per cent in 1971 to nearly 19 per cent in 1979.

4 The proportion of divorces occurring in marriages where one or both partners had previously been divorced rose from 10 per cent in 1974 to nearly 16 per cent in 1980, according to *Social Trends* (Central Statistical Office 1982).

1

The research focus:
concepts and ideas

In this chapter we propose to give the reader some understanding of the ideas and concepts with which we have approached the research problem of seeking help for marital problems. First of all we shall outline our main concepts, which are concerned with the general phenomenon of help-seeking and becoming a client. Second, we shall turn our attention to the principal agencies to which help-seeking was ultimately directed. We shall examine some of the characteristics of these agencies, and particularly the ways in which they are themselves likely to conceptualize and to treat the marital problems of their clients. Finally, we shall return to the substantive area of the study, namely difficulties in marriage for which help was sought and given, and we shall suggest that a framework for the study of seeking help for marital problems must take account of such wider sociological considerations as gender divisions.

There is a general paucity of literature, especially of British studies, on clients of agencies which offer counselling, social work, and psychotherapy. The main body of literature on clients is in the field of medical sociology. Most pertinent is the body of empirical research on health and illness behaviour and specifically what has come to be known as 'help-seeking'. A brief account of some of the findings, particularly those concerning clients seeking treatment for psychological and personal problems from medical and other therapeutic sources, is given in Chapter 8. We shall give some further indication of how far those we interviewed are similar to other client groups when we discuss the characteristics of our informants.

An over-view of help-seeking literature suggests a broad distinction between two main theoretical approaches (Brannen 1980). In some studies the theoretical emphasis is upon the client as actor, on the ways he or she constructs and negotiates the pathways to treatment.

The help-seeker is conceptualized as a decision-maker, and the action of seeking help as a problem-solving activity. The other theoretical approach emphasizes the contextual factors, those events and social situations which surround and impinge upon those who become clients of the 'helping' services, and also the part that is played by the agencies themselves. Here the client is depicted as less obviously a conscious actor initiating and controlling the help-seeking process: the process of seeking treatment is seen as determined and constrained by external forces. However, polarizing the approaches of this research in this way tends to assume that such work makes explicit its theoretical assumptions, which in practice is not always the case. Even so, it is our contention that the tendency for one or other of these theoretical approaches to be adopted is at the expense of understanding the relationship, or rather the interaction, between the two, and that the fundamental issue concerns how far the choices and decisions, which are made by people apparently totally in control, are shaped and structured externally by social situations, events, and beliefs.

The process of help-seeking

One of our central assumptions about help-seeking was that it constituted a *process* and not a single piece of action, and that the various routes and processes by which people became clients could therefore be considered in terms of help-seeking *careers*. The concept of career, originally developed in studies of occupations, was subsequently extended to the field of deviant behaviour. Becker, in his celebrated account 'Becoming a Marijuana User' (Becker 1963) elucidates the advantages of the concept in terms of the notion of 'career contingency': those factors on which mobility from one position to another depends. According to Becker career contingencies include 'both objective facts of social structure and changes in the perspectives, motivations and desires of the individual' (Becker 1963: 24). Additionally, Becker employs the concept of career to distinguish several varieties of career outcome. The application of the concept of career to help-seeking behaviour suggests that the individual concerned must progress through a series of stages which, as Friedson notes, can be observed 'in human efforts at finding meaning in experience' (1970: 240). Each stage is marked by its own set of meanings and actions which are themselves constructed and shaped by social forces. Davis (1963), in his study of the way parents made sense of the onset and course of poliomyelitis in their children, suggests that the parents interpreted and re-interpreted a variety of 'cues', ranging from symptoms to critical incidents. Zola (1973) likewise suggests a series of 'triggers' to help-seeking which, according to Locker (1981), can be subsumed within this conceptual approach: 'The triggers Zola has identified are situational factors taken into account when the meaning of events is being constructed, such that the advent of a trigger leads to a change in the way a problem is defined and a change in the action taken to deal with it' (Locker 1981: 9).

Becker (1963) emphasized the influence of the reactions of others on the deviant's career, especially at the stage where the deviant was publicly labelled. Where the notion has been applied to illness behaviour, although some writers (mentioned above) have emphasized the role of cues and triggers on the help-seeking process, others have focused solely on the choices and options selected by help-seekers in the course of their illness careers. As Locker (1981) notes, this latter approach tends to suggest careers of only one particular direction and type.

Kadushin (1958/59) is one of the few who, while not explicitly using the concept career, isolated stages in the decision to undertake psychotherapy. He distinguishes five stages: (1) recognition of an emotional problem; (2) exposure to the problem within the circle of friends and relatives; (3) decision to seek professional help; (4) selection of an area of professional help; (5) selection of a specific practitioner. It was one of our endeavours in this study both to distinguish the stages in the help-seeking process in terms of sequences of meanings and actions and also to analyse how these were shaped and structured. This we have endeavoured to do on the basis of personal retrospective accounts by a collectivity of clients with marital problems. As the reader will discover, for some people the search for help involved the client taking a very active part, while for others the agencies themselves played a key role, especially at the stage where the marriages became defined as 'problematic'.

Social networks

One aspect of the client's career in which we were particularly interested concerned the social milieu surrounding it: the micro-level of the social network. Since our study group was small and in no way constituted a representative sample of any specific population, we limited ourselves to a micro-structural analysis. Studies such as *The Client Speaks* (Mayer and Timms 1970) have examined how far people make active and conscious choices about seeking treatment in relation to their own social networks. Mayer and Timms suggest that where clients were faced with personal problems which distressed them, they first attempted to solve their problems with the help of family and friends, and that only in the event of a deficiency in, or a total absence of, informal sources of help, did they seek help from agencies. Thus their conceptual framework postulates a uni-directional relationship between informal social networks and formal help-seeking action, suggesting that it is inadequacy in informal sources which leads to an approach to formal sources of help.

In the above study the notion of social network is mainly used to refer to a concrete entity providing social support in times of adversity. It does not apply the notion of social network in its sociological sense, namely as referring to a field of social linkages or relationships *between* persons. In the sociological sense social network denotes a variety of micro-social structures which, according to their structural pattern, act as socializing, constraining, sanctioning, and legitimating forces on the actions and beliefs of their members. In effect, individuals do not act only according to their power to mobilize their social networks, as they are seen to do in Mayer and Timms's study; social networks also act *upon* individuals, constraining their actions and decisions. Social networks can therefore be examined from two conceptual standpoints: first, as resources which individuals draw upon in the course of their help-seeking careers; and second in terms of their influence upon individuals' beliefs, decisions, and actions. McKinlay (1973), for example, applied a social network analysis to a study of the utilization of pre-maternity services, in which he emphasized the constraints of network structure upon the help-seeking actions of his study group, but in a way which did not deny the individuals' power to influence and exert control over their own actions.

In this project we have sought to apply the notion of social network in both senses. First, we have been concerned to see whether and how far social networks constituted a source of informal support for our study group, and we have suggested that the nature and quality of that support depended not only upon the size but also upon the structure of the network. Second, we have examined the influence of networks as structures which affect how people relate to one another in intimate relationships, both in marriage and in confiding relationships with significant others. Third, social relationships form not only a basis for the exchange of goods, services, and communication, but also lend meaning and significance to individuals' actions and to their experience of the world. Moreover, they provide the context in which approaches to agencies occur. Therefore, whether people made use of their friends and kin as sources of help (an interesting question and one which we later investigate in detail) should not be postulated as being simply contingent upon the availability or non-availability to people of such relationships. Social networks provide a backcloth against which beliefs and attitudes about the *value* of confiding problems in others are shaped, and additionally they constrain and sanction individuals' communication and behaviour.

Life events

We conceptualized a second set of factors which we thought might impinge upon individuals' help-seeking careers and might significantly affect the approach to the agency. A number of relevant conceptual approaches suggested themselves: notably, crisis-orientation, psycho-social transitions, and life events. The notion of crisis seemed to have some relevance to an understanding of why and when people sought help, since it conjured up, on the one hand, threat or danger, and, on the other, opportunity or hope. The decisions and actions in seeking help may be seen as responses to circumstances and situations which invoke either or both of these perceptions and feelings. The idea of social transition (Parkes 1971) suggests that both *predictable* events such as life cycle transitions, and *unpredictable* events, require people to make changes in their assumptive worlds, and help-seeking action may be construed as one possible response to such changes. Third, there is the notion of life event, which was developed in relation to explanations about the production of affective disorders (Brown and Harris 1978). All three of these approaches were developed to take account not only of cognitive changes in meaning, but also (and principally) to provide for emotional responses to critical incidents and events. It seemed to us quite likely that critical incidents and events had some relevance to explanations of help-seeking action. Moreover, the emotional state of clients with marital problems is likely to have a highly significant place in such explanations. Thus we hypothesized that if individuals in marital relationships (which most probably were already highly charged) had *additionally* experienced critical incidents or events, these might have some impact on their help-seeking behaviour.

From among the three possible conceptual approaches we finally decided to select and apply the life events approach, largely because of its developed methodology, and despite its general bias towards the negative connotations of life events and their diminishing effects on the individual. In our application of this approach, we endeavoured to broaden its focus beyond the events and persistent difficulties which it would normally cover, to include any positive changes in options and alternatives. We decided to do this because it seemed to us that real or perceived positive changes in an individual's alternatives and options might be equally as important *theoretically* as events of a negative or diminishing nature, in their effects on the ways in which people accommodate, cease to accommodate, and seek help in relation to their marriages. For example, a woman might perceive the possibility of getting a job as a means to some financial independence and, in consequence, as a way out of a difficult and unhappy marriage. However, whether or not those people pursuing such courses of action would actually seek the support of agencies to help them through the painful experience of separation, would depend upon their perceptions of the goals of the agencies. Furthermore, it seemed to us that the perception of positive alternatives to problematic marriages was more likely to be *inversely* related to help-seeking, in so far as help was seen as being mainly concerned with 'mending' marriages.

We considered, therefore, that life events, in a broad sense, might constitute some part of the explanation why certain people with marital difficulties approached agencies. In practice this proved a sensible approach to have adopted since, as it turned out, a high proportion of our study group had initially sought help for individual rather than marital problems. Furthermore, since we applied the life events approach to two kinds of groups, those who sought help specifically for their marriages, and those who did so initially with physical and psychological symptoms, we were able to examine all the marriages within a broad perspective. As the reader will later discover, in a defined period prior to the approach to the agencies, the majority of our respondents had experienced a variety of relatively serious events and problems, some of which were quite independent of their marriage troubles, such as the deaths of parents, and others which were a direct consequence of marital tensions. It can therefore be seen that a 'life events approach' provided us with a framework in which to explore possible linkages between contextual circumstances and the various stages of individuals' help-seeking careers, and was not simply a device for explaining the specific moment at which an agency was approached. As we have stressed earlier, the help-seeking process can be seen as encompassing a variety of stages, from the awareness and definitions of problems to the decision-making stages of whether and which agency to consult. Thus, we considered that a life event might act as a catalyst at any of the stages of the help-seeking process or, alternatively, it might simply engender symptoms of stress for which the 'sufferer' might seek relief. The crucial issue then would seem to concern the way in which the presenting problem is interpreted by the agency; what *kind* of help is given and for *what*.

The agencies

The role that agencies play in defining and re-defining the problems which clients bring to them may be considerable, and has a particular significance for women clients. An abundance of studies show that women report symptoms more frequently than men and use medical and psychiatric facilities more often (e.g. Gurin, Veroff, and Feld 1960; Gove and Tudor 1973). Whatever the significance of this in terms of *true* rates of illness, it is reasonable to conclude that women, compared with men, are at greater risk of being termed sick and especially of being labelled psychiatric cases. Moreover, the doctor plays a crucial role in legitimating illness by the application of a diagnostic label. We considered that an agency's model and 'treatment' of marital problems was therefore a particularly sensitive issue, given the inequality of husbands and wives within marriage; and if, as research on other kinds of help-seeking has indicated, wives tended more often to initiate help-seeking, it was important to explore the agencies' responses to this phenomenon.

Our study embraces clients of very different agencies; it includes, on the one hand, medical practitioners and, on the other, marriage counsellors, volunteers of voluntary agencies. Both groups subscribe to very different bodies of knowledge and explanatory models and they also have different 'professional' allegiances and interests. Thus we considered it likely that these agencies would treat their clients in particular kinds of ways and that, very probably, the different groups of clients would approach and perceive them differently.

Medical practitioners

We considered that the 'treatment' of marital problems was unlikely to be a priority with many medical practitioners; for one thing, few would be able to find the time. However, we thought that explanations for their lack of interest must surely go beyond practical considerations alone and would also be related to patients' perceptions of what is and is not appropriate to present to the doctor, perceptions largely shaped in the first instance by the medical profession. Even the doctors who, in their practice, acknowledge the existence of marital difficulties face this problem. However, a much more intransigent problem for medical practitioners in the recognition and treatment of marital problems concerns the dominance of the medical model. First, the medical model emphasizes the physical rather than the social and psychological. Second, it locates and interprets patients' problems as attributes of *individuals*, and so doctors treat most self-limiting and socially caused illnesses in medical ways. Oakley (1980) has noted the great extent to which there is an emphasis in medical ideology and practice upon successful outcome being judged *quantitatively* in terms of morbidity and mortality statistics, rather than on the treatment experience and the quality of patients' lives.

It has been argued that medicine's failure to acknowledge the social causes of patients' symptoms is systematic and a central feature of the medical paradigm (Stark 1981). Such an argument does not rest upon observations that individual doctors fail to acknowledge the social basis of their patients' problems because of feelings of powerlessness or of 'not being able to do anything'. Rather, it postulates that an integral part of medical ideology and practice is that medical intervention takes place *only* in areas where medicine is likely to gain a monopoly of control. The way in which whole sectors of human experience become subject to medical intervention has been described as the process of medicalization. A number of writers have testified to the wholesale transfer of birth and death, for example, to the control of the medical profession (Illich 1975; Oakley 1980). We do not propose to speculate just now on the question of the medicalization of marital problems, though it is clear that, at present, medicine has no monopoly in this area.

Marriage counselling agencies

The other agencies dealing with marital problems with which we were concerned were the Marriage Guidance Councils. In comparison with the world of medicine, there is much less theoretical and substantive work on therapeutic and counselling services in general, which no doubt reflects their relatively low status and power, their comparative recentness, and their smaller numerical strength. Some therapeutic agencies nevertheless are frequently adjuncts of medical and psychiatric services. Marriage Guidance counselling, however, has no formal association with medicine, except where counsellors have been attached to general practices.

The Marriage Guidance Council was inaugurated in 1937 by a small group of doctors, social workers, clergy, and magistrates (Working Party on Marriage Guidance 1979). It was established largely as a response to fears concerning the rising divorce rate rather than the actual incidence of social problems stemming from broken families. In the previous year, divorce had become legalized on the grounds of adultery, cruelty, and desertion, and a consequent increase in the number of divorces had occurred. Moreover, the Council sought to raise public awareness of this 'threat' (WPMG 1979: 8). The original aims set down by the Council reflect the early political concern with protecting the family and with mending people's marriages. As the report by the working party on marriage guidance notes: 'The pioneers of the Marriage Councils were as clear in their avowed aims as they were prudent, able and persuasive in the pursuit of them . . . They were out to save marriages − to "mend" them not to "end" them' (WPMG 1979: 4).

The post-war years saw a rise in public concern about the break-up of families and the evils that were seen as flowing from this phenomenon, and with the growth in public concern came the consolidation of the Marriage Guidance movement. In the 1940s and 1950s the organization and movement saw itself explicitly as a mechanism for social control: marital disharmony was seen as a 'disease' to be 'diagnosed' and 'treated' (Mace 1948: 50−1). (It is interesting to note the influence of the medical model on the language used at the time to describe this particular model of counselling.)

Since then the aims of the organization and its counselling methods have undergone considerable change. The national organization, the National Marriage Guidance Council, today adheres to much less clearly articulated values concerning marriage and the family. 'The NMGC is concerned primarily with marriage and family relationships and believes that the well-being of society is dependent on the stability of marriage' (NMGC 1975: 8). But, as Keithley (1977) notes, the contrast between such principles, however loosely expressed, and the non-directive counselling techniques which are employed by Marriage Guidance counsellors, must inevitably cause tensions. There has been no research to date which has examined how beliefs about the value of marriage as an institution influence counsellors' views and their 'treatment' of clients' marriages.

Today the counselling methods of Marriage Guidance counsellors are essentially non-directive, with the emphasis on listening and empathy. The conditions under which counsellors work suggest how such methods have come to be adopted. First, counsellors, unlike social workers, have no dealings with material problems and no statutory responsibilities. Second, they are voluntary, and work in organizations which have no formal connections with other agencies and practitioner groups. Moreover, since the entire training of Marriage Guidance counsellors is conducted within NMGC, it is specific to Marriage Guidance organizations and not to the wider area of therapeutic practice. Third, at present the Councils do not offer (nor aim to offer) immediate access to clients in crisis situations. For such reasons counsellors' views of clients' problems tend to be rather one-dimensional, with perhaps a tendency to isolate problems either in the individual psyche or in the psychodynamic elements of the marital relationship, and they thereby run the risk of neglecting the exigencies of the immediate situation. In common with other agencies, they take no account of the material bases of marriage in our society, bases which have specific implications for the distinctive marital experiences of husbands and wives and the problems they encounter.

So far in this chapter we have noted concepts which we, as researchers, have applied to analysing the process of becoming a client. The emphasis on help-seekers as negotiating their help-seeking careers pointed towards a framework which was based upon the actor's definition of the situation. At the same time we stressed the importance of both action itself and the meaning that actors attached to it, being viewed within the constraints of wider structural forces. Next, we turned to the agencies themselves with which clients came into contact. We suggested that their status, and type of knowledge and practice, were also likely to have an impact on clients' help-seeking careers. For our final discussion in this chapter we shall focus on the general sociological issue of gender divisions which, given the focus of help-seeking behaviour and marriage, we thought might emerge as an important variable in the analysis.

Gender divisions

Since marital problems concern both husbands and wives, gender is very likely to be a key variable in any analysis. There is in fact a considerable body of evidence which suggests that marriage is a very different experience for the two genders[1] and the findings of some of these studies point to the concentration of problems among wives rather than husbands (Meyerowitz and Feldman 1968; Rollins and Feldman 1970). However, the concentration of problems among wives is generally conceptualized in these studies as posing problems for the stability of the marriage rather than simply being problems for the wives. In most of the literature on marriage and the family it is evident that this concern with marital stability has tended to deflect attention away from the question how marriage has come to have particular and different kinds of impact upon men and women.

A study of the divorced (Thornes and Collard 1979) noted that divorced women were twice as likely as divorced men to have said that they had perceived marital problems within the first year of marriage. One interpretation of this finding is that women adjust less easily to marriage than men do. On the other hand, it could equally well be concluded that marriage is more problematic for wives than it is for husbands. We believe it to be significant that the question how marriage affects men and women has generally been posed (with only a few striking exceptions) in terms of how men and women *adjust* to marriage. It is only relatively recently that women sociologists have begun the task of overturning the old 'taken for granted' ways of analysing the institutions of marriage and family life. Jessie Bernard (1973) has argued that the institution of marriage is not one but two institutions. Ann Oakley (1980), in her study of childbirth, emphasizes the distinction between what she calls the 'two subjective realities of husband and wife'. Moreover, she also says: 'Any objective reality that is described has to take account of the *discrepancy* [our italics] between the two subjective realities of husband and wife, differently socialized as to gender, and differently encumbered with the reproduction and maintenance of family life' (Oakley 1980: 77). If we consider again such observations as wives perceiving both greater problems in marriage and an earlier onset to them (than husbands), then, in the light of Oakley's distinction, such findings are more likely to emerge as being contingent upon marital experience and not *a priori*.

Even if gender is an important mediating factor of marital experience, it is true that it will have had some earlier significance in respondents' lives. One area in which we were particularly interested concerned attitudes to disclosure. We noted that, in a study of newlyweds, no gender difference emerged in the accounts given by husbands and wives about whether they would disclose marital problems if their marriages were later to run into difficulties.[2] (However, it is of course possible that these accounts reflect respondents' high commitment to a couple ideology at the start of their marriages, something which might not be sustained in practice.) Our study group, on the other hand, exhibited marked gender differences in attitudes to disclosure. One possible explanation for this apparent difference between newly-weds at the beginning of their marriages and our study group, who were experiencing marital problems later, can be found in the inter-vening experience of marriage itself, which distributes power un-evenly between men and women. Given a pattern of inequality both within marriage and in the opportunities available to women in the wider society, it is likely that many women experience the married state as falling far short of the romantic notions which are instilled in girlhood and in the rituals surrounding marriage (Leonard 1980), and which are systematically fostered and sustained by popular ideology.[3]

Overall, our conceptual approach has two important aspects: on the one hand we take account of the process in which people make sense of, define, and ultimately label their marital problems and seek help and, on the other, we seek to analyse the context and factors which structure cognitive changes and help-seeking action. This latter con-stitutes the explanatory part of our approach and we have outlined the sociological concepts we shall apply in the analysis of our material. We noted that socialization is likely to have an impact on people's attitudes towards disclosing and seeking help for their problems and, more importantly in this regard, we have emphasized the concept of social network. The general contexts of circumstances of people's lives (life events), together with the agencies themselves, are also likely to shape the help-seeking process and we suggested that an analysis of gender divisions, especially in relation to marriage and help-seeking, is an essential part of structural explanations.

Notes

1 For findings and a discussion of the division of labour in marriage see Oakley 1974. It is commonly assumed on the basis of Bott's work (Bott 1968) that only working-class couples have segregated marital roles. For a middle-class picture which depicts differences in the marital roles of middle-class husbands and wives see Pahl and Pahl 1972.

2 A study of young newly-wed couples, interviewed three months after marriage in 1979, conducted at the Marriage Research Centre, Central
  Middlesex Hospital (unpublished).

3 An interesting example of such commercial fostering is the current advertis-
  ing campaign by the publishers Mills and Boon, who are endeavouring to
  stimulate sales of their list of romantic fiction. The leitmotiv used throughout is the symbol 'The Rose of Romance'.

2

The project: research design, methods, and characteristics of the group studied

An examination of the literature on seeking treatment or formal help makes the researcher setting out on a study of this phenomenon acutely aware of the very considerable methodological difficulties, especially when the study envisaged is of a retrospective kind. An exploration of what has brought clients to agencies involves disentangling the processes which have taken place in the past — sometimes the distant past — and thereby runs the risk of respondents reconstructing the past from the vantage point of the present (the problem of *ex post* reconstruction). Another and inherent limitation of focusing on client groups only concerns the failure to address the issue how those who seek treatment differ from those who do not. It was with an awareness of these largely insuperable methodological difficulties that we approached the task of designing the project.

Getting into the area and how the research design came about

Our project was considered essentially an exploratory enterprise; our aim was to explore the perceptions and processes whereby people became clients of agencies for marital problems, and the factors which shaped their decisions and actions. At the outset we had no idea or information about the characteristics of the population experiencing marital difficulties, except that we considered it might include most marriages at some point in their duration; second, we did not know anything about the connection between the experience of marital difficulties and the receipt of specialist marital help. Since it did not seem feasible to conduct a conventional piece of research, incorporating a group of help-seekers and a contrast group who had not sought help for such problems, we decided to focus only upon the former. In fact the questions surrounding how people came to be in receipt of specialist marital help provided sufficient challenges in themselves.

The decision of which group of help-seekers to focus on was to some extent made for us. It will be remembered that the organization in which the research was based had a medical setting and was set up and directed by a consultant psychiatrist. This organization was established in the belief that people, when experiencing problems in their marriages, would seek help of some kind from their general practitioners and, accordingly, a clinical service was provided within the organization to which general practitioners in the surrounding health authority areas were encouraged to refer patients. The clinical service will henceforth be referred to as the hospital unit for marital therapy or hospital-based marital service. It was therefore expected that the project would include a group who had sought help from their general practitioners or had been recognized by them as needing help with their marriages. Marriage Guidance Councils constitute a second and more obvious source of marital help in the community, and we decided to include in the project a group of their clients. In the initial stages of the project, other possibilities for obtaining respondents were also considered, most of them to be derived through medical or paramedical channels, for example people whose marital problems came to the notice of health visitors: however, in practice none of these proved feasible.

The initial stages of the project constituted not so much simply a quest for a research design (that is to say which client groups to focus on) as an exploration of the range of channels through which clients *might* present, or were alleged to present, with marital problems. The groups with which we ended up (a group of general practitioner patients and a group of Marriage Guidance clients) may thus be seen as both the outcome and, sadly, the partial failure of this task. In the period following these attempts and forays into the field, we have been reassured however by the failure of others undertaking research in similar areas. For example, Mattinson and Sinclair (1979), in trying to establish the incidence of marital problems of clients of social service departments, found that at the intake stage only a tiny proportion were noted by social workers as having marital problems, and, moreover, that very few were in fact married.[1] It was only when the researchers became involved, at a later stage, in casework studies that marital problems appeared to be particularly significant.

In our study, in order to explore the possibility of general practitioners being a primary source of people presenting with marital problems, the principal researcher spent a period of time with three cooperative doctors in a local group practice, monitoring their surgery consultations, and talking to the health visitors and doctors. Rather surprisingly, only one case which was defined by the doctor as marital emerged during the period of observation. Nevertheless, undaunted by this, and spurred on by the knowledge that a substantial proportion of the clients in the hospital unit had been referred by local general practitioners, we decided to pursue this avenue.

Accordingly, we randomly selected ten general practitioners from those who had referred at least one patient to the hospital unit in the previous four years of its duration. Eight of the doctors agreed to cooperate with us and they all seemed to consider that, generally speaking, they had large numbers of patients whom they recognized as having marital problems. They all expressed willingness to ask such patients whether they would consider taking part in our research project. We left carefully worded letters with these doctors, which they could give to patients at their discretion. In them we explained the nature and purpose of the study, our separateness from medical treatment and marital counselling, and the confidentiality of any information they might choose to give us. The doctors themselves had record slips upon which they were simply to note the name and address of any patient who expressed a willingness to cooperate in the research, which they were to send to us.

Despite the doctors' goodwill and our careful preparatory work, only one suitable respondent was forthcoming in the allocated time period. The other half dozen names we were sent included people whose marriages had long since broken up, and several were surprised and clearly very unhappy that their doctors had put their names forward, seemingly without their knowledge, which, if so, was entirely contrary to our intention. We therefore had to abandon trying to get respondents directly through general practitioners.

However, it was clear that a considerable number of general practitioners did, from time to time, refer patients with marriage difficulties to the hospital unit which formed part of the centre in which we were based. Because we had easy and direct access to these patients, we decided to focus on this group, in spite of the fact that they were likely to constitute a highly selected and atypical group of general practitioners' patients. The reader should also note that the hospital unit for marital therapy accepted referrals from other, though usually medical, sources and we also included such patients.

Our research design eventually emerged when it became clear that we were more likely to pick up people approaching agencies with marital problems in sufficient numbers if we included agencies in which we had direct access to clients (the hospital marital service). However, we also attempted, with some success, to obtain clients of marital agencies where we had no such direct access (two Marriage Guidance Councils). Thus, almost by default, our research approach became a study of two separate groups of people: those referred with marital difficulties by general practitioners (to the hospital unit) and those who sought help with self-defined marital problems (from Marriage Guidance Councils).

Gaining access and getting the respondents

We have already mentioned that we were in a position to gain ready access to the patients in the hospital marital service. The advantages of the researchers being physically 'on the spot', and of having links with practitioners in the field, should not be underestimated for the pursuit of this kind of research. Certainly where we, as relative outsiders, had to forge links with agencies (namely Marriage Guidance Councils) access to clients through the practitioners was much more problematic. Concerning the reluctance of practitioners to cooperate in this kind of research, Mayer and Timms (1970: 18–19) have drawn particular attention to the practitioners' fear of unethical breaches of confidentiality; their fear of the research interview damaging the worker's relationship with the client; and their concern that such research interviewing may prove emotionally disturbing to the client. We ourselves had expected that practitioners might well be impatient with a research project which had no immediate practical implications, and that they might perceive the research as a critical appraisal of their approaches and methods, with the result that we were prepared to experience some difficulty in obtaining clients to interview.

Clients of Marriage Guidance Councils

We tried to conduct our approaches to Marriage Guidance Councils in a sensitive and cautious fashion. In the space between us, as researchers, and the clients of Marriage Guidance Councils, there existed several layers of intermediaries, namely, the national organization, the officers and ethical committees of the Councils, and the counsellors themselves. The national organization of Marriage Guidance Councils (NMGC) was favourably disposed towards our endeavour but, since each of the individual Councils is an autonomous body, we had to make separate approaches in each instance. The chief officers of the two Councils we approached were in fact very cooperative and helpful, and we had to rely largely on them to communicate with the counsellors face-to-face. Moreover, the counsellors themselves were dispersed over a wide area and worked in many different places. We sent written material to each Council concerning the aims of the research, so that each counsellor could consider it at leisure.

In each Council we were able to talk informally with volunteer groups of counsellors in order to discuss the research further, and to answer any questions they might care to ask us. These meetings were very challenging, and some strong misgivings were expressed, especially about requests that the counsellors mention the research to new clients at very early counselling sessions. Our suggestion was that the counsellors should give their new clients details of the research, and that we should collaborate with the counsellors in developing the most acceptable method to contact the client. Those counsellors whom we met agreed in principle to give information produced by us concerning the research to all their new clients within a specified period but, in the end, we had to leave it to the counsellors to decide whether and when to give the information to the clients. The chief officers of both Councils agreed to pass information to all the counsellors and piles of leaflets outlining the research were left in the waiting-rooms of the central premises, beneath eye-catching posters, for clients to read. Clients were given the information on the research together with stamped addressed envelopes and brief forms on which they could indicate whether they were prepared to take part (and which they could return to us).

The fact that we were only able to meet a small proportion of the counsellors, and that some of them were clearly unhappy about what they perceived to be the intrusiveness of the research into a very contained and protected client–practitioner relationship, was reflected in the client response rate. Since we had had little idea in advance of the likely response, from either the counsellors or the clients, we tried to include a degree of flexibility in our research methods. We intended to conduct detailed interviews with clients and had already piloted the schedule but, because of our limited resources (at that time one full-time and two part-time researchers), we were prepared to make use of a postal questionnaire should the response be too great for the three of us to conduct interviews. We need not have worried, however. Overall, during the specified time period, we received only eighteen replies from individual clients and couples, of whom we eventually interviewed fourteen.[2]

Counsellors were also supplied with forms on which they could record the number of new clients and whether they had given them information concerning the research and so forth, but sadly only a very few returned them. We were, therefore, unable to estimate accurately whether the poor response rate reflected a disinclination to be interviewed on the part of the clients, or a reluctance to mention it to clients on the part of the counsellors, although the latter looks the more likely.

The selection of a representative group of clients was simply not possible. It is now clear to us that the only way of achieving this aim is through direct contact by the researchers with the clients themselves, a method that was entirely possible in the hospital marital service which formed part of the centre where we worked. Operating through a chain of intermediaries, however cooperative and sympathetic to the research, deprives the researchers of the control necessary in meeting the requirements of systematic investigation. Behind the protectiveness displayed by counsellors towards their clients lies a strong defensiveness about their status as counsellors and their counselling practice. This is very understandable given Marriage Guidance counsellors' lack of professional status and the fact that they are workers in voluntary organizations. As Keithley has noted: 'The paradox is that marriage counselling which . . . could be said to be the epitome of a certain model of "professional" work practice, is carried out not by highly trained and highly paid professionals, but by voluntary, part-time people, with limited training' (Keithley 1977: 35).

Reflecting these more general fears, counsellors expressed great reservations about one of our research requirements, namely that we sought to interview clients as early as possible in the counselling process. We had very strong reasons for wishing to do this. Since the main aim of the research was to explore the range of perceptions and processes whereby people became clients of formal agencies, it was essential that we located people who had only recently sought such formal help. Focusing on clients shortly after their initial contact with an agency would ensure freshness of recall; moreover, it would minimize the effects of the counselling which, as it progressed, would tend to influence clients' perceptions and feelings.

Clients of the hospital marital service

After we decided to focus on people referred to this service, the secretary sent out letters, giving information about the research and requesting cooperation, to all new 'patients', as they were called, the majority of whom had been referred to the service by general practitioners in the area. The letters made it clear to these clients that the research had no connection with the therapy, and was entirely optional. When the clients came to the hospital unit for their first appointments, they were seen by the principal researcher with no therapist present. Of all those seen by the researcher, almost no one refused to be interviewed. The researcher arranged with the clients for the interviews to be conducted in their own homes, at times convenient to them, and as soon as possible after their first appointment. This source provided us with thirteen marriages, and we interviewed both partners in almost every case.

The researchers were able to invite both partners at the same time to participate in the research, since the service operates on the basis that both partners attend together. The service is run by a psychiatrist who is considerably involved in marital therapy, and all new referrals were seen by him or by a second male psychiatrist, also a marital therapist. Although the initial therapeutic interview was conducted in the spirit of the medical 'diagnostic' model, clients were subsequently frequently referred to non-medical therapists in the unit for 'treatment'. However, one of the two psychiatrists retained the medical responsibility for them as general practitioners' patients, wrote diagnostic letters after their initial appointments, and usually wrote letters of 'discharge' at the end of therapy. Although the approach of the therapist was not essentially medical, psychodynamic and behaviourist models being preferred, it can be seen that the management of the patients was nevertheless largely within a medicalized framework.

Methods

The interview schedule

We interviewed each partner separately, with one researcher doing the interview and another observing, save in those instances where both partners were to be interviewed at the same time in which case only the one interviewer was present at each of the two interviews, which were conducted simultaneously in different rooms in the respondents' home. Our schedule was of the 'non-scheduled standardized' type; questions were standardized but the researcher was allowed latitude and flexibility in probing (Richardson, Dohrenwend and

Klein 1965). We first of all piloted the schedule with clients at the hospital unit. The main areas covered were:

1 *Demographic and background questions*
2 *Formal help-seeking*
   (a) Where respondents had considered they might go for help.
   (b) The decisions which led to the first contact with an agency.
   (c) Respondents' pathways to and through particular agencies.
   (d) Respondents' expectations and experiences of each agency.
3 *Critical events and problems*
   (a) Events and problems which respondents had experienced in their adult lives, with particular attention to the eighteen months prior to the initial approach to an agency. Respondents were asked systematically about the following topics: health, role changes, leisure and interaction, employment, housing, money, crises/emergencies, etc.
4 *Social networks and consulting*
   (a) Respondents' monthly social contacts, their context, and interconnections.
   (b) The persons, in order of preference, to whom respondents felt closest or most attached.
   (c) Whether respondents turned to or consulted anyone over the three critical events and problems which had most affected them (normally in the eighteen months period) and which were elicited in 3 above. Respondents were asked to whom they talked and turned, over these and their current marital difficulties. In the case of each person mentioned, respondents were asked why they had turned to them, what they had got from doing so, and whether these people had ever turned to *them* at any time.
   (d) Perceptions of social integration and isolation.
   (e) Attitudes to the disclosure of personal and marital problems.
   (f) Perceptions of the marriages of significant others.
5 *The marital relationship*
   (a) Attitudes towards marriage and divorce.
   (b) A brief description of their marital problems as they saw them. (Attention was paid to the ways in which these had changed over time.)
   (c) Amount of satisfaction and dissatisfaction with various areas impinging on the marital relationship: housework, child care, leisure, money, talk, affection, arguments, and sex.

6 *The media*

   (a) Respondents' interests in radio phone-in programmes, maga-
       zine, newspaper, and other media material concerned with
       sexuality and interpersonal relationships.

In practice the order of these topics was such that the interview
flowed remarkably well, with each subsequent section reached almost
spontaneously by the respondent. Overall, we felt that the interview
achieved considerable coherence for the respondents. Each interview
lasted some three hours or more and, in some cases, we were not able
to complete the interviews in one session. Second visits were, however,
almost always arranged within days of the first visits.

Altogether, between the period between November 1978 and June
1979, forty-eight interviews were carried out, with twenty-six wives
and twenty-two husbands. These included twenty couples where both
partners were interviewed, and a further eight marriages where it was
possible to interview one partner only, either because the other
partner was unwilling, or because he or she had left the household
and was unable or unwilling to be contacted. We did, however, interview both partners in two marriages where separation had already
taken place.

All the interviews were tape-recorded, which was beneficial for
several reasons. It freed the interviewer from strenuous note-taking
and enabled the interview to proceed naturally; it also allowed the
interviewers to concentrate on gesture and mien and to give their
individual attention to people who were disclosing very intimate kinds
of information and very personal feelings.

In addition to the material provided by the interviews, we have
made use of other sources of data. As we have mentioned, the
principal interviewer spent some time as an observer in various agency
settings. We have applied the insights we have gained through our
connections and our many encounters with workers, both in Marriage
Guidance and in other therapeutic settings. In addition, we examined
the records of the hospital unit and the referral letters of general practitioners who referred patients to it.

The interviewing

The field-work was conducted by three people, two women (the
present authors), both of whom are sociologists, and one man, a psychiatrist. We introduced ourselves to respondents as researchers,

and presented ourselves in an informal and neutral fashion, making it clear that we had no connections at all with their status as clients. Save in the instances where both partners were being interviewed simultaneously, there were two researchers present at each interview, one conducting the interview and the other observing, a method which proved extraordinarily useful.

Throughout the field-work we had imagined that we were conducting ourselves according to the text-book paradigm of interviewing, combining the necessary rapport for obtaining our respondents' co-operation with the requisite detachment for treating them as primarily a source of data.[3] While this was no doubt to some extent true, we now think that our own interviewing had other important ingredients. The problem concerning our interviews was the reverse of that which is usually described in the literature, where the interviewer is instructed in the importance of gaining rapport on the assumption that significant barriers to disclosure exist. Our respondents were people in crisis, and any questions we asked them almost inevitably provoked very painful feelings. Moreover, because they were in crisis they were only too ready to talk to someone who was uninvolved and was not unsympathetic. Thus our strategies as interviewers served to trigger respondents' responses rather than to overcome barriers to communication. Such a situation made it extremely important for us to stay with, and to see through, the discharge of our respondents' feelings arising from their efforts to describe their situations, and it was essential therefore to preclude the possibility of any embarrassment by either party. We were supported in this often difficult task by our own therapeutic experience, and by the knowledge that most of our respondents had recently become clients of 'counselling' agencies.

At times, and almost contrary to our expectations, the very presence of a second person seemed helpful, both to the respondent and to the interviewer, easing the intensity of the one-to-one interaction. The second researcher remained silent and retiring while the interview was under way and did not disturb the rapport, but at the same time his or her presence seemed to exert some kind of 'holding' balance or safeguard of the emotional boundaries, for both the interviewer and the respondent. It seemed to give courage to the interviewer to pursue areas which he or she might well have avoided as too awkward or sensitive, and to give reassurance that there was someone else to hand if necessary. To the respondents, it seemed to give permission to disclose as freely as they wished, and at the end of the interview they could turn to the second 'silent' researcher in a different vein, having discharged to the first what had been so strongly felt. Since these interviews were inevitably searching and deep, it was crucial for us to be able to promote and maintain a sense of balance and containment, and this arrangement proved most useful in this cause.

Interviewing people when they are in the midst of some kind of crisis in their lives presents special kinds of problems for research. For the interviewers it can be extremely stressful, and some therapeutic experiences and training (which we ourselves had in some measure) is undoubtedly invaluable in enabling the interviews to be conducted in a sensitive and yet relaxed way. It was clear that, especially for the men in the study, this kind of disclosure was either a totally new or a rare occurrence, and it was therefore important for the interviewers both to be, and to appear, neutral and confident, in order that they could facilitate and handle the situation. It is important to remember that almost half of our respondents were men. The fact that the typical respondent in much of this kind of research is female has perhaps tended to obscure some of the issues surrounding the methodology of interviewing. But in no way were people coerced into revealing anything they did not wish to reveal. Moreover, it was often the case that once people had overcome the initial barrier of agreeing to be interviewed, they proceeded very much under their own steam, and it was left to the interviewer to insert the key questions, at critical moments, without interrupting the flow of the respondent.

The second and most important issue concerns the respondent. Although the interview is not a one-sided affair and constitutes an exchange of interaction, its ultimate purpose is for the benefit of the researcher, and this has to be openly acknowledged to the respondent. However, at the same time it should be recognized that the interview can, for some respondents, have a cathartic effect. It enables them to express themselves in a relatively full and uninterrupted way to impartial and uninvolved outsiders, who are nonetheless genuinely interested and who give them their full attention for some considerable time.

The third problem for research on people in crisis, concerns the kinds of analysis imposed on the data. Attention must be paid to the frequently conflicting and ambivalent attitudes and feelings expressed by such respondents, and care must be taken in unravelling perceptions and in taking account of feelings. The recognition by the interviewers of the ambivalent nature of many attitudes and feelings is crucial to an understanding of marital problems. Moreover, it is useful for the interviewers to prompt respondents into describing their feelings and perceptions in relation to specific events and time periods. A particular sensitivity to the language used was also fruitful in interpretation and analysis.

In a later chapter (Chapter 11) we note that, to our surprise, a number of respondents mentioned the research interview as being the ideal situation for the disclosure of marital problems, and we shall consider there the ways in which it may have fulfilled some of respondents' conditions for full and optimal disclosure. In the present chapter we shall confine ourselves to some of the possible dangers for researchers in interviewing people in crisis. For it seems to us that our penetration into the clients' personal and social, worlds, our tacit invitation to open up to us in a situation where we had very defined limits of commitment, meant that we needed to be especially aware of our status as investigators and careful not to be drawn into the role of counsellor. Sometimes we were specifically asked for help or for our opinions. We always managed to stand firm and to explain clearly the boundaries of our positions; on occasion this was extremely difficult, and certainly we were at times affected by our refusal. We found it was important to end each interview with care, and indeed the structure of the schedule was such that it finished with a relatively non-emotive section to do with respondents' interest in the media. Moreover, having a second interviewer present as 'observer' proved valuable especially in the closure stage of the interview encounter. The second person was less likely to be drained and could step forward at such a point and lighten the proceedings. On the rare occasions where only one interviewer was present in respondents' homes and, at the end of the interview, the other spouse appeared, the situation was likely to be emotionally charged and somewhat difficult to handle.

The exploitative character of the research interview is probably inevitable, which makes the integrity of the interviewer that much more important. The receipt of confidences, divulged by people with such high degrees of trust, in the setting of their own homes, brings with it a weighty responsibility. It was therefore important that the rapport we established was governed by our being non-judgemental in approach, and fairly neutral, though sympathetic, in manner. We certainly tried in every way to keep our promise of confidentiality over the interviews; code letters were used on all the files, transcripts, and tapes, and, in the writing up we have changed not only respondents' names but also their occupations.[4] In some parts of the text of this book, because information given by respondents might make them more easily recognizable, we have not attributed the quotations from the interviews. In one or two cases we also erased certain sections of tape-recordings before they were transcribed.

The research benefits of this type of interviewing are immense and do not need to be emphasized. Such interviews can be an affecting experience, and we were sometimes deeply moved by the ways in which people strove to express, with such honesty, their inner feelings and to describe their personal worlds. But we do wish to emphasize the necessity for safeguards, since, in undertaking research interviews, people reveal and render themselves vulnerable. It is therefore crucial that researchers should handle the respondents and information they impart with respect and integrity.

The analysis

All the tape-recorded interviews were transcribed and typed up. This was extremely helpful to us in our modes of analysis, which were various. Our method of analysing involved the progressive formulation and reformulations of our analytic categories. Thus we started off with general hypotheses and gradually, as we developed new modes and categories for analysing our material, we generated more specific hypotheses. Because of the very small number of cases in any one category of our analysis we have not applied any statistical techniques to the data. Moreover, since our study group does not constitute a systematically derived sample of a defined population, it would have been pointless to attempt to make any *statistical inferences* or generalizations. By this we do not mean to suggest however that what we have found in relation to our study group has no general or wider implications.

The ways in which researchers make sense of long in-depth interviews, and the vast number of variables involved, need to take account of the considerable subtlety of the data. However, at the same time, the researchers must keep in view the totality which each interview provides, and the interconnections between the various components of the analysis. This latter possibility is indeed one of the great strengths of a small-scale study. The methods researchers adopt in this type of project, which involves dealing with very large amounts of qualitative data, are inevitably individualistic and somewhat makeshift. Just as numerically computed data are processed, so it is possible to deal with qualitative categories in quantitative ways. The fact that there are only relatively few tables in the book reflects the small size of the study group (which was in any case, again, split into husbands and wives) and not the nature of our material.

The process of developing analytic categories which made sense of our data was very time-consuming. The first stage of analysis involved listening to each interview in conjunction with the typed transcripts, in order to ensure a correspondence of meaning between the two. Detailed information and quotations were transcribed by hand on to large sheets and index cards, each of which related to a different component of our analysis. For example, on the 'events' sheets, we distinguished certain characteristics of events and problems (in terms of the material given to us by respondents concerning the context of events) from their emotional impact upon respondents, and any likely connections with an approach to an agency, the marriage, and so forth. We also had sheets on which we systematically noted all the data concerning social networks, and respondents' consulting behaviour in relation to particular events and difficulties which they had experienced. We also compiled sets of index cards on which we recorded respondents' comments concerning, for example, their pathways through the agencies, their attitudes to disclosure, and so on.

The second stage of analysis involved the development of particular categories and typologies which fitted each section of the data. Having developed a particular typology we tested it on different cases and tried to find a negative case (see Becker and Geer 1960). In this process the categories were gradually modified and refined. For example, in the analysis of respondents' social networks we translated the data into diagrams and various numerical measures, and developed a typology of three types of social network, which seemed to make some theoretical sense. With the events material, we tried to make systematic judgements in the spirit of the existing methodology (see Brown and Harris 1978) on the basis of a set of prior criteria relevant to our own project.

The second stage of the analysis was the most challenging. We developed fairly detailed and subtle categories from the various aspects of the data in which we were most interested, and we then began to examine the different components of our analysis in relation to one another. Although often difficult, it was a possible and meaningful exercise because, by then, we were so well-grounded in the interview material. Moreover, the connections that began to emerge made some theoretical sense in terms of our general impressions and initial hypotheses. As others who have done similar kinds of research have noted, the constant contact we had with our data, from collection to analysis, enabled us to be sensitive to the whole range of explanations within the data (see Oakley 1980).

The characteristics of the study group

We selected respondents on the basis of only two criteria: first, that they or their partners had approached or had been referred in connection with marital difficulties to specific agencies; and second, that they had but recently become clients of these agencies. We did not impose any restrictions about the legal status of respondents' marriages, and we included those who were separated, so long as the separation had only recently occurred. We shall now briefly outline some of the characteristics of our respondents.

The spread of the ages of our respondents at interview is broad; over two-thirds were aged between twenty-five and forty, with a further quarter who were older. On the basis of both husbands' and wives' occupations, three-quarters of the marriages may be regarded as middle class and one-quarter working class.[5] Non-manual occupations appear to be over-represented in our study group, that is if we compare estimates of it with the population of Marriage Guidance clients. However, in the National Marriage Guidance Council's estimates of the social class distribution of their clients, it should be noted that a fair proportion of them was not assigned to any socio-economic group.[6] Nevertheless, despite many of our respondents' apparent middle-class status, almost half of the husbands and wives in our study group had no formal educational qualifications beyond school-leaving examinations and only a handful had been to a university or had completed a professional training. A few of the husbands had had a technical training and some of the wives had done secretarial courses. The wives, however, had left school at a slightly older age than the men, and half of them had stayed on at school after the age of sixteen, compared with approximately only a quarter of the husbands. The fact that just under two-thirds (17/28) of our respondents were buying their own houses is also suggestive of a middle-class imbalance.

On the characteristics of respondents' marriages, we were interested to find that the distribution of ages at which respondents first married almost exactly corresponded with the national distribution.[7] Concerning differences in the ages of the partners in the couples, in only four marriages was there a very marked age gap. Contrary to expectation, there was a broad and even spread in the duration of respondents' marriages with no particular length of marriage being more vulnerable to problems than another. Moreover, and also contrary to expectation, life stage was not significant either. In fact the smallest proportion of respondents' marriages had a child under five; the remaining three-quarters were divided equally between those whose youngest child was of school age and those who had no children or whose children had all grown up.

The most noticeable feature of the marriages in our study was that a very high proportion of the couples had been married previously. In ten of the twenty-eight marriages one or both partners had been married before: in five both were previously married and in five only one partner was. Given the high incidence of second marriages in the study group we were surprised to find that there was so little mention of this, both in respondents' own accounts, and in their explanations why they approached agencies, or the manner in which problems were presented. In fact remarriage did not distinguish between help-seeking patterns at all; half of those in second marriages did not present at an agency with self-defined marital or sexual problems, and in two of the other five, the previously married partner did not initiate the approach to the marital agency.

There are only two further characteristics to which we should like to draw attention. The first concerns place of birth and upbringing: in six of the twenty-eight marriages, one partner had grown up either in a different culture or in a European country outside the British Isles. In some cases the respondents had come to Britain at marriage, and had experienced difficulties (such as learning the language) which appeared to have had some negative consequences for their marital relationships. The second characteristic is that a considerable number of our respondents (11/56) had lost, either by death or by separation, one or both parents by the age of fifteen. Moreover, a third of the study group had lost one or both parents, by death, by the time of interview which, as we shall show later, was likely to have had some effect upon the support available to respondents during their difficulties, and especially so where they had few other significant ties.

Notes

1 A study of a year's referral of nearly 1,200 cases to an area office of social services shows that just under one-quarter of these involved a client who was either married or had married parents (Mattinson and Sinclair 1979).

2 We excluded several potential respondents on the grounds that their marriages had broken up several years before.

3 Ann Oakley (1981) provides a critique of the text-book recipe for interviewing, in an account of her own experiences as an interviewer.

4 We selected new occupations which reflected the original ones in terms of the social class classification which we used (Registrar General).

5 Table 2(1) *Social class breakdown of the husbands and wives in our study.*

Registrar General classification	Husbands' occupations %	Wives' occupations %
Social classes I and II	13 ⎱ 75	4 ⎱ 76
Social class III non-manual	8 ⎰	12 ⎰
Social class III manual	5 ⎱ 25	— ⎱ 24
Social classes IV and V	2 ⎰	5 ⎰
Housewives	—	7

According to a manual/non-manual breakdown, therefore, three-quarters of our study group can be considered middle class and one-quarter working class. Taking both husbands' and wives' occupations into account together, it is interesting to note that husbands in manual and non-manual occupations almost always had wives in similar categories.

6 In a survey of Marriage Guidance clients, Heisler (1975) found that 38 per cent of men clients and 36 per cent of female clients had non-manual occupations (i.e. social classes I, II, III NM (Registrar General)) whilst 42 per cent and 14 per cent respectively had manual occupations, (III M, IV and V). However, a further 20 per cent could not be assigned, and likewise 10 per cent of female clients. (Moreover 40 per cent of female clients were housewives.) But, since wives were more likely to be clients, it is not clear from this analysis what effect this could have had on the class distribution if women clients had been assessed on their husbands' occupations.

7 In our study group, 31 per cent married (i.e. the first time) when they were under twenty, 46 per cent between the ages twenty and twenty-four and 23 per cent at twenty-five and over. This compares with 21 per cent, 49 per cent, and 30 per cent in the general population according to the Registrar General.

3

Attitudes to the disclosure of
personal and marital problems

It is our belief that, in order to make sense of the process by which people became clients in respect of marital problems, exploration must begin much further back, and for this reason we asked our respondents about their general orientations to the disclosure of personal and marital problems. It seemed to us crucial to have some awareness of how respondents felt in general about turning to others over such matters, since these basic attitudes would surely influence, and be reflected in, whether and how they chose to seek formal help.

The research literature on self-disclosure in general suggests that women are more likely to self-disclose than men (Jourard and Lasakow 1958; Cozby 1973). Although some of the evidence is contradictory it is perhaps indicative that no study showed men with higher disclosure scores than women (Cozby 1973). One study of disclosure between husbands and wives, principally concerned with the value-laden question whether disclosure strengthens or weakens the marital tie, revealed an association between high self-disclosure and the presence of marital satisfaction, though only with the revelation of positive feelings (Levinger and Senn 1967). Another study found no correlation at all (Shapiro and Swensen 1969). One might deduce from the evidence that attitudes and patterns of self-disclosure within marriage are to some extent shaped prior to it, and that they are a consequence of other factors, and not simply products of the quality of marital relationships. Predictably, the few studies which have investigated these questions have tended to focus on the wives' reports only (Rainwater, Coleman, and Handel 1959; Mayer 1967).

There is not much evidence in the literature on the disclosure of personal problems and even less on marital problems. Moreover, as Cozby (1973) emphasizes, disclosure behaviour has been studied often on the value premise that self-disclosure is something to be fostered and encouraged. Thus the need for people to have privacy and discretion, and the social forces which inhibit disclosure, have been somewhat disregarded and neglected as topics of enquiry.

A study by Mayer (1967) which investigated disclosure patterns concerning the marriage difficulties of a representative sample of middle-class and lower-class wives, found that husbands were the main recipients of communication, with friends and relatives constituting the rest. Mayer also found that lower-class wives talked most openly and frequently to relatives, with the middle-class wives being marginally more likely to talk to friends. Moreover, both Mayer's study and other larger-scale studies found that informal others were more widely consulted than all the agencies combined (Gurin, Veroff, and Feld 1960; Mayer 1967). Although such studies give little idea of the value and importance that their informants placed upon self-disclosure, they suggest that disclosure of fairly intimate matters is not uncommon, an impression which contrasts rather sharply with the evidence from studies of friendship. For example, Babchuck and Bates (1963) in a study of middle-class couples, found that close friends did not exchange intimate confidences despite contact over a period of years. The apparent discrepancy between these findings no doubt reflects the different foci of the studies: Babchuck and Bates (1963) explored the ritual patterns of everyday life, while Mayer questioned respondents about more profound and less commonplace dissatisfactions and frustrations. In a study of newly-weds, it is interesting to note that there appears to be no very great difference between husbands' and wives' expressed attitudes to the disclosure of hypothetical marital problems.[1]

Issues concerning disclosure patterns, behaviour, and resources will be discussed in later chapters in this book. In this chapter we propose to concentrate on the general orientations towards disclosure of our respondents, all of whom were experiencing marital and personal problems at the time of interview.

Orientations to disclosure

When we were investigating general orientations to disclosure among our own respondents, we tried to avoid what we felt was a common pitfall of most studies of clients: namely, the assumption that people always do turn to someone for help with problems, and if not to agencies, then most likely to family or friends. Accordingly, we posed general questions designed to elicit attitudes to disclosure, and we also asked respondents how they had felt and what, if anything, they had actually done in terms of turning to others, about a range of major, and usually adverse, events and problems which they had earlier told us had happened to them in their lives, including the current problems in their marriages. We hoped that the detailed contextual material might usefully augment and validate the wider attitudinal questions, and on the whole this proved to be the case. Thus, although respondents' overall orientations towards disclosure were principally derived from replies to the question 'What do you think about turning to others with (your) personal problems?', they were additionally substantiated by data from other parts of the interview schedule.

It soon became clear that there were two principal orientations among respondents, the first generally positive towards turning to others, the second predominantly reluctant or negative. Both sets of replies yielded interesting features in terms of the vocabularies respondents used to describe them. However, it must be emphasized that even those who were favourably disposed towards disclosing personal problems nevertheless expressed a variety of reservations concerning to whom, and under what circumstances, they would be prepared to do so.

Negative orientations

Just over a half of all our respondents held negative views, but it was very striking that the vast majority of the negatively orientated replies came from the men. Of the twenty-two men interviewed, eighteen can be categorized as having a negative attitude towards disclosure, whereas this attitude was found in only seven of our twenty-six women respondents. It thus seemed as if gender might be a strong influence.

Most of the men tended to couch their reasons for not disclosing their personal problems to others in normative and moral terms, expressing such beliefs 'One should not be a turner to people for help', 'Sort out your own problems', or 'Keep a stiff upper lip', 'Soldier on'. The strength of such a view was exemplified by Mr Hull (aged 41, a fitter) who said:

'I've never sought help at any time in my life. If *I* can't solve a problem then I can't see that anybody else can do anything for me. Now that is my attitude.'
'What about in general?'

'In general I wouldn't do it — I am of the old school — I believe if you can't solve your own problems then no one else can.'

Overall, the men's accounts of their attitudes and feelings about revealing private areas of the self to others suggest that, for many of them, non-disclosure constituted an unchanging, central, and even fervent part of their identities. Some of their accounts reveal a recognition of the importance of the role played by their early socialization in shaping these attitudes and practices.

Mr Rugby, aged 37, fitter:
'I was told from young: you stand on your own two feet, your problem's *your* problem. So get on with it sort of thing.'

Two men attributed their attitudes to having failed to 'get close' to their parents when they were young.

Mr Frome, aged 32, systems analyst:
'I personally find it very hard to go to anyone at all . . . I never felt close to either of my parents in that way, so I tend to keep it to myself. I certainly wouldn't discuss it with friends.'
'*What about personal problems?*'
'I would just keep it boxed up. I have very deep feelings but my feelings are mine and I don't want to share them, so they obviously led to problems.'

Mr Luton, aged 30, sales representative:
'I wouldn't talk to anybody. So we just learned from a very early age that anything that worries you is in there. You don't talk to people about them.'

In many cases men's comments were tempered by references to deep-seated feelings of being unable, unwilling, or not needing to communicate personal troubles to other people. Frequently these attitudes to self-disclosure seemed to be sanctioned and sustained by a sense of inner precariousness or insecurity about the possible consequences of their weaknesses and failings becoming known to others. Some men seemed to fear they might become, in Goffman's terms, stigmatized persons with 'undisclosed discrediting information' (Goffman 1968: 57) so that, for them, disclosure would risk serious loss of status, dignity or esteem. It is therefore not surprising that the central issues in self-management and self-presentation were: 'That of managing information about his failing. To display or not to display; to tell or not to tell; to let on or not to let on; to lie or not to lie;

and in each case, to whom, how, when and where' (Goffman 1968: 57). As Goffman points out, and as we ourselves came to recognize, this problem may be particularly acute for those whose marital problems were such that they 'had their effect chiefly upon intimates, frigidity, impotence and sterility being good examples' (1968: 72). The fear of disclosure in such instances would inevitably be very great because self-esteem would almost certainly be under threat.

It is interesting that among our own respondents, a dominant theme, particularly among those men who had problems connected with the sexual aspects of marriage, was that of the risk and embarrassment posed to their self-identities if they were to be disclosed. As one man remarked:

'Well . . . I suppose one doesn't like to admit that things aren't quite right. So I suppose one does with trepidation.'

In the following extract a man voiced his fear of losing face if his problem became known to others.

Mr Crewe, aged 31, sales clerk:
'I like to keep things to myself. Even though I'm aware people will listen, I couldn't tell them anything.'
'So in general what do you think about telling other people personal problems?'
'I can't . . . well . . . I don't mind telling them to completely neutral people.'
'But the thought of telling people you know . . . How do you feel about that?'
'Very embarrassed . . . I get the feeling it would reflect on me because they would then go and pass it on and even if they hadn't then I'd think they had and I would be walking around the office thinking "He knows about me . . .".'
'What about personal problems in general?'
'I couldn't tell hardly anybody any problems of mine.'

Misgivings about people's propensity to spread such knowledge and that they themselves would lose control over it, were expressed by several respondents.

Mr Ripon, aged 53, entertainer:
'I don't think I would (tell anyone) because generally they would tell someone and *they* would tell someone else — people do like to know things about other people.'

In so far as the men were disinclined to risk admitting to problems, they were also unlikely to define such matters as problematic. As one of the above quotations indicates, a problem may simply consist of something being 'not quite right', a somewhat diminished description of an objectively serious situation which helped make the problem more acceptable to the respondent in question. The comments of several other men suggest that for them problems could only be allowed to exist when solutions were available. There is an internal logic in the idea that a problem can only be so defined if a solution can be found, and which may at the same time act as a rationalization for not disclosing something which risks or threatens self-esteem.

Male respondents' perspectives on problem-solving were frequently couched in mechanistic terms. Mr York (aged 45, civil engineer) did not admit that any of his wife's complaints about their marriage presented problems for him. Throughout the interview he was unable to grasp the idea of an emotional or personal problem. He kept returning to a mechanistic model.

'Now personal problems involve cars breaking down, other trivia of that sort.'

Eventually after more than usual probing he admitted:

'The problems of the nature you are discussing are difficult to solve.'

Mr Ripon (aged 53, entertainer) said he would not like other people to know his problems and, as far as voluntarily disclosing personal problems to others was concerned, he was prepared to make only one concession:

'I don't think I'd mind asking if I wanted advice how to build a cupboard.'

The attitude was one which also found echoes in the views expressed by Mr Mold (aged 53, self-employed plumber) who quite unequivocally stated:

'I would go for advice if I wanted some mathematical problem worked out or if there was something I wanted in my car repaired or something like that . . . but I can't see really how − unless somebody is a genius − how they can sort somebody's marriage out in two or three easy lessons.'

One male respondent had begun to perceive the rational problem-solving approach as an unsatisfactory way of dealing with problems in his marriage.

> Mr Bath, aged 59, retired middle manager:
> 'I would apply . . . a statistical approach to it. In other words, was it the right thing to do and what the alternatives were and how they were likely to come out . . . and of course I unfortunately found you just can't apply it to human beings in the same way as you can apply it to a system.'

What seemed to be an extension of this kind of reluctance towards discussing problems was the fairly common attitude, amongst the men, that it was only worth discussing personal troubles if help could be given of a purely *practical* kind. Two working-class men subscribed to notions about the importance of material help, particularly in terms of the exchange of goods and services amongst kin. Moreover, they regarded kin as the only appropriate source of such help. But it was not only a male characteristic to emphasize the instrumental aspect of support, namely material help, and to question the expressive side. At least two women said that they did not see the point of telling friends about their personal troubles, but they were clearly frequently in the habit of doing so. However, those men who subscribed to the notion of keeping problems 'in the family', if only in terms of material help, were in practice unlikely to disclose very much to anyone at all.

> Mr Mold, aged 53, self-employed plumber:
> 'When it comes to family problems, the only people to work it out is family, I think, unless they are absolutely stupid . . . If I needed anything or [my brothers] needed anything — if they need financing or anything like that or if there was any trouble — I know they would help me.'

To people like Mr Mold who regarded material help as governed by the rules of reciprocity 'within the family', friendship was not seen as being bound by similar ties or obligations. Mr Wells (aged 39, small shopkeeper) likewise said he did not expect to turn to his friends with his troubles although, at one point in the past after his first marriage had broken up, he had been looked after by his friend's family. He regarded that instance as atypical, and justified their help in terms of acting 'like family'. On the whole he displayed a very cynical attitude towards friendship:

> 'You only know a friend in adversity and how often are people in that situation, when they can be seen for their true self . . . I don't have much trust in people's judgement because you've got to pay for it you know . . . You've got to make your own mind up about something.'

It seemed as if the men largely rejected the notion of family or friends as appropriate to turn to, for those of the men who did contemplate disclosure at all seemed on the whole to prefer a more impersonal setting: 'a little more distance, a little more anonymity'. Several cautiously referred to this as a possibility.

> Mr Crewe, aged 31, sales clerk:
> 'I don't mind telling them to completely neutral people, people who aren't associated with me.'

> Mr Dover, aged 28, computer operator:
> 'I prefer to talk to somebody who is neutral — who does not know too much about the situation. In that way I can be more honest, whereas with friends from the past I tend to cover things up, or tell them white lies, not the exact truth.'

These replies do not immediately suggest the idea of 'the luxury of an intimate disclosure to a stranger' (Eliot 1958: 29); they were more in the nature of a cautious consideration that, were disclosure to happen at all, one would be *more likely* to open up to a stranger. Nor, as the reader will discover in Chapters 9 and 10, was there unanimity of welcome for the notion of disclosure to professionals.

In general, however, it does seem fair to say that men gave accounts which led us to categorize many of them as having non-disclosing orientations and their own descriptions suggest various levels of explanation for their genesis. The major theme of their accounts seemed to concern the early internalization of ways of behaving which have been continually reinforced by normative pressures. One man suggested that the kind of society in which he had been brought up had been largely responsible for shaping his attitudes to disclosure.

> Mr Flint, aged 44, clerical worker:
> 'Because as I say it's been all in my upbringing as a kid and early life, that you keep problems to yourself and sort them out within the family if you can. This modern idea that there is a society that

can cure everything, help everything, is alien to the way I was brought up. There's a society for everything these days, Shelter, Amnesty, everything under the sun, which didn't exist when I was a young man. It wasn't there. The area I lived in was a very poor area and of course I lived my childhood through a war as well. You lived in your own close-knit community and sorted things out yourself and that's stuck with me.'

Positive orientations

We said earlier that the majority of women in our study (19/26) were positively orientated towards disclosing their personal problems to others. However, as if qualifying this overall positive approach, the evidence from both what they said and what they did shows that they discriminated carefully over the issues which they were prepared to disclose and the people whom they were disposed to tell:

Mrs Ripon, aged 40, shop assistant:
'You don't walk about with your heart on your sleeve . . . it depends how personal the problem is and . . . how close the person is you are telling it to.'

Mrs York, aged 34, a school teacher:
'I don't like people who have problems to talk about it too much. At school there are people who are always talking about their problems . . . I keep it to very close friends.'

In addition to the importance of the 'closeness' of the confidant, many women emphasized that it was important to choose with care, to select people whom they could trust and who would not gossip.

Mrs Bude, aged 30, secretary:
'As long as you don't talk to every Tom, Dick, and Harry and spill your heart out and tell people all your problems . . . then I think it's a good thing . . . if you turn to people that you know you can trust. But I wouldn't go telling everybody my problems that I felt would be relayed to everybody else.'

Most women in the study who had close female friends clearly preferred to confide in them. Only a small minority of women, all of whom were middle class, were disposed to confide at all in male friends. Those women who lacked friendship networks were more likely to disclose to husbands or to family members, although usually to a much more limited extent.

The comment made by Mrs Cowes (aged 22, housewife) illustrates what a number of women in the study also said:

> 'I think it's good to talk to friends. Not for them to sort it out for you but I find just to be able to talk to somebody makes you feel a lot better afterwards. But friends, I think it's good, if you've got close enough friends that are not going to spread all the details around.'

The importance of the selection of the right person was a constantly reiterated theme among the women. Mrs Ascot (aged 32, media consultant) put it this way:

> 'It's got to be the right people otherwise it's no help.'

Another issue which seemed relevant to respondents in deciding who would be helpful as a confidant concerned reciprocity. In Mrs Ascot's case, a very close friend of hers appeared to her to have an untroubled marriage. This she said made it difficult for her to confide in this particular friend over her marital problems, since it seemed to her unlikely that this friend would ever be in the situation of confiding over similar issues. She said:

> 'Yes, I think that between people who have close friendships there is a sort of defined limit to the bounds of which you can go. My friend Liz, for example, whom I miss a lot now, I think she is very happily married, and although she might tell me she has had a row with Bill it was always in the context of a very happy marriage and I didn't want her to know somehow that I wasn't so happily married. And I felt that if I told her anything about it, I would present it in the same way as a row within the context of a very happy marriage.'

The need for discrimination in the choice of a confidant, and the importance of being able to feel that the person had at least a sufficiency of life experience to render her cognisant of the respondent's own situation, was brought out by Mrs Tenby.

Mrs Tenby, aged 42, housewife:
> 'You must choose carefully − people who have a good knowledge of life. It's no good going to somebody who has no experience of life whatsoever, only from books . . . they are academically very good but in life they don't know any blasted thing.'

There is an assumption which was shared by several of the women that only those who had lived through a comparable, if not identical, experience could be helpful. The converse of this notion, noted and described by Timms and Blampied (1980) in their study as 'the projected inability to help', may well bedevil much formal and informal help-seeking.

A range of caveats about disclosing to others expressed by the women referred to reservations and fears that relationships might be damaged or people might be shocked. Another theme concerned the fear of external interference. One woman declared herself reluctant to confide in her extended kinship network in case they became over-involved and interfered in her affairs, as had happened in the past. In many other instances women said they were reluctant to confide in particular people, especially in parents, for fear of shocking, upsetting or overburdening them.

A common notion in women's vocabularies about disclosure concerned 'shielding', especially children and older members of the family, an aspect of confiding we shall be considering in more detail later in Chapter 7. This was particularly the case when the information or personal problem to be confided represented a threat in some way to the family, as a marriage problem often did. But it is striking that the women usually described the threat posed by the disclosure of such information in terms of its effects upon others and only rarely upon themselves. Mrs Epsom was generally in favour of disclosing personal problems but was at the same time concerned about over-burdening other people with her troubles. Her husband had walked out without warning and had never returned or subsequently communicated with her face to face.

Mrs Epsom, aged 48, executive director of small family business:
'Well, I think it'd be very helpful if you feel there is someone you can trust to turn to. I also feel it's a little bit selfish because I realize, looking back, what I was doing to my sister. That was one of the reasons I was glad I had a counsellor to go to. But it is good to have someone to talk to, I mean, now I can talk to her in a different frame of mind.'

Another dominant theme concerned a fear of being disloyal to their spouses which permeated *women's* attitudes about disclosing matters, particularly those connected with their marriages.

Mrs Ascot, aged 32, media consultant:
'I don't feel that most people can help. I think they can lend a sympathetic ear. But for a start, if I turned to a friend they couldn't hear both sides. Now that's why I quite like talking to Susan, because I know she likes Michael, and because she likes him I don't

feel I'm being disloyal to him, I wouldn't like anybody to sit and say "Oh! isn't he dreadful" and agree with everything!'

We see here a confidant who was chosen because she had a favourable rather than an unfavourable attitude towards the respondent's husband, and this choice was made in part to mitigate the disloyalty and unfairness Mrs Ascot felt she would be committing towards her husband by confiding her marital problems to her friend.

In the very few instances where women were *not* in favour of disclosing personal problems to others, it is perhaps significant that they rationalized their attitudes in terms of the deleterious effects such disclosures might have upon *others* and especially upon their husbands. It thus emerges that the attitudes and rationales of non-disclosing women had more in common with the attitudes of disclosing women than they did with those of non-disclosing men.

A non-disclosing wife commented:
'I feel it is admitting failure to tell people I've got a problem . . . I think that well, other people might be hurt if I start discussing things you know.'

The sexual problem in this respondent's marriage came to the attention of the general practitioner after she became ill with acute stomach pains and was referred to a hospital department for tests. She subsequently went back to her general practitioner for the result and was told that nothing organically wrong could be found. Eventually, under questioning from the general practitioner, this wife acknowledged a sexual difficulty in the marriage. She described to us why she had previously felt unable to disclose or even mention these problems to anyone:

'I think if I'd discussed our problems with any of my friends, I think Joe (husband) would have been very hurt. He had confidence in me not to tell anybody else and I wouldn't break that confidence . . . especially because *he* would feel a failure.'

This woman was in general a non-discloser and, like the women disclosers, she said she had been deterred from disclosing her problems by the fear of hurting *others*, and especially of being disloyal to her husband. Unlike men non-disclosers, she was apparently unconcerned with losing face or self-esteem. Even so, she indicated that she might herself have approached the doctor if things had become even more desperate. It is also worth noting that she had been married for less than two years when this happened which, in itself, may have effectively deterred her from disclosing or seeking help at the time.

Unlike the men in the study who couched their rationales against disclosing personal problems in terms of the deleterious effects upon themselves, when the women expressed reservations about disclosures they were invariably principally concerned with the impact upon others. We are not necessarily suggesting that women were unconcerned about the impact upon themselves, but our focus here is the *way* constraints upon disclosure were described and experienced by women respondents (where they were said or seen to reside). It seems to us to be the case that each gender described and experienced different sanctions against disclosure. Men indicated they were reluctant to disclose their personal problems because of *internal* constraints of self-identity and women because of *external* constraints of significant others. Since internal constraints arising from the processes of socialization are generally more effective than those associated with external agents of social control, it was not surprising, therefore, to find that men in the study were likely to be opposed to the disclosure of personal problems, both in principle and in practice, and that the women were in favour in principle although not always in practice.

This evidence, one explanation for which might be that the genders internalize different norms about disclosing personal problems prior to marriage, also suggests that husbands and wives differ in their *need* to disclose within marriage. Husbands generally said they did not feel a need to disclose in marriage, or could not bring themselves to do so; wives tended to see themselves as 'needing to confide' either because they felt it important to tell others how they felt about their problems, or sometimes because they felt a basic urge to release pent-up feelings.

Mrs Hythe, aged 25, typist:
'I find it easier to talk to somebody about (a problem) rather than just keeping it to myself. If I don't talk to anybody I just bundle up inside me and feel more upset and anxious.'

As we shall go on to show in Chapter 4, women were much more likely to say that they had recognized problems in their marriages early on, and also to have defined them as such. Many husbands simply did not experience their marriages as problematic for themselves. By denying the existence of problems, or by avoiding the subject altogether when confronted with their wives' dissatisfaction, husbands effectively prevented the marriages from becoming subjects for debate. The frustration of such a stalemate situation is likely to have added to their wives' feelings of stress and desperation, and further increased their need to confide in others.

Mrs Leeds, aged 32, unemployed library assistant, admitted:
'(It was) something I started doing in desperation . . . if somebody was prepared to listen it let the pressure off.'

Although it can be argued that talking to others may be a characteristic way of coping with personal problems for many women, it must also be emphasized that, far from freely disclosing their problems to others, the women required certain conditions to be fulfilled before doing so. They were also fearful of gossip, a risk which they tried to minimize by selecting the right person in whom to confide. They stressed the importance of assessing the seriousness and gravity of the problem on the one hand, and the degree of their desperation on the other. In contrast, the men tended to be concerned with the issue of whether or not a matter might be said to constitute a problem in the first place.

The following comments made by Mrs Rugby illustrate the fine balance between a number of constraints which she saw as impinging upon her; on the one hand, the societal norms which favour loyalty within marriage and, on the other, her own feelings of desperation and the consequent need to disclose problems in her marriage to women friends, especially to those who had been through similar experiences. Mrs Rugby had recently taken out a court injunction against her husband for violence.

Mrs Rugby, aged 40, school and play-group worker:
'If I've got a problem that I mustn't tell anybody, I'll talk to my friend type of thing, but I mustn't talk to anybody else because, well, it's not on. And I think if they did, you know, people wouldn't need to go to the doctor and take pills. People seem to bottle their things up don't they? They're not so friendly. They don't want to talk to people . . . If you feel that desperate, then go and talk to somebody. I'm the sort of person that will do, if I'm depressed, I will still talk.'

In suggesting, therefore, that women reveal their troubles to others, especially to friends, it is important not to overlook the extent to which they also feel constrained by the fear of gossip, by the value society places on presenting an image of marital bliss to the outside world and on preserving the confidences of the inner sanctum of marriage. It seems that the majority of the women in our study, unlike the majority of the men, did not subscribe to or to abide by the dictum of 'keeping one's problems to oneself'. In spite of these very different disclosure orientations, it seems that in our society the above dictum is a laudable goal and is associated with a certain kind of moral superiority and constitutes part of widely held beliefs. Nowhere is it likely to have greater potency than in the privatized and exclusive area of a monogamous relationship which is bound and constrained by ties of sexual loyalty. Mrs Ascot (aged 32, media consultant) painted a middle-class picture of the pressure to appear to have a successful marriage in the eyes of the world, and even to one's friends. She said:

'We live in an artificial age where we all have to pretend we're so ecstatically happy. There are all these books and things. Everything in society is somehow geared to successful people and I'm sure most of the people in the world or in this society aren't nearly as successful as they pretend to be. But somehow we are conditioned to present this veneer of everything being under control and smooth. There's a stigma to saying there are things going wrong and I feel it's a terrible problem . . . There are some people for example, if you've had a row and things are pretty bleak between you, there are some people who knock on your door and you immediately pretend you haven't had a row. And then you start making the coffee and doing the right bit. There is sometimes an atmosphere that people can sense but we are very good at playing those kind of games.'

If we sum up our argument in this chapter, it is that men and women both experience constraints in marriage against the disclosure of marital and personal problems. However, those constraints are differently felt and expressed, and are reproduced in very different orientations and attitudes towards disclosure. This is not surprising since, as we shall go on to suggest in later chapters, both the ways in which men and women experienced marriage and the ways in which they related to significant others, to agencies, and to the wider society, differed significantly. Moreover, respondents themselves did not refer to these marked gender differences in disclosure orientations, which strongly suggests that the distinction is a 'taken for granted' one.

Notes

1 In a study of young newly-weds, interviewed three months after marriage (undertaken at the Marriage Research Centre, Central Middlesex Hospital) it was found that 19 per cent of the wives and 16 per cent of the husbands said that if they were ever to have any marital problems they would not turn to anyone at all.

4

Marital problems: the ways they were defined and attributed

In this chapter we are concerned with how husbands and wives made sense of the difficulties they encountered in their marriages. Our contention is that the ways in which the partners in the marriage accommodated (or failed to accommodate) to marriage troubles are related to the processes by which they constructed accounts and made attributions of their problems. These interpretations and attributions were, as we shall see, subject to transformations which were gradual and subtle and in some instances considerable. The ways in which individuals reacted to changes in their marriages, whether or not they themselves were instrumental in bringing those changes about, may be usefully viewed therefore as developmental processes, with each change posing new problems or challenges which generated a search for new interpretations and definitions of the situation.

We propose to set this discussion in the context of one way in which the marital relationship may be usefully understood in theoretical terms. Our point of departure is that the experience of being married is differentiated by gender and that this affects the relationships of men and women in marriage and whether and how they define their relationships as problematic. Bell and Newby's (1976) theoretical discussion of the marital relationship in terms of the 'deferential dialectic' is germane to our discussion.

A central theme of a recent commentary on marriage in Britain (Dominian 1980a) is that a marked diminution of the exercise of authority by the husband over the wife has taken place in this century. However, we would argue that the writers who concur with this view have failed to recognize the subtle and covert ways in which structures of power are maintained and managed. Bell and Newby (1976) have made a perceptive analysis of what might be described as 'the couple ideology' – the growing normative emphasis and paramountcy of the psychological and social needs of the couple — in terms of the concept of deference.

Central to their concept of deference are relational and normative elements. The relational element concerns both the person who defers and the person who is deferred to, and applies particularly to situations in which traditional forms of authority are exercised. The normative element refers to the way in which the power of superordinate and subordinate parties of the deferential relationship are legitimated. Bell and Newby (1976) further note that deference is the most *stable* form of legitimation of authority. However, the process by which a husband's legitimated authority prevails over the wife is seen by Bell and Newby as essentially dialectical and consists of two opposing elements, differentiation and identification. They suggest that the norms of the marital relationship have changed considerably, with greater emphasis being placed today upon the 'affective identification' of the couple, whereby the spouses perceive their partnership as a cooperative enterprise and not as a relationship between *morally* subordinate or superordinate individuals. Nevertheless significant areas of activity and responsibility, both inside and outside the domestic sphere, continue to be differentiated hierarchically according to gender, except perhaps in a very small minority of dual career professional families (Rapoport and Rapoport 1976), and as a consequence of this the greater power of husbands remains relatively undisturbed (Stacey and Price 1981).

Key areas of power in the marital relationship have traditionally been, and still remain, economic resources and sexuality. The home, security, the family's standard of living are still largely organized around the husband as breadwinner. Wives' income from employment may be increasingly important to family income in our present society but there is very little evidence to suggest that women are catching up with men in gaining equal and similar opportunities and rewards in the labour market (Hakim 1979). Housewifery and caring for children, still largely the responsibility of women, are economically invisible and remain undervalued areas of activity, and the fact that few men have moved into these areas of responsibility in any major way may be significant (Oakley 1974). It is currently widely argued that women have acquired equal *rights* with men, at least in legal terms, and especially in relation to divorce legislation. However, as Brophy and Smart (1981) point out, this argument takes no account of the wider economic structures which impose dependency upon women. Thus they argue that, although some legislation has improved the position of women as wives and mothers, where divorce is concerned 'legislation has failed to contribute in a material sense to the economic viability of the mother/child unit outside of a family structure; whilst celebrating motherhood the law has retained the economic dependency of the mother on either a "wage-earner" or the state' (Brophy and Smart 1981: 12).[1]

In the sexual sphere it is true that certain changes have taken place in the twentieth century in the mores which govern women's sexuality. The most notable change has been the recruitment of women into *active* participation in heterosexuality (Campbell 1980). The enjoyment of sex within marriage has increasingly come to be defined as a right of wives as well as husbands, and the notion that sex is a duty that wives perform for their husbands has become unfashionable. But, as Campbell (1980) emphasizes, women's sexuality has continued to be regarded as inherently problematic. Moreover, the solution to what is still commonly seen as the problem of women's passivity and unresponsiveness ('frigidity') has been defined as requiring greater resourcefulness and virtuosity on the part of men, or at least this is the stance taken in many sex manuals. However, in spite of a shift in emphasis concerning sexual manners, which can be detected in some of the current popular literature on sex, the male orgasm continues to be depicted as the centre and 'pinnacle' of sexual action between men and women. As Campbell has noted, 'the quintessential moment of heterosexuality remained penetration, the Sexual Act' (Campbell 1980: 11). So, in the sexual sphere (as in the economic) the marital experience remains dissimilar for men and women, with the emphasis still very much on the rewards to be gained by men.

Returning now to the question how partners define difficulties in their marriages we wish to emphasize two points. First, these definitions arise within a relationship that is historically embedded in a system of power which significantly discriminates against women both inside marriage and in the wider society. Second, the inequality between husbands and wives is largely stabilized by the deference of one partner (the wife) to the other (the husband).

It is therefore very interesting to consider how far this deferential relationship between husband and wife is called into question when the marriage runs into difficulties, or is for some reason required to undergo a major change. We hope to be able to throw some light on this larger question in the course of examining how husbands and wives defined their marital difficulties and to what they attributed them. First we shall consider the patterns of attributing blame between the partners with regard to their difficulties. Second, we shall examine the areas of relationships which each partner regarded as problematic. In both cases these perceptions usually refer to the time at which an agency was approached. Third, we shall examine respondents' accounts of how they made sense of their difficulties in the past, and how they accommodated to their marriages. Fourth, we shall show how these accounts were transformed over time as respondents' situations changed and their marriages came to be defined as problematic.

Patterns of blaming between the partners: who blamed whom for the problems

The notion of one or both partners being to blame was present in most accounts of marital difficulties given by respondents. It has been possible to distinguish three typical patterns of ascribing blame between the partners. During the interviews themselves, we were particularly attuned to the evidence indicating that respondents' definitions of their situations had changed over time. We were also careful to take note of any recent involvements they had had with agencies which could have influenced their perceptions of their problems. We have tried here to delineate the 'state of blaming' between the partners at the point where the first contact with the agency was made (usually by one partner, the wife) and to exclude as much as possible from this analysis any subsequent influence which contact with the agency might have had upon respondents' perceptions or the ascription of blame for the marital difficulties.

The most striking feature of the attribution of blame is that there were no marriages in our study in which both partners apportioned blame equally to each other, with each accepting a similar share, and this seemed true both before and after the initial intervention of agencies. There were three definable patterns of blaming. The most common pattern consisted of husband and wives each putting the blame on to the other partner, which we call a pattern of conflict. This pattern was found in five of the twenty couples interviewed, and in five of the eight marriages where only one partner was interviewed.

The second most common pattern was one of concordance, with one partner putting the blame on to the other and the other partner accepting the blame. (This happened in seven marriages.) The pattern of concordance, with the husband blaming the wife and the wife blaming herself, was notably more frequent than the converse.

Moreover, even where the husband had come to attribute blame to himself at the point where an approach to an agency was made, we noted further evidence of the same deferential pattern: for example, husbands presenting at their doctors with sexual impotence appeared often in the past to have blamed their wives for this condition, and several wives stated that sometimes *they* had felt themselves responsible.

The third pattern concerns the situation where the wife tried to blame the husband and the husband had either ignored the wife's complaints, or had denied the legitimacy of the wife's definition of a problem. (Here there were six marriages in all.) These different patterns of attributing blame will be illustrated in the next section where we shall give the reader some idea of the areas in the marriages which respondents said had caused the problems and for whom.

Areas in the marriage perceived as problematic

Two of the most problematic areas of marriage in our study concerned sexual activity on the one hand and communication and demonstrativeness on the other. Husbands and wives were almost equally likely to mention sex as constituting a significant difficulty (although there were some important and subtle differences in emphasis). Moreover, even where respondents did not mention specific sexual difficulties as part of their problems, it seemed likely that there were difficulties. Sexual activity appeared to be infrequent for most couples in the study, a situation with which many respondents were clearly unhappy. Women emphasized lack of communication and demonstrativeness more than problems in sexual activity *per se*, although not surprisingly sexual difficulties were almost always implicated in the problem. It was significantly wives and not husbands who complained about the spouse's lack of communication and demonstrativeness.

'When would you say you first noticed this?'

Mrs Luton, aged 28, secretary:
[Pause.] 'I think it's always been there. It's just a question of when you're first going out, there are things that mask it . . . when we first went out we were always out with people and at clubs and parties and all the rest of it . . . To find out that I was married to somebody who wouldn't open themselves out at all came as a shock, whereas I am naturally . . . basically I'm demonstrative and my

parents have always shown affection to each other and to me openly. He's never received much affection or given much affection . . . or spoken to people openly. That *did* come as a shock. I think that was the main problem because I think the others have stemmed from that.'

Mr Luton's side of the story corroborated this. He had come to acknowledge the existence of problems in his marriage only as a consequence of his wife's actions. She had gone to the doctor with a relatively minor complaint. The general practitioner previously (and unsuccessfully) had questioned the husband about the marriage, and he took up the matter with the wife when she next came to see him. She admitted to considerable dissatisfaction with the relationship and agreed, at the doctor's suggestion, to persuade her husband to go with her to a marital therapist.

Mr Luton, aged 30, sales representative:
'Communication that's our biggest problem, not being able to sit and talk . . . It's times when we'll be sitting here and we'll have some music and we may be drinking . . . It's a lovely feeling to feel total unity but when the subject of personal feelings and emotions comes into it, it starts to go to pot. It's not been so bad recently because she asks me a question and I try to answer it truthfully.'
'When do you think you first noticed the lack of communication?'
'I suppose I didn't really notice it until she told me about it. I mean it's not something one really notices.'

Returning to the significance of the sexual arena in marital problems, it seems to us more likely that complaints about sexual activity constitute part of a *hidden* agenda for wives in their communications with their husbands. For one woman the expression of feelings to her husband about issues other than sexual assumed a disproportionate significance.

'Well if I was upset about other things, other than sexual things, which were very close to me, very intimate — so I didn't, I was inhibited, I didn't give out. But *other* things, yes I would show my feelings which I thought was *right*. So that he would know and understand me and maybe react differently in the future. But it didn't seem to help.'

Wives in our study were more likely than husbands to have defined their marriages as problematic. There were six marriages where husbands had successfully denied the existence of problems or had avoided any confrontation over them. Wives were also more likely than husbands to blame their partners' personalities and behaviour in areas other than the sexual, whereas the husbands tended to focus on sex. We will show how these findings relate well to Bell and Newby's notion of deference (Bell and Newby 1976).

Earlier we suggested that the economic and the sexual are key arenas where husbands are most dominant. The following case of Mrs Tenby suggests the extent to which women in general become economically dependent when they give up their jobs to have children. For Mrs Tenby the power of the purse became the major issue in her marriage. She was born and brought up in a foreign country. She married an Englishman with a secure professional career, gave up her own interesting job, and they came to live in England in a stockbroker belt just outside London. She lived a particularly lonely and isolated life as a housewife, with few friends and no kin. In addition, she had some language difficulties and lacked a car in a neighbourhood which had no public transport, and where most households had two cars. But most importantly, she lacked control over and access to money. At the time of the interview her older child had started school and her younger one was at a nursery school. When we interviewed her she was beginning to consider the possibility of finding a job and of making a new life as a single parent.

Mrs Tenby, aged 42, housewife:
'My husband is somebody who wants to keep everything under his control which you cannot do with an adult woman. So everything I have to ask first, everything. I have to ask for money and I have to do it in a very polite way. I must say "Please can you give me some money?" And if I don't say "please" I don't get it, and this sort of thing. I will accept that I've always been afraid of my husband in a way but that is finished now.'
'How do you mean afraid?'
'Well when I came here I was a very independent woman, afraid of nobody. I came here and completely collapsed . . . it was my downfall. I was nervous. I got afraid of my husband. He treated me as a mere nothing. But now I got out of it . . . and now I am not afraid of anybody.'

Complaints by wives about their husbands in the sexual sphere were not usually as overtly stated as was Mrs Tenby's complaint about her husband's control over economic resources. Significantly, for some women the uncertainty about whether or not *they* really had a sexual problem, and thus the discovery of where the explanation for this problem might lie, in fact constituted part of the problem.

> 'I think there has always been a sexual problem but I hadn't known about it until I had this affair.'
> *'When you say a sexual problem could you say a bit more?'*
> 'Yes, my husband does nothing for me sexually. He doesn't turn me on at all.'
> *'Did you have sexual intercourse?'*
> 'Oh! yes, all the time. We had a regular sexual relationship and he was always apparently satisfied but I didn't know what it was to feel it, you see. I didn't know what it was to enjoy it really. I just used to make sure that he was always happy because I didn't want him to go anywhere else and I didn't know that *I* was supposed to enjoy it.'

Men's sexual problems fell into two groups: in some cases problems arose from their own 'impotence' and, in others, husbands spoke of problems stemming from their wives' unresponsiveness. For those men who defined their impotence as problematic and had approached an agency, usually a doctor, they regarded it as an unavoidable breakdown in functioning. This makes sense, in that none of these men consciously wished to be impotent and had taken steps to put it right. However, others with the same problem had not defined their impotence as problematic at all, and therefore did not consider it legitimate for their wives to do so. In these cases impotence usually came to be recognized as a problem for the marriage only *after* the intervention of a general practitioner who was already treating one of the partners for something else. In one rather remarkable instance, the husband had been impotent for the entire duration of the marriage, which had lasted four years. Throughout that time the wife had been treated both by a hospital psychiatrist and a general practitioner for repeated overdoses and depression. Just before we interviewed these partners, it appeared that a *locum* general practitioner, with a fresh viewpoint, had made a new assessment of the problem and had suggested to their own doctor that he refer both the husband and wife to a Marriage Guidance Council, since he saw the problems as going beyond the psychological problems of the wife.

Throughout the interview this particular husband made frequent and graphic reference to his wife's depression as being the sole problem in their marriage. But towards the end of the interview (and after a direct question), he acknowledged his own sexual difficulty. He commented:

> 'We don't have intercourse at all. Now that doesn't worry us really. It doesn't worry me because I think sex is vastly overrated and it's not on my list of, you know, desirable things in life.'

The wife's side of the story was rather different:

> *'Was this your reluctance or his reluctance to have sex?'*
> 'Well, I think he partly knew [about his impotence] before we got married and was covering up and blaming my illness for it. So consequently I was making myself ill and taking overdoses and to me that was what it was all about, that it was my fault.'
> *'And when was that?'*
> 'Well we got married in the June and then I went to the GP and then I was under the psychiatrist more or less straight away.'
> *'When did you begin to see the lack of sex as a problem, how long after the marriage was that?'*
> 'Well it was more or less straight away but I said nothing. I sort of . . . It was making me all sort of tense and nervous. Eventually the GP sent me to a psychiatrist but of course he kept saying "If you are a psychiatric patient, you *get* all tense and nervous." He sort of blamed me entirely, but then they realized I was calmed down and was back to normal and was all right, having been treated. Then he realized that—[husband] was covering up all the time and I was much better then.'

We recognize that this marriage had unusual and deeply complex features we have referred to it here because we think it illustrates several points worth emphasizing. First, it suggests the way the problem, itself chameleon-like, is tossed to and fro between the couple and adapts to each new coloration. Second, it indicates the imbalance of power between the sexes, and the role that agencies may unwittingly play in reinforcing that imbalance. Third, it demonstrates how each of the partners in the dyad may take upon him or herself either of the two poles of avoidance and depression which, according to Parkes (1971: 10) are 'two main alternatives to the acceptance of reality'. It is obvious that these two alternatives are antithetical; the main component of depression is passivity and powerlessness (Brown and Harris 1978) whilst the practice of avoidance requires the individual actively to exert power and control. We believe that the association (in the above example and in similar cases in our study) of the wife with depression and the husband with avoidance, has a wider significance, and that it is structured and mediated by gender. Others have observed similar patterns, with Lieberman and Hyde for example suggesting that wives 'seek an outlet to an unhappy marriage through the development of neurotic symptoms while equally dissatisfied husbands fail to develop similar pathological symptoms' (Lieberman and Hyde: unpublished).

In general, in our study women were much more openly self-blaming towards their own sexual unresponsiveness than husbands were towards their sexual difficulties. Furthermore, men were rather more deprecatory about their wives where they were sexually unresponsive than they were about their own lack of sexual inclination. This, we would suggest, is because there has been a strong normative emphasis, until recently enshrined in the marriage service itself, on the duty of women to submit themselves sexually to their husbands, and on the husband's right to expect them to do so. Although these beliefs are perhaps not at the forefront of respondents' current attitudes towards sex within marriage, their earlier socialization is nevertheless likely to have been greatly shaped by such traditional beliefs. Indeed many women, especially those married to manual workers, still appear to regard sex as a marital duty.[2] The views expressed below by one young wife suggest the centrality of sex within her marriage, the 'price' as it were, that she expected to pay for her husband's love, regardless of the fact that she herself did not find sex pleasurable. Her comments suggest that the importance she placed upon sex was determined by its exchange value within the marital relationship and not by her own set of beliefs. This of course reflects the historical pattern. The sexual and property rights of husbands over their wives have been at the heart of monogamy in our patriarchal society; women thereby became dependants of their husbands and were granted in return protection and security, which in practice may not have amounted to much.

'Any sexual problems or difficulties?'
'I don't know if we've got a sexual difficulty or not. Everybody seems to think we do. The psychiatrist I saw turned round and said I've got a guilt complex, because I've never been satisfied with sex, never had an orgasm or anything . . . It has been a problem because it's got to the stage where my attitude was that I had to make an appointment with my husband because he didn't seem to be that interested . . . I used to think that sex was love. I've always thought

that. If a bloke was making love to you, he had to love you. I thought, well, my husband couldn't have loved me that much because he wasn't making love to me any more.'

We have stated that women were much more likely to blame themselves for sexual difficulties in their marriages, even when their husbands seemed to be the ones who had the main difficulties. (The converse situation of husbands blaming themselves or taking initial responsibility for wives' sexual difficulties is significantly absent.) The following self-deprecating comment by a wife illustrates this finding:

> 'We haven't got a sex life at all . . . he doesn't appear to be able to get an erection, but I don't think it's a medical condition . . . I think it's a mental condition . . . I think the problem is not physical with him and that the cause of the problem is *me*. Because I was so critical of him when he did try "That's not right!" "This hurts!" I didn't realize, being stupid, that you just don't do that. There are so many things that you learn after the event. If only someone had said. Only how can anyone say, because no one knows anyway.'

The readiness of women to take the blame upon themselves when things go wrong in marriage, is reinforced by popular mythology. That a husband's impotence is somehow automatically the wife's fault, for example, is a common enough joke amongst men in our culture.[3] One man in our study put it this way:

> 'You always have some sort of a sexual problem with a woman don't you? [Laugh.] Unless you get married to an extra-sexy girl.'

Another husband in our study sent his wife to the family planning clinic to check whether her intrauterine device was interfering with and diminishing his sexual performance, even though he had previously experienced identical sexual difficulties after his first marriage had broken up. In spite of the clinic's assurances that the coil could not produce these effects, the husband sent his wife back to the clinic.

> '*And when you went back the second time, did you still feel it was the coil that was causing the trouble?*'
> 'Yes, because it was. Because Tom [husband] said he could still sort of feel the coil there anyway. *Now*, I don't think so. But after I had it done [the string shortened] the second time, I did. Before he went to his own doctor I thought there was more in it than he had actually told me as well . . . and then he went to the doctor, I thought it must be more than the coil anyway for Tom to go to the

doctor . . . because usually he would sort of leave it. So I knew it
was more serious than what I thought it was.'

On the basis of our assessment of the separate interviews conducted
with the partners in this marriage, we concluded that the husband's
strategy of blaming his wife's coil had served to deflect attention on to
his wife and away from his own hidden extra-marital activities which,
as it later emerged, he suspected might have caused the problem to
occur and about which he had very mixed feelings.

   This brings us to another theme, that of conflict in blaming. In ten
marriages[4] each partner attributed all the blame to the other and frequently stressed difficulties in the partner's personality. However,
there were markedly different outcomes to this process in terms of
which partner sought help. Wives were much more likely than husbands to approach agencies, both for marital and for individual problems. In practice, therefore, women often bore the responsibility for
marital problems either in the sense that it was frequently they who
sought outside help, or in the sense that they accepted at a cognitive
level the definition of the problem in terms of themselves as
individuals (or in both these senses). In between a third and a half of
the marriages (11/28) in our study, a re-definition in marital terms of
the initial presenting problem was made by an agency, usually a
general practitioner. Moreover, in these cases there is evidence of
negotiation between the partners over the definition of problems. The
theme of husbands attributing the problem to the wife in terms of her
depression, for example, is set in the context of a dynamic process of
negotiation between the partners. However, the balance is tipped
towards the husband in a way which suggests some underlying structural bias. As we have already suggested, women were more likely
than men to attribute blame to themselves, even in the absence of a
blaming other. Thus where women were not exposed to pressure from
their husbands, they were often subject to their own socialization,
which had led them to see themselves as more or less subordinate.
There are, therefore, elements of complementarity and tension here
between the two social processes of social control and socialization,
with one sometimes reinforcing the other.

   We have already mentioned the husband who, together with the
reinforcement of medical agencies, had successfully deflected attention away from problems within their sexual relationship on to his
wife's depression. In another marriage, a crisis provoked by the
revelation of the husband's long-term friendship with a woman

threatened its stability. This husband indicated the way in which he had previously viewed the relationship with his wife.

'Did you have any awareness of a problem between you?'
'No, not as serious as it developed to be. I thought it was just a phase *she* was going through and that she would get out of it. I thought it was just post-natal depression.'

In a further example, the husband, after a year of illness and misfortune, both in his own and his wife's family, eventually tried to end his life. His wife had had bouts of severe depression throughout their relationship and also in the preceding year and he focused on this.

'And have you been able, or wanted to discuss your relationship with anybody?'
'Well, I have recently, November or thereabouts. [*After* the suicide attempt.] Well, yes. I didn't know or realize there is anything wrong with *my* side of things, you know, because I thought it was all *her* depression.'
'And so before that you hadn't actually talked about it in terms of both of you to anybody?'
'No, if I had talked about it, it was in terms of her only.'

In talking about how he had earlier rejected his wife's advice to go to the doctor, just before his suicide attempt, he described his state of mind at the time.

'How did you feel? Reluctant or the feeling that the GP wouldn't have anything useful to say?'
'I think it was *me*, because it was quite easy for me to think that really. I wanted to, because Ann [wife] had had one or two psychiatric problems in the past and I suppose quite honestly the easiest thing was to blame her for it, not entirely fair, but that is probably what happened.'

He went on to describe what had happened after his admission to hospital.

'We realized that we had some sort of problem . . . the doctor in the hospital was obstructive and said it was completely irrelevant to consider my wife in the matter. And though I agreed that I may well have individual problems and so may she, nevertheless they must interrelate to some extent. He was completely arrogant and unhelpful about it . . . and so I said that we could deal with it by ourselves and so we went to the GP.'

The general practitioner subsequently referred them to a marital agency which was actually within the same hospital and both partners received marital therapy. In each of the above cases it was made clear that the marriages had been poor for a number of years in terms of communication and expression of feelings, but it was the wives who were more likely to acknowledge this and who tended to complain.

In this section we have examined the areas in which husbands and wives located their problems, and the dynamics of the attribution process in terms of who blamed whom (at the point when help was sought from an agency). We wish to argue that any consideration of the processes of problem definition must take particular account of gender, and that there is a socially structured bias which on balance appears to favour the position of husbands in these processes. At the beginning of this chapter, we suggested that the key arenas which exemplify the power division between the partners in marriage are the sexual and the economic. Although we found a number of instances where marital conflict was being acted out in the economic arena, the sexual arena assumed greater importance for both husbands and wives in our study. Since there were fewer working-class than middle-class respondents in our study[5] it is possible that money was less of a problem. However, it was clear from one middle-class couple we have quoted, that patterns of money management within marriage were likely to affect the economic power of wives.

We have illustrated some of the uncertainty which shrouds the sexual arena for wives, noting women's greater tendency (in comparison with men in the study) to blame themselves for sexual difficulties, and the lesser importance they seemed to place upon their own sexual satisfaction compared with greater emphasis upon their husbands'. We noted earlier a general trend towards a more active participation by women in heterosexuality. But, in so far as men have been historically dominant in heterosexual relationships in our society and culture, this trend has by definition taken place under the auspices of men's legitimation and their continuing dominance in the economic sphere. Sexual behaviour combines both real and symbolic aspects of marriage, so that it is therefore not unexpected to find sex as a central focus of respondents' vocabularies about their marriages (although not always fully articulated). We also noted the emergence of another theme in our data, namely the relatively greater power of husbands in deflecting 'the problem', however defined, to the wife, with the result that it was she who was most likely to seek help. Moreover, in a number of cases, the definition of the problem in terms of the wife's depression was a strategy that perpetuated a state of play which favoured the husband and this especially so when it was additionally reinforced by agencies.

Making sense of problematic marital experiences in the past

In a later chapter we shall be suggesting that critical events and problems influenced when and how respondents defined their marriages as problematic and that, alternatively, they may also have constituted part of the difficulties themselves, or the background against which these difficulties occurred. There are, however, insuperable problems endemic in a retrospective study in distinguishing the impact made by events at the time they happened from the way people eventually came to regard them. Nonetheless, people's accounts and interpretive frameworks, if read and scrutinized with care, can and do provide some important insights into the processes whereby people initiate and accommodate to change. Respondents' interpretations often revealed subtle shifts of meaning over time of which they themselves appeared only rarely to have been fully aware. The gradual and subtle nature of the transformation of the meaning of events and situations over time reveals the way in which the tension between continuity and change was 'managed' at the level of individual consciousness, in order that an individual might avoid the discomfort of confronting disjunctures and contradictions. Thus, in our study, respondents often 'reasonably' explained, or explained away, marital 'hiccups' that had occurred in the past. However, at the same time, because by then their marriages had been defined as problematic, they felt constrained to reinterpret the past in the light of the present and, in some instances, the earlier marital 'hiccups' came to be seen as early warning signals or omens for the subsequent turns of events.

We asked respondents when they first *noticed* or were aware of marital difficulties and when they first perceived them as *problematic*. This was partly a common-sense distinction on our part but it was also one which other research had suggested might be useful (Thornes and Collard 1979) and it seems to have been meaningful for the majority of our respondents who readily linked these perceptual distinctions to different events and/or times when they occurred. Two-thirds of respondents said they were *aware* of some kind of incongruity between themselves and their partners from the very start of the relationship itself, whilst a quarter actually regarded such matters as *problematic* from the beginning (even though they may have discounted this in other parts of their interviews). However, as we have already hinted, there is a dynamic aspect to the process of what constitutes the problem and 'who blames whom', which makes it exceedingly difficult to say definitively what exactly respondents' timing of the start of the problem referred to. Respondents' accounts of their troubled marriages (obtained through a close reading and review of the whole text of their interviews) suggest two sets of interpretations. The first concerns how respondents made their past difficulties intelligible to themselves *at the time they occurred*. The second set of interpretations derives from respondents' new accounts of the past *in the light of current developments*, a past which it is also clear they had previously explained to themselves rather differently. These sets of interpretations may serve to illuminate the interesting sociological question how it is that the majority of people accommodate to their marriages most of the time, as well as the quantitatively smaller and more specific issue why some marriages are in the process of breaking up some of the time.

Accommodating to problematic marital experiences

In many cases in our study, respondents had only recently reappraised their marriages. However, as we have indicated above, new appraisals were not necessarily pre-conditions for seeking help, especially for those who initially presented at an agency with an individual and not a marital problem. In such cases, where the method of accommodation had been to focus on an individual problem, this way of accommodating to past marital difficulties tended to persist right up to the moment at which the agency intervened and redefined the individual's problem (at least in part) in marital terms. In these cases, certain strategies for accommodating to troubled marriages seemed to be particularly persistent. One partner would deny the existence of difficulties or would turn a blind eye, thus avoiding the definition of a problem altogether. Alternatively, and sometimes additionally, one partner would project blame on to the other. Yet another strategy was to take the blame upon oneself. Strategies of denial, evasion, and blaming were particularly likely to persist where an agency reinforced the location of the problem in a particular partner, and accounted for the problem in terms of one partner's 'sickness'.

In those cases where respondents had themselves already arrived at reappraisals of their marriages as problematic by the time they

approached an agency, other ways of accommodating to their problematic marital experiences were apparent. One particular strategy
adopted in the past was the practice of attributing problematic
marital experiences to events or situations extraneous to the marital
relationships. This meant that anything which might have been
regarded by either partner as posing a threat or problem to the marriage was often seen as a consequence of external circumstances, over
which (in our estimation) neither partner usually had much control.
We do not wish to suggest that these external events did not have a
causal impact, nor that they did not constitute *real* problems for the
individuals concerned, because they clearly did. On the contrary, we
want to make the observation that respondents' accounts focused
principally on the *externality* of these events rather than on their
control of or adaptation to them, thus deflecting 'causality' from
themselves and the marital relationship and enabling them to maintain that there was nothing intrinsically wrong with their marriages.
In the following extract the husband regarded his former account of
his marriage difficulties as some kind of rationalization of another
problem which he now believed lay underneath. Mr Ascot (aged 32,
surveyor) talked about how he and his wife had viewed their marriage
in the past:

> 'We seemed to feel that there was something wrong with our life
> style. It was pre-empting our happiness and as I said the house we
> had before was very cramped . . . I suppose we just felt we didn't
> have the proper nesting instincts . . . We would say "Things are
> going to be all right once we get things sorted out." When we got
> things sorted out, they didn't really get better. Then you see, *now*
> looking back, I realize that we went in for fostering another child
> and now we've got something else to blame it on. We've got another
> problem . . . another problem to blame it on.'

In the next example Mr Luton described difficulties at the beginning of the relationship. His account contrasted sharply with his more
recent view that he and his wife did not have a marital problem. However, the apparent contradiction between his two accounts makes
some sense in so far as he regarded his difficulties as the consequences
of certain events which would, he thought, given time 'work themselves out' or go away. That the discord in the relationship had not
gone away had led him to avoid defining his marriage as problematic:

> 'I mean, three months after getting married I was made redundant.
> We had rented accommodation and we just didn't seem to have any

money. I was as insecure as hell, emotionally, financially, and job wise . . . well, until this new job. She was disappointed in me in as much as I couldn't offer security which she'd always had. I was disappointed in that she was not backing me up. She couldn't see that it was having the same effect on me, being unable to provide. She was earning more money than I was. It's only this last year . . . things haven't got better in the marriage, but having a job I liked, *that* was working out.'

The next account, given by Mrs Rugby, suggests that while her own and her husband's lives were governed by and devoted to the needs of their child and the wife's sick father, the couple were able to achieve a form of marital accommodation. Both she and her husband focused on the subsequent death of the wife's father as part of the explanation for their disrupted marriage.

'We were all right until my dad died. Jean was nearly three and I think things deteriorated. It seemed that while we had plenty to do and were occupied with the child, with bottles and napkins, I suppose we didn't have time to row or think what was going on. Well, we were seeing to a baby and a sick person. No, once dad died, friction started, because mum used to come up every evening . . . and that got on his nerves. I don't know, it was all silly things.'

Our last example of a respondent who accommodated to her marriage by making sense of the difficulties in terms of an 'outside event' is Mrs Derby. She connected her husband's bad temper, their deteriorating relationship, and the misfortunes of their social and economic situation with her father-in-law's death some six years before the interview.

'The problems were there but they were not too bad, but after my father-in-law died my husband tended to expect a lot more of me . . . The good times were up until my father-in-law died . . . He'd have a half day or one in three weekends off, but since his father died he's been set up in business on his own . . . Ever since my husband has been struggling and envying the fact that other children have made good since he left school. Since his father died he hoped to step into the partnership but the other person excluded him and he feels very bitter. As you know, big multiples do well and the small man is slowly being squeezed out. It does affect him. He is terribly emotional and it does affect his general attitude, which I have tried to understand and cater for. But he does fly to extremes.'

Mrs Derby suggested that the father-in-law's presence was also important for *her* in that he acted as an effective sanction against what she regarded as her husband's unreasonable behaviour. Thus it is clear that in this marriage, problems predated the father-in-law's death, but that accommodation to them had taken place because of his presence. She still lacked this kind of support and regretted the loss of it:

> 'Earlier, I could phone my father-in-law and say that my husband was being beastly . . . sometimes he would come over and he would tell my husband to curb his temper . . . I felt at least there was one person which he would listen to . . . Since then there is not one single soul I know of that could tell my husband.'

In these examples we have illustrated how respondents attributed marital difficulties to adverse or unpredictable circumstances which they saw as being extraneous to their marriages. However, respondents also connected their marital difficulties with 'normal' and predictable events, such as the birth of a baby. It is clear that in many of these cases respondents regarded their marital difficulties, like the events themselves, as commonplace and transient. In the following quotation, a woman described how she was able to attribute sexual difficulties over thirty-five years of marriage in part at least to the vagaries of using the safe period as a method of birth control:

> 'Physical demonstration of love hasn't got the same priority with me as it has with my husband.'
> *'When did you know or realize this?'*
> 'More so as we've got older. Thinking about it now, you know I was always very busy and always worked hard when the children were younger. [Pause.] I was brought up a Catholic. My husband became a Catholic and you didn't practice birth control if you were a Catholic, when we were younger anyway . . . We tried to use the safe period, so that caused its own stresses and strains. Anything that went wrong on the physical side of our marriage was automatically blamed on that . . . and being the wrong time of the month you didn't feel in the mood and that kind of thing . . . so until that was out of the way it really put a different reason for it.'
> *'Can you say when you first saw this as a problem?'*
> 'The last few years really, since my husband hasn't been so well and has been unable to do all the physical activities that he normally does, deprived of them.'

A second woman, Mrs Ascot, also attributed the lack of a good sex life to having become a mother:

> 'Having a child takes a big chunk out of your life. Yes, you feel you are justified in not having a very lively sexual life or not being responsive. It gives you a good excuse and you forget. You can forget you've got a problem.'

Reinterpreting problematic marital experiences of the past

Not unexpectedly, the ways in which people explained their marital difficulties of the past often provided them with cues to any subsequent reinterpretation. Mrs Epsom described how she had increased her work involvement in her brother's family firm at the same time as her husband had gained promotion and greater financial rewards in the world of big business. It was only from the vantage point of her husband's sudden disappearance — he walked out during a family party and never returned — that she came to perceive her own increased work as having had a significance for the marriage.

> *'Have you increased your hours at work as your daughter has grown up?'*
> 'Yes, I have increased my hours over the years. *Funnily enough*, that brings me back to my marriage. As my husband went more into *his* business, I filled my time more by doing more work in my business and I was glad of it. I thought "Well what am *I* supposed to do?" In fact I used to say to him "It's lucky I've got the business to take an interest in, because you're so occupied."'

Later in the interview, thinking about her own marriage, Mrs Epsom reflected also upon her parents' relationship and in particular upon their habit of going everywhere together, which contrasted greatly with her own marriage. In the context of these thoughts, Mrs Epsom remembered a warning given to her by her mother many years before and which she had ignored at the time. It was significant that it was only since the break-up of her marriage that she had come to regard the warning as a signal of what had subsequently happened:

> 'My parents pop in, they go everywhere together, my mother and my father. She wouldn't let him off the leash for a minute. Funnily enough, she always used to say to me "I don't like it. Bill is away too much." And I used to say "Oh, Mum! Don't be so old-fashioned." But in a way she hit the nail on the head.'

In the next passage from the interview, Mrs Epsom described how she had noticed her own unhappiness in the latter days of her marriage and how she had put it down to the pressures of her husband's job. But it was only since the break-up that these work pressures, and notably her husband's promotion to the board of directors of the company he worked for, had assumed a different kind of significance for her.

'*Can you tell me, did you ever notice problems in your marriage?*'
'Yes, I noticed things. For the past few years I was getting unhappier and unhappier. I couldn't sense why.'
'*You didn't see them as a problem?*'
'No, I thought it was going to be overcome.'
'*Well, what did you notice?*'
'I noticed a lack of interest at home, a lot of irritableness.'
'*When do you think it was worse?*'
'I think in the last year I had a very bad year. I, . . . just nothing. There was no happiness. It was all unpleasant, thoroughly unpleasant and I started to say "Look it's not worth working so hard." I was putting it all down to work you see, but I didn't know what it was.'
'*Were there any sexual difficulties for example?*'
'Oh! yes, there were.'
'*Can you tell me when you noticed that first of all?*'
'Well I would say probably from the time he became a board director. Over a period of ten years it went from bad to worse until it became non-existent. He seemed to get more and more remote. I put it all down to work pressure.'

In the next example, a husband (Mr Mold, aged 53, self-employed plumber) described how a frightening experience (an extraneous event) led him to see his wife in a different light, which in turn provoked a deterioration in their marriage. Whether or not his wife's behaviour or attitude towards him actually changed a great deal at the point in time to which he referred was less important to him than the significance of the event and the new meaning it cast for him upon his relationship with her.

'I told you I slid down off the roof and nearly broke my back and nearly killed myself. My wife never turned a hair and that was twelve years ago. That was when I realized that my wife was taking me for granted and you see that is when the marriage really started to go wrong . . . It just deteriorated from that time, when I faced death or being crippled. I just couldn't understand that my wife didn't understand what I was talking about.'

From this time on Mr Mold began to place considerable significance upon his wife's apparent lack of concern for him which culminated in his view and treatment of her as 'mentally deficient'. This in turn led to a new pattern of accommodation in the marriage. We believe there is some significance in the fact that in this couple it was, most unusually, the husband who volunteered for the research interview and that, despite our efforts, we were unable to interview the wife.

> 'As I say the marriage deteriorated from that time until I saw that she was really mentally deficient, and from that time on I wanted to look after her and take care of her . . . If you keep a dog and you feed it . . . if it suddenly turns round and bites you, you say "What have I done this for?" And that's the same with my marriage. I married my wife and I looked after her. In every way I took care of her. I worked every hour that I could work and I went on a roof ladder and slipped down a roof and . . . I saw terror in my face and my wife didn't want to know it!'

In the last two cases the respondents had reworked the past in order to make sense of a *loss*. For Mrs Epsom it was the actual loss of her husband, and for Mr Mold it was his assumptions about the appropriateness of his wife's demeanour towards him which had somehow been seriously called into question. Marris (1974: 41) puts forward the view that where a dominant feeling of loss is provoked the person is precipitated into a struggle, akin to mourning, between 'attempts to retain the past and to escape altogether from its consequences'. The process is essentially concerned with evolving a new meaning within the context of the past.

For some respondents the occurrence of 'normal' events, like the birth of a first or second child, were retrospectively regarded as significant moments when their marriages started to go wrong. There appears to be no systematic pattern of meaning associated with births of children in our data, only perhaps a generalized sense of loss. As Oakley (1980) has propounded, childbirth involves both losses and gains. It is possible that women's sense of loss at particular births was *heightened* by a sense of loss or disappointment connected with their marriages. For some respondents a birth seems simply to have signified a way of dividing up the years and of marking the 'normal' passages of married life, whilst for others a birth had a special and unique significance.

Other respondents, in the process of reconstructing and reinterpreting what had gone wrong or was lacking in their marriages, focused on the sexual arena. Interestingly, several people had come to regard the state of being legally married as inherently problematic. In the following quotation the losses involved in getting married came to be seen by the respondent as outweighing the gains. Mr Hove had been married for less than a year when his wife suddenly, and with only two days' warning, left him. Until that moment Mr Hove had not regarded his marriage as problematic. In the following passage he favourably compared the period of cohabitation with their subsequent marriage.

Mr Hove, aged 35, partner in a small firm:
'I think before we were married there was more sex than there has been since we were married . . . When you live with somebody, you are both on your best behaviour all the time because there is no piece of paper. There is no actual commitment. You can both say "Well I'm buggering off" and that's that! Once you get married, one side can easily sort of slip and not bother and it's very difficult if the other person isn't capable of bringing the other person up to scratch again, whereas if you don't live with somebody before marriage, you don't know what they are going to be like after. I think the most valuable thing I could say is that, having lived with two women and then married them, both changed after marriage, and maybe I changed as well, got sloppy, got lazy. Strong words maybe, but one expects that things will be the same when you get married and that's why you go on getting married. You think it's good while you're living together. If she wants to get married and he wants to get married, fair enough! It isn't going to change the relationship. But it *does*, with a capital D. It certainly does. One thing our parents' generation didn't have was living together. I think this is an undoubted reason why divorce is getting more prevalent, because people live together and find it's different when they are married. So when you get married you say "Oh! well, I didn't realize it would be quite like this" and you get on with it, but when you live with somebody you know what it's like before and you can't accept that change.'

In this chapter we have suggested four characteristic strategies adopted by individual respondents for making sense of their marital difficulties.

1 Respondents attributed the difficulties to themselves or to their partners.
2 Respondents turned a blind eye or denied there were any difficulties at all.
3 Respondents attributed the difficulties to adverse or unpredictable circumstances and events extraneous to the marriages.
4 Respondents regarded the difficulties as transient and part of the 'normal' course of events.

We have also examined how some respondents, once their marriages had been defined as problematic, came to a *post hoc* understanding of what had 'gone wrong' in their marriages, what Timms and Blampied (1980) have termed 'the cognitive thrust'. We suggested that this process was frequently tied up with making sense of a loss and the process of adjusting to it. In reworking the past respondents were endeavouring to construct new meanings. Thus, for many, a characteristic way of coming to terms with a marriage which they had come to regard as problematic or under threat was to reinterpret the significance of a particular event of the past in the light of subsequent developments in the marriage. In short, individuals' frames of meaning gradually changed as they made sense of their altered situations and the losses they had sustained.

Notes

1 Dependency on another wage-earner in Brophy and Smart's (1981) terms means upon their husbands and/or another man, since women's lack of equality in the labour market prevents them from themselves earning an adequate wage. If women become dependent on the state, they must suffer major constraints upon their sexual practices and on what they may earn from employment.
2 Personal observation made during some field-work amongst wives of manual workers in an inner London borough.
3 Trevor Griffiths, in a play called *The Comedians* (1976) analyses different kinds of humour. He suggests that one type of humour relies on the reinforcement and perpetuation of crude stereotypes. Amongst his examples of racist and sexist jokes is one which reinforces the notion of male sexual invulnerability − with the husband's impotence being 'all the fault of the wife'.
4 In five of these marriages, since we were only able to interview one partner, we do not know the other partner's view.
5 Moreover, given the diversity and complexity of the ways in which people

sought help for marital difficulties, it is difficult to assess how far the class bias in our study accurately reflects a social class imbalance (i.e. in favour of middle-class people) in the two populations of help-seekers from whom our research group was drawn (Marriage Guidance clients, and general practitioners' patients referred to the hospital-based marital service).

5

The context of the
help-seeking process:
critical events and problems

In Chapter 4 we examined the ways in which people explained and made sense of difficulties in their marriages, both at the time they first began to be affected by them and subsequently when their marriages became defined as problematic and help was sought from agencies. In this chapter we propose to focus upon the critical events and problems which took place in the eighteen months preceding the moment when respondents first approached agencies. We have selected this focus since one of our initial ideas concerning this research project was that the reasons why people approached agencies at a particular moment in the course of their difficulties constituted an important part of the story of how it was that people became clients.

One of the main distinctions in this study is between those who themselves defined their marriages as problematic and those where the definition was made by the agency. This distinction is only partly an artifact of the two agencies from whom we chose to derive research subjects, namely general practitioners and Marriage Guidance Councils. Of the twenty-eight marriages in the study eleven were defined as problematic by a medical agency whilst, in the rest, the partner defining the marital problem approached the agencies, which included both Marriage Guidance Councils and general practitioners. The analysis of our data suggests that respondents who approached agencies with self-defined marital problems had generally experienced a *marital* crisis usually directly prior to their approaches to agencies. Conversely, in the other eleven marriages an approach to an agency was preceded by an *individual* crisis or by a symptom experience, either physical or psychological, and usually located in only one of the partners. In one instance, the symptom was present in the child of one of the couples and provoked contact with an agency which ultimately led a second agency to define a marital problem. The general practitioner referred the child to a hospital children's department, where the child and the mother were eventually seen by a child psychiatrist who offered to refer the parents for marital therapy.

In considering marriage troubles defined by doctors as a consequence of other kinds of problems having been presented to them, we are not necessarily assuming that some kind of 'displacement' took place, whereby marital conflict was projected on to other life crises and problems, nor are we saying that symptoms were really marital problems in disguise. To do either of these would be to deny the existence of more than one level of reality: the external reality of the life circumstances of the individual and the internal reality of the way each person experiences and perceives his or her own situation. Nonetheless, we believe that it is useful to examine how far respondents experienced critical events and problems before approaching an agency; what they were; the bearing which they had upon one another; and the ways they put stress on individuals.

The theoretical framework developed by Brown and Harris (1978) in their work on depression in women was an important influence upon the ways in which we began to conceptualize and examine the relationship between marriage and critical events, and problems in general. In Brown and Harris's model of depression, the quality of the marital relationship emerged as one of the principal factors which put women at risk from depression, but only when they had first experienced a severe life event. A marriage difficulty, or in their terms a 'non-confiding relationship', does not form an *a priori* premise of their model which is a causal one, since the essential or necessary component is the presence of a severe life event. Moreover, they contend that the quality of the marital relationship is only *one* important influence on whether a woman who has experienced a severe life event is protected from, or vulnerable to, a depressive illness.

One of the advantages of relating Brown and Harris's model of depression to our research project, with its different substantive and conceptual issues, was that it helped us to examine respondents' marriages in a wider perspective than simply the connection between marital difficulties and the approach to agencies. We did not wish to apply the ideas of Brown and Harris about provoking agents and vulnerability factors to our model of help-seeking, since we did not propose to develop a causal framework. Our aim was to elucidate the stages of the help-seeking process and to seek to identify the factors which affected each stage. Nonetheless, the structure of their theoretical model has helped us more clearly to pose the question why help was sought at a particular moment in *time*, and also to focus on the circumstances in which people were actually seeking help, and what they sought help in relation to. Our attention was thereby shifted away from practitioners' preoccupations and assumptions about the state of clients' marriages on to the reality of the clients' situations as they experienced them, and how it was that they became clients.

We therefore decided in this project to examine, in a systematic way, our respondents' life situations: we asked them about any critical events and problems that they had experienced, particularly in the eighteen-month period prior to contact with an agency, and we also enquired about the *major* events and problems which had occurred previously in their adult lives. We could not test the hypothesis that critical events and problems precipitated approaches to agencies, since our study was by definition a study of help-seekers and their partners. We are therefore unable to say how far a group of people with marital difficulties who had no contact with agencies would have differed from our study group. However, on the basis of studies done in the community, it would seem that a fairly high proportion of women suffering from depression, for example, of whom the great majority had experienced severe life events, did not visit their doctors (see Brown and Harris 1978). Our aim was to explore how far (if at all) the help-seeking actions of people experiencing marital difficulties were preceded by critical events and problems. In this way we thought it might be possible to see whether help-seeking action was provoked by stress-related factors and if so, of which kind.

'Life events' methodology

The method of eliciting from respondents critical events and problems occurring in a given time period has been developed by Brown and Harris (1978). It involves a structured and detailed interview, in which attention is focused on the timing and contextual circumstances surrounding the events and problems. The principal aim of this methodology is to control for sources of bias.[1] This is done by asking the respondents specific questions about each area of their lives in turn, and by assessing the impact of events on the respondent in terms of the average person's reactions in those particular situations and circumstances.[2]

The 'life events' methodology has been developed in the process of empirical research on the aetiology of disease. Thus in order to demonstrate the role of life events in bringing about a depressive disorder, for example, Brown and Harris regarded it essential to show that the events themselves did not depend upon or arise from the disorder itself. In our study, such issues were not important, since we were not concerned with matters of aetiology but with the ways in which people came to define their problems and act upon them. However, it was nonetheless important to examine how far critical events and problems were independent and how far they were associated with the marriage troubles.

We adapted the Brown and Harris 'life events schedule' and methodology for our own purposes and for the following reasons: the definitional nature of marital problems, the exploratory nature of the study, and the small size of the research team. Respondents were not asked to recount in detail their feelings about any critical events and problems which emerged in the course of the 'life events schedule'[3] but, at a later point in the interview, they were asked to select specific events and problems, preferably from the eighteen months before they contacted an agency, which they considered had affected them considerably at the time they occurred. We, as interviewers, tried to ensure that all recent and relatively serious events and problems were covered. Our aim here was to explore respondents' coping strategies and consulting and disclosure patterns in relation to the critical events and problems respondents had experienced, and not only the marital ones. We therefore gathered a great deal of material about the range of critical events and problems which respondents had experienced and the impact these had made upon them. In collecting and analysing this data we were very aware of the problems inherent in retrospective recall, and therefore tried very hard to disentangle what people had felt and thought about the critical events and problems *at the time they occurred* from how they *subsequently* came to view them.

Our threshold for the inclusion of critical events and problems was to be lower than that of Brown and Harris (1978), particularly for some groups of events. This was because we were concerned with outcomes related to how people saw their problems and how much they were in fact affected by them, which varied considerably both in type and intensity. Moreover, it soon became clear that critical events and problems might be important at *several* stages in the help-seeking process, and not simply at the point of the decision to approach an agency, for they might also have influenced when people began to experience the marital difficulties in the first place, or when they perceived and defined them as being problematic.

Critical events and problems in the eighteen months before respondents approached agencies

Before we explore some possible linkages between critical events and problems and help-seeking for marital difficulties, it may be useful to consider the range and incidence of problems and events which our study group had experienced in the eighteen months preceding help-seeking.

In *Table 5(1)* we included all major health problems, including those for which medical help was sought when marital problems were also identified, unless the problems were actually trivial. We also included all instances (some of which were not strictly events as such) where there was evidence of very strong feelings of dissatisfaction or disappointment with employment and unemployment, and also with full-time housewifery, and retirement. We decided to include in *Table 5(1)* some of the 'normal' and transitional events which respondents had experienced during the period (despite their not always having been problematic for the individual concerned), but we have grouped them separately (*Table 5(1)*, item 12). In those instances where such events *were* problematic, they would already have been included earlier in the table under the relevant heading; for example under a child or health problem. We have also noted (included separately in *Table 5(1)*) a category of positive events for, in a few instances, these had considerable effect on the help-seeking process; the main impact they made was that of enabling respondents to perceive *alternatives* to continuing in their troubled marriages.

On the basis of this classification, it appears that each partner in the study had experienced at least one fairly critical event, serious problem, or major dissatisfaction in the eighteen months before agencies were approached. The average number of such critical events and problems (*excluding* transitional and positive events) was 3.8 per marriage.

One of the more striking and obvious features of *Table 5(1)* is that the vast majority of items have as their *focus* either the respondents themselves, their partners, their children, or close ties in their families of origin; not friends, more distant relatives, or the wider world. Second, and rather obviously, a major impact was upon the respondents themselves. Unfortunately, we cannot say whether this rate of critical events and problems is particularly high, although this would seem likely in common-sense terms.[4]

It was not surprising to find a high incidence of marriage-threatening

Table 5(1) *Kinds of critical events and problems in the eighteen months before an agency was approached*

Kinds of critical events, problems, etc.	Total no. events etc.	No. marriages	No. men	No. women
1 Employment events and situations producing strong dissatisfaction and disappointment (including unemployment, retirement, and housewifery)	21	17	13	8
2 Events involving the revelation of relationships with the opposite sex	6	6	4	2
3 Problems stemming from respondents' relationships with kin	16	14	7	12
4 Deaths of respondents' parents	7	6	5	2
5 'Acting out' behaviour, e.g. overdoses, heavy drinking	6	6	6	—
6 Violent behaviour of husbands towards wives	5	5	5	—
7 Serious mental and physical health problems (specific sexual problems for which help was sought are included here)	20	16	10	9
8 Behaviour and health problems of respondents' children	8	7	—	—
9 Separations/departures of one spouse. Also threats of separation (e.g. solicitor consulted about divorce)	11	11	6	5
10 Material difficulties (e.g. bad housing)	4	4	—	—
11 Other negative events (e.g. respondent's father's serious heart attack)	5	5	—	—
Total no. events and problems	109			
Average no. per marriage	3.8			
No. of individual spouses involved	52			
No. of marriages	28			
12 Life stage transitions (e.g. marriages and childbirths)	11	8	—	—
13 Positive events (e.g. trip round the world)	4	4	—	—

Note All critical events and problems had occurred principally to one individual partner in the marriage unless otherwise stated.

events among those seeking help for marital problems. However, since we had not anticipated the various ways in which marital problems would be presented to agencies, we were surprised to discover such a strong association between help-seeking and health problems. One of our early hunches had been that people with marital problems might be under stress in a number of other areas of their lives as well as in their marriages. There was some evidence in support of this general hypothesis; for example, in almost a quarter of the marriages, one of the partners (and in one marriage both partners) had lost parents through death in the eighteen-month period. Second, a high proportion of people either had encountered employment, kinship or material problems or had experienced major dissatisfactions with these areas of their lives, very few of which, in logical terms, could have been entirely provoked by their marital difficulties. There remain however a large number of items, especially health problems, where it was much more difficult to estimate the extent to which they were related to the marriages. In some marriages both the marital and the health problems had persisted for so long that it was difficult to say which had occurred first. For some of these there was the possibility that the marital próblems emanated from problems which the partners brought with them from their respective pasts. Nonetheless, even in these instances it was clear that respondents and their marriages were under considerable stress which arose from a variety of sources. In those instances where respondents' marital problems were identified by the agencies and not by themselves, it could be argued that the stress response seemed to be encapsulated in the health problem they presented to the agency. But whatever the relationship between these problems and the marital difficulties, we would argue that there is significance in the fact that the great majority of marriages in our study had recently experienced at least one major critical event, problem, or dissatisfaction. These were likely to have depleted the emotional resources of the individuals concerned, which in turn was likely to have made coping with marital problems more difficult.

Events and problems which directly provoked help-seeking

We were concerned in this study with two distinct help-seeking groups: those whose approaches to agencies were characterized by a marital focus, and those whose initial approaches concerned individual problems. (We have included those who went to their general practitioners with sexual problems under the rubric of a marital focus.) We noted earlier the rather obvious finding that those who approached agencies with self-defined marital or sexual problems[5] had generally experienced critical events connected with their marriages in the period immediately before they approached an agency. These classes of critical events characteristically involved an action by one partner which the other perceived as posing a threat to the marriage. Thus, the definition of the marriage as problematic usually came about when one partner perceived the action of the other as putting the relationship in jeopardy. The 'erring' partner was seen by the other as having transgressed a set of 'taken for granted' rules which generally also had a legitimacy beyond the perspective of the individual. Moreover, when these marriage-threatening events occurred they tended to provoke a rapid reaction from the 'offended' partner, part of which often was to approach an agency. In this sense it is therefore useful to talk about these critical events as marriage-threatening. Marsden (1973), in his study of mothers alone, described their marriage break-ups in similar terms. He notes that the end of the marriage was not brought about by a gradual process of talk or of progressively firmer decisions, but by the occurrence of a sudden crisis or opportunity: 'The two were not distinct: a crisis such as the discovery of her husband's VD clinic card might bring at last the resolve to separate, with the offer of legal evidence and an offer of accommodation from a relative' (Marsden 1973: 92).

However, it was not always the case that a critical *event* provoked an awareness of the marriage as problematic. The following case concerns a woman who initiated the break-up of her marriage not because of any actual critical event or change in her situation, but because of a changed awareness of its possibilities. It was in the consideration of these *possibilities* and alternatives that she came to view her marriage differently. Although this change cannot be attributed to the advent of any critical event or problem as such, it is nonetheless of interest and indicates the definitional nature of marital problems. Mrs Hove (aged 25, secretary) described her sudden decision to leave her husband with whom she had lived for four years, but whom she had only recently married, in terms of what she stood to gain:

'I went away somewhere I hadn't been before and I wandered around and I walked and went to the shops and thought "Well, what would it be like by myself?" It felt a bit empty really, empty because there was nothing familiar, but take all those things away and there was just me, bare, which I thought was a good thing. I thought a lot about what *I* was and what *I* wanted and not about the existing situation that I'd got myself into, but about what was *going* to happen and where I *wanted* to be . . . I sat down and thought "There isn't enough. I can't see enough ahead. I don't think there's any future. I don't think he understands me . . . what I want and feel" . . . I couldn't sort of settle and accept things as they were, like it was. No, because I wanted to make progress, to build, grow, learn . . . I suppose I was trying to make our marriage go forward and really it was me that needed to progress. Perhaps I should have gone further along the path of developing myself before I sort of gave myself and lost myself in this situation, marriage situation, where we do have to give a lot of ourselves, an *awful* lot . . . Things about me seemed to sort of wake me up suddenly. We'd been together for four years, wrapped up in love and each other and planning and superficial things. I was at a superficial stage, I was young. I didn't know what the other layers deeper down meant. I just took the level to be exciting. There was always something happening. It's youth . . . you don't have to look very far or very deeply at things. Maybe there's tomorrow and maybe there's not. You just enjoy every day. You don't analyse things somehow.'

In our study it is interesting to note that there was a general absence of options or opportunities, either real or perceived, particularly among the '*offended*' partners and that, in the event of marriage-threatening crises, these individuals had sought help from an agency in often vain attempts to prevent their marriages from breaking up irrevocably. This absence of options may indeed suggest an important difference between those who seek help and those who do not when their marriages are under threat.

We identified two main types of marriage-threatening event. The most common event amongst those seeking help with self-defined marital problems was one partner either leaving the household or threatening to do so by, for example, consulting a solicitor about divorce. The second was the revelation of a close, though not always sexual, relationship with a person of the opposite sex. These types of events, namely desertion and adultery, have long been regarded as unequivocal transgressions of rules governing marriage in our society. It is interesting to note the absence of husbands' violence towards wives as an acknowledged marriage-threatening event. The still equivocal significance of such behaviour in our society is perhaps reflected in the fact that, in our study, husbands' violence was never followed by a *direct* approach to a marital agency such as Marriage Guidance. Four of the five women who incurred violence from their husbands consulted their doctors shortly afterwards, some for their injuries and some for other things. Three of these women were eventually referred for marital help. In another case it was the husband who approached a marital agency, in order to gain some recognition from the court that he could be seen to have sought help with his marriage when his wife tried to divorce him. Two women attempted to take some 'public' action when their husbands were violent. They called the police, who refused to do anything at all, and so they continued with their lives as if their marriages were relatively stable and undisturbed. Thus, in our study, violence was not seen by respondents as a sufficient and 'legitimate' reason for seeking help from marital agencies. Moreover, with the exception of the women's refuges, agencies do not appear to encourage women to approach them when their husbands act violently towards them.

In the group who initially approached agencies with what we have termed an individual focus, marriage-threatening events, such as actual or threatened separations and affairs, were on the whole absent. Some of the individual problems for which people sought help from their doctors presented as crises, such as suicide attempts and acute stomach pains, whilst other respondents presented chronic health problems for which often they had been in treatment for a long time. Chronic physical health problems included a severe pelvic infection, a period of illness provoked apparently by a virus infection, and a case of high blood pressure. The psychological problems all involved depression. In one instance a woman approached the doctor with great trepidation, with no specific symptoms but a general feeling of inertia and malaise. In another instance a woman presented a relatively trivial physical condition for treatment.

An approach to an agency with a health problem does not appear to be simply a function of the distribution of health problems in that group. Just over one-third of those who approached agencies with self-defined marital or sexual problems were also likely to have consulted a doctor, often for something fairly serious, in the eighteen-month period. There is therefore a *capricious* element in the fact that a group of respondents who presented with individual health problems were identified by agencies as having marital problems. Nonetheless, irrespective of how problems were presented to, or taken up by, the agencies, it is significant that in both groups there was a fairly high incidence of critical events and problems in the eighteen-month period we investigated in detail. This high incidence suggests the extent to which the people in these marriages were under stress, whether or not they defined themselves as having marital problems.

So far we have suggested that all events or problems with a marital focus, together with certain problems with an individual focus, have a crisis flavour and precipitate approaches to agencies. However, it is clear from our respondents' accounts that only some of them explained their approaches to agencies in these terms. It was more common for respondents *not* to comment on the contextual circumstances surrounding their approaches to agencies, at least in response to the direct questions about their help-seeking which we asked them at the beginning of the interview. Moreover, it was clear that in many cases the process had been so complex and affect-laden that respondents themselves had often not been able to see clearly the chain of events and decisions which had led them there. Thus judgements about the factors which precipitated help-seeking actions were often far from straightforward. It was of considerable methodological importance, therefore, to have given careful attention to the time-ordering of events and problems, and to their interdependence, especially since this was a retrospective study. We will now discuss these critical events in terms of their constituting the context of the help-seeking process.

Events and problems surrounding the help-seeking process

We suggested at the beginning the importance of distinguishing the different stages in respondents' help-seeking careers. The stage at which a person became *aware* of the existence of a possible problem in his or her marriage needs to be analytically distinguished from the stage at which he or she *defined* it as a marital problem, and also from the stage at which he or she *decided* to approach an agency. In a retrospective study these stages, which entailed cognitive changes, were not always clearly distinguishable in every respondent's account of his or her reality, but nonetheless the analytic concept was generally elucidative. However, its application became further complicated since the help-seeking process involved couples and not simply individuals. Even so, despite the inherent difficulties, we have tried to examine the role of critical events and problems in relation to particular stages in the help-seeking process. Our data suggest that sometimes the contextual events and problems may have been impli-cated in the marital problems themselves. In other cases they may have served to bring about respondents' awareness of possible prob-lems in their marriages, or they may have provoked the definition of marital problems or decisions to seek help. It is also possible that they may have been significant for more than one stage of the process. Furthermore, as well as influencing how people saw and defined their situations, such events and problems are also likely to have affected how they *experienced* them. As we have said, a serious critical event or problem was likely to increase the stress on individuals and to put strain upon their coping resources and strategies, with the effect likely to be correspondingly greater if their marriages were in difficulty at the same time.

The following discussion of these issues will take the form of specific examples. In order to bring the data to life we will use respondents' own words wherever possible, but it should be remembered that our decisions about the significance of events and problems rested *primarily* upon data concerning the contexts of the events and problems and not upon how people said they felt.[6]

The role of events and problems in provoking the definition of marital problems

It is perhaps useful to distinguish between those events and problems which had almost inevitable consequences for the marriages, and those which did not. The most clear-cut case of the former concerns a couple (the Hoves) where the wife announced 'out of the blue' her decision to leave her husband. Both parties, who were living apart when we interviewed them, told us that there had been no prior or overt warning that there was anything wrong in the relationship. Both said that neither of them had previously discussed with the other any difficulties between them, nor had there been any conflict that was at all 'out of the ordinary'. The only inkling that the husband received of his wife's impending departure was her sudden decision to go away for a weekend on her own, which she promptly did. She returned on the Sunday night and announced then that she was going for good.

Mr Hove, aged 35, partner in a small firm:
'Oh yes, it happened – unfortunately I had two squash matches, the first at six o'clock and the second at nine o'clock and I played the six o'clock one and when I came home still in my gear and literally just to sit for two hours and have a cup of tea prior to

recuperating for the second match, she announced that she felt unsettled and we then started to discuss it . . . we discussed it fully and I didn't really get what I considered to be the right kind of answers from somebody suddenly announcing they were leaving. If she had said "I'm sorry I'm in love with somebody else," that is a good reason, you know. For her to say "I need something else in my life. I feel unfulfilled, unsettled" didn't seem to me to be . . . My first reaction was I suppose slight annoyance. Why, if you felt so strongly that you are going to leave . . . why not have discussed it before now, instead of just buggering off?'

Mrs Hove's decision to leave and her subsequent departure two days later, which together constitute the marriage-threatening event, precipitated a definition of the marriage as problematic, which neither partner was able to reject or dissent from.

In this last example the event which provoked the definition of a marital problem also precipitated the approach to the agency. We wish to emphasize that one should not necessarily be seen as the corollary of the other.[7]

The contribution of events and problems to the marital difficulties

What we have in mind here are those events and problems which were inextricably linked to the marital difficulties. In our study two specific types of problems seem to have been especially significant in this respect, namely those related to kin relationships and those related either to the health of the partners or of very close and significant others. Economic problems also contributed to marital difficulties in certain cases, being predictably more significant for working-class respondents. The following case is an example where kinship and economic difficulties combined.

Mr and Mrs Cowes, aged 23 and 22 respectively, both belonged to large working-class families, and their ties of kinship were additionally reinforced by ties of neighbourhood. As teenagers, the couple had lived together for several years in the home of the husband's mother, who was separated from Mr Cowes's father. Some of the husband's sisters lived with them, whilst other siblings had set up their own households in the neighbourhood. The couple had moved into poor-quality housing and, one year before the interview, they had been rehoused by the council in a flat which, to the families' surprise, was immediately above the flat belonging to the husband's mother. At the time of the interview, they had a child who was a year old and they had only recently been formally married. In a sense it seemed as if this couple had only just become a separate and distinct family unit, through the acquisition of their own flat, the arrival of the baby, and their subsequent marriage. However, two factors conspired to under-mine their 'separateness': the close proximity of the husband's mother and the continuing unemployment of both partners. Both of these features of their situation clearly played a considerable part in the marital problems that eventually developed, and which the couple described in terms of persistent arguments and quarrels. Mrs Cowes (aged 22, housewife) talked about the friction between herself and her husband's family:

'There is a lot of friction between us . . . this is partly because she [husband's mother] is by herself and Alan has got two older sisters who are a year or two older than me and one of them has got two kids. We all got on okay but, I know it sounds a bit bitchy, but one gets a bit jealous if the other visits me or I go and visit them . . . now and then there is a little stirring and trouble starts and everyone gets accused of being two-faced.'

Comparing her own family with her husband's she said:

'Well, we didn't sort of talk a lot in my family. We talk but not, you know, you couldn't sit down and discuss everyone's problems. Obviously my mum might say to me "What's happened?" or she'll talk about something. But we don't really sit down and delve into everyone's problems and work them out . . . You see this is the dif-ference with Alan's family. I would like to be able to talk but you can't. It's either got to be the whole thing or nothing at all . . . I'd rather just say talk for a couple of hours about something and then forget it, but you can't. It's either "Tell me the whole story" and everyone is told or "Don't say anything". So I tend not to say any-thing any more.'

She talked about the mother-in-law's interference in their marriage and her bias towards her son:

'I just saw it as her picking on me and going for me all the time . . . Well, obviously he is her son but I just wished she wouldn't. I'd rather her not say anything at all, just sort of go on with her normal life, and if we had an argument I wished she'd not say anything. Like she says "Have you been arguing and why are you arguing and what's the problem?" I can't think of a good example – Oh yes! My sister Sandra, she's always saying "Why doesn't Alan get a job?" and I said "Well at the moment he's doing a bit of wood-work and so he might as well finish and what's the point of getting a job that he's not going to stick at." Better to go to college. I told Alan's mum and she said to me "Bloody cheek, what a cheek Anne should say that. If anyone should say it, *I* should!" [Laughs.] And I said "Why you? It should be me!" And somebody else said to me that I'm married to two people!'

The above example illustrates the more general point, that the effects of events, and particularly of persisting problems, upon people's marriages may be construed at a number of different levels. At the level of the individual, it is possible to interpret this couple's difficulties in terms of their *failure* to separate adequately from the mother; they were constrained because they could not find work or move further away. At a micro-social level, the difficulties in the marriage may be understood as both a product of a particular struc-ture of kinship relationships which, at the same time, may also have acted as a constraint against excessive conflict or violence in the marriage. Third, the marriage difficulties may be seen against a background of structural economic disadvantage.

The role of events and problems in relation to respondents' coping resources and strategies

We have in mind here those events and problems where there was little evidence to suggest that they had directly provoked the marital problems or respondents' decisions to seek help, or even that they brought about the definition of the marriages as problematic. Respondents did not connect such events and problems to their marriages, save sometimes in a very tenuous fashion. This is hardly surprising, since many of them had no 'common-sense' connection with the difficulties in their marriages. What principally character-ized these events and problems was their ineluctable character: the things that happened in the external world over which respondents could exert little control. Examples of such events and problems were the deaths and illnesses of close and significant others, structural unemployment and redundancy, and boring and monotonous jobs.

Most of the events and problems that are relevant here clearly post-dated respondents' awareness of their marital difficulties and, as we have said, did not occupy a position in respondents' accounts of why or when they needed or sought help. Nonetheless, by the very fact of their seriousness and their timing within the eighteen months prior to help-seeking, such events and problems seem likely to have depleted respondents' emotional resources and to have taxed their coping strategies, especially given that their marriages were already in trouble. The following example suggests how an external event, the death of a parent, can affect the individual concerned and ultimately the marriage.

Mr and Mrs Rugby both said that their relationship had been marked for a number of years by persistent quarrelling and unhappiness. Some years before the interview they had been seen unsuccessfully at a Marriage Guidance Council. The difficulties between them eventually reached a second peak after the husband's mother's death. Mr Rugby described himself as being unaffected by her death at the time. He discounted it in terms of their poor relationship over the years and thought himself to have been affected by his wife's refusal to go to the funeral or to help him with the arrangements, for which he alone was responsible. Less than two weeks after this event, over a bank holiday weekend, a violent row took place between the couple, after which the husband took an overdose. Mrs Rugby next took out an injunction against her husband for assault and the court banned him from the home for a month. We interviewed them a few months after the husband's return to the home and shortly after the wife had accepted an offer from the general practitioner to refer them for marital therapy.

In this case, a parental death appeared to have put considerable pressure on Mr Rugby's coping stategies which reflected his non-disclosing attitude. Moreover, the structure of Mr Rugby's social network, which was of the truncated type,[8] testified to his attitude and practice. At a later point in the interview, Mr Rugby began to describe, in addition to his anger at his wife's refusal to go to the funeral, the old hostilities in his family of origin and his feelings of loss and ambivalence towards his mother's death.

Mr Rugby, aged 37, fitter:
'What about when you learned your mother died? Did you talk to your wife about it at all?'
'No, I didn't. My actual feeling of mother to son was negative . . .'
'Did you mention the fact that your mother had died to anyone else?'
'I had to phone my governor at work to tell him I wouldn't be in.

I phoned [friend and workmate] and he more or less said "I'm sorry to hear about your mum but your mum was ill wasn't she?" And I said "Yeah".'

'Was that — ?'

[Loudly.] 'I had to phone in to tell him that I wouldn't be in to work . . .'

'And how did you feel when you told him?'

[Pause.] 'Well, just — I felt inside me, because I never broke down . . . Something that I lost, but I didn't break down because there was nothing strong between my mother and myself. My brother's the same as well. There's nothing strong there at all . . . When I went to see my dad after my parents separated [R was seventeen at the time] nine years later, I knew what my dad done [he was violent to his mother] but then again I had a better communication with my dad — he died nine years ago and I understood a bit more. I understood what he had gone through as well in respect of being married to my mum. She was very discontented as a person . . . always moving around and everything like that. [Pause.] But I never, not really deep down, never really felt I had any strong ties towards my mum, not in that respect. The thing that really bothered me was the horrible business of going and doing the funeral arrangements and maybe facing my brother because there was one particular time when my brother didn't have any money. There was some argument about what my mother was going to leave . . . and I thought there would be a big argument about "Well, I'm going to have this and I'm going to have that" and I didn't want to go through that.'

After the marital crisis (in which he assaulted his wife and was banned by the court from the home) some change seems to have taken place in Mr Rugby, and an indication of that was a new attitude towards disclosure and help-seeking. Because he was banned from his home Mr Rugby *had* to seek help from a friend in finding somewhere to stay. He described how the retired couple, with whom his friend had found him accommodation, encouraged him to talk about his marriage:

'I gave in to my feelings, in respect of talking about it to somebody, and more or less somebody really understood the way I felt, and what I'd gone through. I realized that afterwards, even when I first went away from Jan [wife] the first week and a half, after the injunction and stayed with the old-age pensioners. . . . They're quite lively and the person that I sat down and spoke to about my married life . . . I said to them "I don't want you to take sides or be a referee. You can talk about it and think about it." There was one night when we were sitting down watching television, the world cup was on and we were football mad. I mean we would stay up till 2 a.m. watching football and talking. But he did, he spoke to me and said "That's the worst thing you've ever done." [Referring to the assault on his wife.] He said I should have come and spoken to somebody . . . He said "What's happened to you, you've got every emotional feeling as sheer frustration within yourself and it's exploded like a bomb." And he said "What's happened is you've taken it out on the next, the actual one that's been beside you, your wife . . . And she's done the same to you".'

We have suggested in the previous example that an external event affected a person's ability to cope. We would argue that such an inability to cope effectively was rooted not simply in a lack of social support, but that it was also a consequence of a particular type of coping strategy which is ideologically reinforced (i.e. men do not, at least overtly, seek support from other people). As we have seen, many husbands feared that by turning to others they risked loss of face and, as we have argued earlier, such attitudes are concomitant with men's structural domination both within marriage and within society in general. In the case of Mr Rugby, it is significant that a crisis emanating from the state of his marriage and his mother's death led him in some degree to a re-evaluation of his past ways of coping. But it remains to be seen how far such a re-evaluation could lead automatically to a new coping strategy, given the already limited resources of his social network.

The fact that those who had limited social networks (which we later term truncated) were either bereft of social support, or chose not to rely on what little they had, must be considered in the light of another of our findings, namely that those with truncated networks were also less likely to have defined the existence of a marital problem (see Chapter 6). As we shall later suggest, this group of respondents was likely to be highly dependent on their partners, and in a fashion that would not easily brook the exposure of differences between them. It is our contention, therefore, that critical events and problems, experienced by people whose marital relationships were already in trouble, were especially likely to have a severe effect upon partners who, either by choice or circumstance, had to depend exclusively upon the other partner or rely upon their own *internalized* methods of coping.

As the reader will already have gathered, certain kinds of behaviour which might be described as 'acting out' (such as suicide attempts, heavy drinking and violence) were more common amongst husbands than amongst wives in the study. A high proportion of these husbands were reluctant to admit to problems in their marriages and, significantly, most of them belonged to truncated social networks. As we shall show later (Chapter 6), where such husbands had wives who likewise had very limited social networks, there was a particularly strong likelihood of marital problems *not* emerging; such wives tended rather to present at their doctors with individual problems of a psychological or physical nature. This suggests that where a critical event or problem occurred to a partner whose marriage was already under stress, its effect upon him or her was likely to be mediated by the type of network structure and the extent and nature of the support provided. Thus the presence or absence of social support outside the marital relationship may in turn have had some influence upon the way in which the stress induced by the event was manifested. It seems highly likely therefore that those kinds of people, whom we later designate as belonging to truncated social networks, were more vulnerable to individual or internalized crises, and also to health problems, when under stress from their marriages and other sources. By contrast, those respondents with other network types were more likely to express their stress and conflict in overt ways, and to bring their marital problems out into the open. Of course one explanation why many of the truncated group did not bring their marital problems into the open may be that these did reach really critical levels because agencies had intervened at a relatively early stage.

In examining critical events and problems as the context in which people sought help, a somewhat complex picture has begun to emerge. Certain classes of events and problems seemed to have pre-cipitated particular kinds of help-seeking: marriage-threatening events provoked people into approaching marital agencies, whereas health problems led people to the doctor. However, many events and problems had little or no connection with help-seeking action. An examination of the part played by events and problems in our data suggested their importance at a number of different stages in the help-seeking process: in the production of the marital problems them-selves; at the stage when people became aware of a potential problem; or later at the problem definition stage. Alternatively, their major impact was simply to add to the stress which respondents were already experiencing in their marriages. The impact of events and problems on the help-seeking process thus depends both upon their nature and also upon the way people viewed and reacted to them. A key factor which intervened between the problems and situations people encountered and the ways in which they defined and acted upon them is the structure of people's social relationships. It is to the subject of our respondents' social relationships that we shall turn in the following three chapters.

Notes

1 There are two main sources of bias which Brown and Harris's life events method seeks to exclude. The first concerns differential reporting by the respondent. In estimating the impact made by an event at the time it occurred, any subsequent reconstructions made by the respondent (what Brown and Harris call 'effort after meaning') needs to be excluded. A second source of bias relates to the reporting by the researcher and, since he or she already knows 'the outcome' in a retrospective study, the life events method is designed to prevent over-inclusion of events on the basis of known outcomes (Brown and Harris 1978).

2 Any material concerning the way in which respondents described the impact of events (i.e. in 'affective' terms) is then excluded from the researchers' judgements about whether or not to 'include' an event as severe and therefore as likely to bring about depression. A rating of the *likely* impact of events is thereby made 'independently' and is carried out in a 'consensus' meeting by other researchers in the team who are only given the 'contextual' material (Brown and Harris 1978).

3 We used the schedule as laid out in Appendix 5 in Brown and Harris 1978.

4 It is not possible to compare our rates of events and problems with those of Brown and Harris. In our study we included as single events and problems all those which were contingent upon our respondents' situations and actions. Thus a partner announcing that he or she was leaving, and doing so some time later, was included as *one* event, and this was the practice so long as the 'event' happened before the first approach to an agency was made. The criteria concerning the definition of an event in Brown and Harris's study are different from this and appear to produce a higher rate of events.

5 Some of those who presented with sexual problems fit our general conclusions about people presenting with marital problems while others do not. However, since this group is so small we shall not consider them in great detail.

6 This was done in the spirit of the life events' methodology of Brown and Harris.

7 It is often the case in our study because our study group consisted of help-seekers. However, as we shall show, it was the wives who were more likely to make the approach to the agency, even when the husbands took part in the definition of a marital problem.

8 In the next chapter we shall define the main social network types to which our respondents belonged. For the purposes of this chapter, the reader should simply note the three types: (1) the truncated type (which provided few ties); (2) the close-knit kinship type (with a relatively large number of ties and interconnected in structure); and (3) the differentiated friendship type (with a relatively large number of ties with each sector of the network being relatively discrete, i.e. compared with (b)).

6

The marriages and
their social networks

The notion of social network was first applied in a systematic way to the study of marriage and family life in western urban society by Bott (1968). She found that the networks of the families in her study varied in the degree of connectedness: 'the extent to which the people known by a family know and meet one another independently of the family' (Bott 1968: 59) and she found that these variations were particularly evident in informal relationships between friends, neighbours and relatives. Bott's major conclusion was that the degree of segregation in the role relationships of husband and wife (including for example the extent to which emotional 'satisfaction was sought by each spouse in the other) varied directly with the connectedness of the family social network in which the couples were enmeshed. It is not appropriate to consider here the various criticisms that have been levelled at Bott's analysis, nor to review further research which has sought to test the relationship between networks and conjugal roles. The reader who wishes can find detailed discussions elsewhere (see e.g. Lee 1979).

More recently, attention has been paid to the notion of social network within the field of medical sociology, although in only a very few studies has the network aspect been emphasized or systematically applied. Some researchers have begun to take up this concept within a social-psychological perspective and have emphasized the importance of network as an expressive resource or emotional support for the individual, and especially as a buffer against mental illness (Henderson *et al.*, 1978, 1980). However, there is already an established tradition in social anthropology, and to a lesser extent in sociology, concerning the structural aspects and implications of social networks for beliefs and social action (Mitchell 1969). The concept of social network may prove to be particularly useful in the field of illness behaviour; for example, it has already been shown to be an important mediating or intervening variable in explaining why some groups of people seek treatment from formal services and why others do not (McKinlay 1973). We shall now briefly refer to some of this work and suggest its relevance to marital problems, their genesis and definition.

In much of the social-psychological work there is no emphasis on social *network* as such. Instead the focus is on the impact of groups of intimate others who are seen to constitute resources in the maintenance of an individual's psychological integrity. Caplan (1974: 7), for example, has suggested that such groups provide individuals with 'an enduring pattern of continuous or intermittent ties' which serve to maintain individuals' psychological and physical integrity over time. Others, such as Weiss (1969) and Bates and Babchuck (1961), without actually addressing themselves to the notion of network, have pointed to presence of kin and close friends in providing 'the individual with an understanding of reality, moral values and a sense of self' (Weiss 1969: 37). Several studies have found a link between poor mental health and the absence of close intimate relationships (Henderson *et al.*, 1978, 1980). One study found that the absence of many casual less intimate friends was also associated with high symptom levels (Miller and Ingham 1976).

Weiss (1969) examines and rejects the hypothesis that the mere quantity of social ties is of salient importance in producing emotional support. He suggests that different kinds of relationships have different kinds of functions and effects so that, for example, friendship cannot be a substitute for marriage nor vice versa. He goes on to suggest that particular relationships become specialized in the needs they provide so that marriage for instance tends to provide the individual with an opportunity for intimacy and emotional integration whilst kin relationships provide material help.

One of the problems with Weiss's conceptualization is that it takes the relationships and the needs and supports they provide as given, and so fails to take account of how individuals define and act upon them. In short, the important issue of how far potential resources for social and psychological support are co-terminous with people's *strategies* for coping is largely ignored. Weiss's contentions therefore need to be restated in a way that takes account of the *meanings* of social relationships for the individual. For example, the assumption that marriage meets the needs of husbands and wives in identical ways is questionable if one accepts that there is a high degree of differentiation in the experience, expectations, and structural position of each conjugal partner.

Research in this field based upon a sociological rather than a social-psychological perspective has rather different concerns. Social network here refers not simply to concrete entities such as groups of kin and friends, but also to conceptualizations of the ways in which social structures socialize, sanction, constrain, and legitimate the actions and beliefs of the individual. It has provided some explanation of people's actions and decisions in terms of the constraints of social structure, whilst at the same time throwing light upon people's power and latitude to make decisions, but only within the limits of the social situations and structures in which they find themselves. The application of network analysis has yielded explanations why certain groups and individuals (and not others), seek help and services from agencies and services. Some have suggested that they do so according to their power to mobilize their social networks (Mayer and Timms 1970). However, a sociological perspective suggests that social networks also act upon individuals, constraining their actions and decisions.

McKinlay (1973) explored the utilization patterns of pre-maternity services by lower working-class women, and found that where women were members of highly connected networks they were unlikely to use the pre-maternity services. He argues that the networks to which these women belonged provided them with readily available systems of lay knowledge and beliefs about pregnancy, and that the close-knit structure of these social networks acted as an effective constraint on women to make use of the lay referral systems rather than the pre-maternity services. In contrast, he found that women with loose-knit or differentiated networks were more likely to use the services. He suggests that this is because the women belonging to loose-knit networks had more latitude in their decision-making; they could make a choice whether or not to act on the advice of their network members since the sanctioning by loose-knit networks was less effective than by close-knit networks. In utilizing the concept of network, McKinlay was able to go beyond an examination of the value system of a particular social class about consulting medical agencies, and he suggested that, irrespective of values, which may not vary very much within the lower working class (with which McKinlay was concerned) the structured complexity of interpersonal relationships is likely to have a highly determining influence on whether or not an individual seeks formal help.

Each of these two rather different interpretations of the impact of social networks on the individual (that which we have rather crudely termed the social-psychological and sociological) has a different theoretical focus. Notions about the importance of intimate relationships as a source of psychological well-being and emotional support are fundamentally individualistic in orientation and usually assume that all individuals have similar and essential needs. Such notions therefore are not concerned with the issue of how the social fabric creates and meets those needs. The sociological perspective, on the other hand, tends to neglect the emotional aspects of social relationships, being principally concerned at the level of structures, beliefs, and conscious action. It does however raise questions about the genesis of so-called essential needs and suggests the possibility that society may meet needs in a variety of different ways, thereby injecting ideas which allow for a dynamic element in the nature of social relationships and the structures they create.

The idea of social network is relevant to a study of troubled marriages and the search for help. First, it would seem to offer a way of analysing the immediate social *context* within which people live out their marital relationships, define the problems they encounter and seek help, both formally and informally. Second, the notion of social network as an expressive and instrumental *resource* which people may mobilize to a greater or lesser extent, and in a variety of ways, in their efforts to cope at times of trouble would seem to be useful. Finally we would emphasize the importance of the *emotional* aspect of social network both as a context and as a resource.

There have been relatively few studies which focus on how people cope at times of difficulty and crisis, and even fewer which have examined this question in relation to the impact of family, friends, and the structure of these relationships.[1] In the literature on friendship, for example, there is little to suggest that friends play an important role at times of adversity (see Babchuck and Bates 1963). It is possible that although in the 'normal' course of people's lives friendships have a fairly superficial impact, at times of crisis they may be activated rather differently and assume a more important role.

One of the aims of this study was to explore the effects (if any) of people's social networks on the ways in which they coped when they had serious marriage problems. However, in order to carry out this task, we felt it was important to address ourselves to two issues which have been neglected in the literature. First, we sought to examine the *structure* of relationships in which emotional and social support was present (or absent). Second, we were clear that where supports were present, we could not assume that they had a constant effect on all those for whom such potential support was available. In short, we have tried to explore how far the presence of significant others (as social network members) is co-terminous with how people define and act upon it. Thus Weiss's (1969) assumption that specific social relationships provide particular kinds of support needs to be tested, both in itself and especially in relation to the particular structures of people's social networks.

In this chapter we propose to examine the resources in terms of significant others — family, relatives, and friends — who were *potentially* available to respondents as supports at times of trouble. In addition to estimating the number and range of persons available, we are concerned with the structural contexts of respondents' significant relationships. To this end we have utilized the sociological notion of social network, both as a concept and as an analytical tool, and we have restricted social network membership to significant others. We will begin by describing three distinct types of social network that we have identified in this study and the criteria by which we have differentiated them.

Respondents' social networks

We asked respondents to list members of their households, their families, relatives, and friends and we gave them the following additional criteria for inclusion: '. . . people you see for more than just a chat, people you make a point of spending some time with, either in person or on the 'phone. We are interested only in those contacts that take place at least once a month. Can you include persons to whom you write letters at least once a month?' The interviewers also elicited further information: the number of contexts and situations in which the respondents knew each member of their networks; whether the respondents' spouses were usually present; whether any of the network members met each other independently of the respondent.

The average size of our respondents' networks was seven and a half members. This figure is similar to the estimation of Horwitz (1977), whose study concerned people being treated for psychiatric problems and whose bases for estimation were similar to ours. Like Horwitz, we found differences in network size between men and women; women in our study had an average of eight and a half members and men an average of six and a half. In our estimates we included respondents' spouses but not their children, unless they had already left the household. We excluded children living in the household partly because we were not primarily interested in the kinds of support provided by children at home but also because we did not wish automatically to inflate the network size of couples with children. We found that women in the study had more contact with friends, especially with friends of the same sex, than the men did. Women also had more multiplex relationships, that is they knew and met network members in more than one social context. However, for both sexes the proportion of multiplex relationships over all relationships was low.

By simultaneously taking three measures of network into account, namely size, membership and connectedness, we were able to distinguish three 'ideal types' of network in our study group. However, two points need to be borne in mind concerning our classification. First, since the cut-off points for each type were of necessity arbitrary, respondents' networks must be regarded as only approximations of these three ideal types. Second, it is important to regard respondents' networks as dynamic rather than static, and it is quite clear from our data that a few of our respondents' networks had recently changed from one structural type to another as their life stages and circumstances changed. It is important to note that we were concerned with measuring respondents' networks at the time of interview, and that where respondents' networks had radically changed as, for example, over the period of a marital break-up, we had to make a rough estimation of their former structures. We shall now briefly outline the three network types.

1 We have termed the first and most predominant type of social network in our study *truncated*, because of its truncated and attenuated structure and its relatively few ties. The main features of networks in this category are as follows: (a) a relatively small number of members, ranging from two to seven; (b) a tendency for members to be limited to the family of procreation and to the family of origin; (c) a small number of friends, three or fewer; (d) an absence of cross-cutting ties between network members, apart from between family members. The highest proportion of respondents in our study fall into this group (21/48). It includes thirteen men and eight women, amongst whom there are seven couples.

2 We have termed this second type *differentiated friendship network*. The characteristics of these networks are: (a) a relatively large number of members (that is compared with the truncated type) ranging from eight to thirteen members; (b) a larger number of friends than the truncated, that is four or more; (c) a varying degree of connectedness between members. A slightly smaller

proportion of respondents fall into this category than the above (17/48). It includes six men and eleven women amongst whom there are four couples.

3 The third type we have termed *close-knit kinship network*. The characteristics of these networks are: (a) a relatively large number of members, similar to the differentiated friendship type; (b) a tendency for ties to be based on kinship, by blood or by marriage; (c) a high degree of connectedness between members; (d) a tendency for ties to be reinforced by similar religious or ethnic affiliation. The smallest proportion of respondents are in this group (10/48). It includes seven women and three men amongst whom there are three couples.

We believe that these three network types make some theoretical sense. Both our close-knit kinship and differentiated friendship network types relate directly to the network types conceptualized in other research. Bott distinguished between close-knit and loose-knit networks, and in the families in her study close-knit networks were based on ties of kinship (Bott 1968). McKinlay (1973), in a study of the role of lay consultation in the use of health and welfare services, distinguished between the undifferentiated and differentiated networks of readily available relatives and friends in the lower working class. In our study, close-knit networks (which roughly correspond to McKinlay's definition of the undifferentiated type as well as to Bott's close-knit type) appear to be strongly based on ties of kinship, whilst differentiated networks are more closely associated with friendship. We can make some claim to originality in delineating the structural type we have named the truncated group. The nearest approximation to this type is probably to be found in studies concerning the relationship between social bonds and mental disorder. In one study, respondents with high rates of mental disorder were found to have very few social bonds. (Henderson *et al.*, 1978, 1980). However, network structure *per se* was not investigated in these studies.

In addition to constructing respondents' networks we also explored their perceptions of what it was like to live in them. Some people were rather defensive in response to these questions, tending to insist they were quite satisfied with the number of people they knew, whilst others more readily and easily expressed satisfaction and dissatisfaction. However, spontaneous statements made by respondents about such characteristics of their networks as the extent of their contact with others in general matched our own objective measures of net-work type and structure.

In the rest of this chapter we shall briefly consider the relevance of network structure to three aspects of marital relationships. First, we shall examine its effects upon the types of investment, particularly in an emotional sense, that respondents made in their marital relation-ships. Second, we shall explore network structure in relation to the extent to which respondents perceived the marriages of the members of their networks as having problems. Third, we shall see whether network structure has any bearing upon the ways in which respon-dents defined their problems. In the two subsequent chapters we shall examine network structure in relation to both informal consulting and confiding.

Types of investment in marital relationships

Behavioural description of respondents' marriages was limited to an examination of how far they consulted spouses and others over the major life events, problems, and marital difficulties which they had experienced. It was not one of our principal aims to describe day-to-day patterns of marital interaction but we did question respondents about satisfaction with specific aspects of their relationships, such as talking to one another, decision-making, the showing of affection, and the sexual side of their relationships.

On common-sense grounds, given the restricted number of people available to respondents in truncated networks, we might expect a greater degree of emotional involvement and social interaction between partners in marriages where both belonged to this network type, compared with those with other types of network. Likewise, given Bott's finding that segregated conjugal roles were associated with a close-knit network structure (Bott 1968), we might expect low consultation between partners with close-knit kinship networks. How-ever, in our study, it was not uncommon for both partners in a marriage to belong to different types of network, which makes for further complexity. Moreover, all marriages in our study were by definition experiencing a certain amount of difficulty, so that in con-sequence it would have been surprising if communication between the spouses had not been seriously affected.

One of the main themes which emerges in this study concerns wives' dissatisfaction with their husbands' unwillingness openly to acknow-ledge and discuss problematic aspects of the marriages. The converse of this (husbands' dissatisfaction with wives' communication) is significantly absent. Moreover, this theme figures not only in the wives' complaints about their husbands but is also present in what the husbands had to say about themselves. The following comments made by a husband and wife in the study are fairly characteristic.

Mrs Frome, aged 31, housewife, differentiated friendship network: 'I can want to say something and he'll either be watching TV or consulting a technical magazine . . . he tends to study an awful lot and be very into it. It's quite hard to say "Yoo hoo, I'd like to say something now" . . . There is a reluctance on my part to say anything very much because I think "Well, I won't bother him with that because he's doing something else". Or he's been on courses and things like that and been away from home and so on. I sort of think that it's a bit small to worry him with and so I don't bother. But that is a mistake I can see now.'

Mr Frome, aged 32, systems analyst, differentiated friendship network:
'Do you feel you can talk as easily as you want to?'
'*Now*, since the counselling yes, before no. I found it *very* hard to talk to her . . . I couldn't. I wanted to and couldn't. She wanted to and felt she couldn't and would get angry about it. So when she finally did start talking, she'd be angry and then she'd get me angry.'

In the next chapter, one of the issues we shall consider concerns the extent to which the couples consulted and confided in one another over a range of major events and problems including marital ones. Without anticipating the next chapter too much, it is apposite to summarize some of the findings from this data which suggest that social network may be a critical indicator of the extent to which respondents invested emotionally in their marriages. First, we found that, compared with respondents with other network types, respondents with truncated networks (and particularly where their partners also had truncated networks) more frequently turned to their spouses in adversity, rather than to other people. Second, more respondents in the truncated group had spouses as confidants.[2] Third, where respondents in truncated networks confided in their spouses, they were likely to do so exclusively. Nevertheless, overall, those in truncated networks were less likely than those in other networks to turn and confide in any one at all, and, when they did consult others, it tended on balance to

be their spouses. However, over the marital difficulties, those in truncated networks (although this was a feature of the men rather than the
women in this group) were less likely to define their marriages as having problems in the first place, and hence were unlikely to discuss
these with their spouses.

Moreover, it appears that the quality of communication between
spouses experienced by the majority of respondents in the study was
poor. But for one group in particular (i.e. the truncated group) the
absence of significant others meant that, in spite of serious difficulties
in communication and in showing feelings, they were forced to be
mainly dependent on the other spouse for these things. A second consequence of this pattern of marital relationship was that such couples
did not actually define the problems in their marriages. These two
characteristics were most likely to exist where both partners had truncated networks. As we shall show later, in those marriages where the
husband had a truncated network and the wife had a differentiated
friendship network, the wife was more likely to define a marital problem and to mobilize some form of support from significant others.
Thus it seems that where spouses had only each other they placed considerable importance on presenting, both to themselves and to others,
an apparent consensus, for fear that recognition or definition of an
underlying conflict or rift in their relationship might threaten the
little security they had in their lives, namely one another. Thus it may
be that those whose marriages were in difficulty, but who depended
more or less exclusively on one another, tended to keep their worries
and dissatisfaction *within* each of themselves, because they feared the
uncertainty and danger of being thrown upon a world which was, in
reality, bereft of significant others. If this is so, it would not be surprising to find such persons more at risk of mental or even physical disorder (Henderson *et al.*, 1978, 1980).

A number of studies have delineated different types of marital
relationships. For example, Horwitz (1978) classified his informants'
marriages according to four types. The first of these types is marked
by conflict, and the second concerns couples who have already separated. A third type of marriage is characterized by a marked lack of
involvement between the partners, and the fourth type, the only relatively healthy marriage represented, is described as 'mutual' and is
suggestive of a cooperative partnership. It is of interest to us here that
Horwitz found that those with mutual relationships had a low rate of
consulting kin and friends, and that those with conflictual and separated marriages had relatively high rates of turning to kin and friends

and received low support from spouses. In our study we found considerable variation in the extent to which people with poor marriages turned to family and friends. Moreover, we would suggest that an apparently 'mutual' relationship may not necessarily be an untroubled one, and that mutuality in itself and especially under adverse conditions, may *preclude* the expression of conflict, because it is based on an exclusive interdependence between the partners. Such relationships might well be described as 'pseudo-mutual'.[3]

Of course, it is by no means clear that social network structure *in itself* generates particular types of marital relationship. Nonetheless, in some cases the lack of a pool of significant others, as where previously important kin are now dead for example, is likely to be a significant *predetermining* factor. In such cases it is possible to envisage people turning to their spouses simply because they were the only people there. Second, the fact that a large proportion of respondents who had truncated networks were *men* might in itself be more significant than network structure *per se*, in which case the structure of the wife's network perhaps becomes the more critical factor for the marriage. However, even if men's disinclination to disclose to others is assumed to be an important influence upon the structure of their social networks, attitudes to disclosure cannot be seen as the only predetermining factor, since relationships with kin at least, unlike friendships, are generally ascribed and not achieved. But whatever the full explanation why certain respondents, and men in particular, had such stunted and limited networks, those situations where *both* spouses in such marriages had truncated networks[4] seem likely to have had important implications for their marital relationships.

Amongst those with truncated networks, another marriage pattern, in addition to the 'pseudo-mutual', emerges. This second type relates to marriages where husbands had truncated networks but whose wives had other types of network. We have described these marriages as 'uninvolved' (see Horwitz 1978), since in them the husbands did not consult their spouses at all, and tended not so much to avoid conflict as to pre-empt the possibility of it ever arising. We think that, in some of these cases, it is likely that the personalities of the husbands may have rendered them unable easily to form intimate relationships.

Thus, borrowing Horwitz's (1978) definitions, we suggest that there are four types of marital investment exhibited by respondents in our study, all of whose marriages were in trouble. Moreover, we believe that these can be partly distinguished on the basis of network structure. In the truncated group we found that where both partners belonged to this network type (and they formed the majority of this group) the marriages displayed mutuality or, in some cases, what we have termed pseudo-mutuality (14/21) and that, additionally, several of the husbands' marriages in this network group can be described as uninvolved (5/21). In the differentiated friendship group, there is an absence of mutual or pseudo-mutual marital investment. Over half of respondents' marriages in this group were marked by overt but not necessarily continuous conflict (9/17) and some had broken down altogether (5/17). In the close-knit kinship group, the majority of the marriages were marked by conflict (8/10), and two respondents were already separated at the time of interview.

Perceptions of problems in others' marriages

Before we go on to describe and illustrate the relationship between respondents' social networks and how they defined their problems, we shall first discuss an interesting association that we also found between the types of networks to which respondents belonged and their perceptions of others' marriages.

Marriages are in many respects highly privatized relationships. Nonetheless, it may not be unreasonable to expect some variations in the *visibility* of marital problems among those bound by ties of closeness and intimacy. One of our conjectures at the outset of the study was that network structure might to some extent influence whether or not respondents saw the marriages of significant others as also being in trouble. Seeing others' marriages as unproblematic might lead people to feel isolated and alone in their difficulties, whereas seeing relatives or friends as also having marital difficulties might lead respondents to compare themselves with others, and so might lessen some of the anxiety of feeling unique in these situations. Moreover, since the normative emphasis on having a happy marriage is so strong in our society, failure to perceive the unhappy reality of some other people's marriages might in itself lead to an avoidance or denial of problems in one's own. It is of course possible to argue the converse, namely that avoidance of marital problems in the first place is likely to influence respondents' perceptions of others' marriages. The direction of influence is by no means always clear in our study but it seems likely that respondents' perceptions of others' marriages reinforced, even if they did not determine, their perceptions of their own situations.

Over half of the people in our study saw their friends or relatives as having marital difficulties. These responses were obtained by a direct question to all respondents. Breakdown by network type reveals that three-quarters of those who belonged to truncated networks did not see either relatives or friends as having marital difficulties, whilst all but two respondents in the other two network types perceived some marital problems amongst their family or friends. Here are some of the comments people made:

> '*Do you see your relatives or friends as having marital or sexual difficulties?*'

Mr Crewe, aged 31, sales clerk, truncated network:
'No, not really. I can't think of anyone who has. If they have they are better actors than I. I think they must be covering up really if they have.'

Mrs Luton, aged 28, secretary, truncated network:
'No. None of the friends I have ever give me the impression that they have any, but whether or not, God only knows . . . But then I should imagine *we* present a pretty even face as well.'

Mr Clare, aged 45, junior manager, truncated network:
'No I've never seen much of my friends' home life.'

Mrs Frome, aged 31, housewife, differentiated friendship network:
'Oh yes . . . And we're all the same, to a greater or lesser degree.'
'*How does that make you feel?*'
'Marvellous . . .'

Mr Wells, aged 39, small shopkeeper, differentiated friendship network:
'I know of only one marriage that I can recall, that I'd say is stable.'

There are a number of points to be made here. From the structural point of view, it seems highly feasible that those with truncated networks saw fewer problems in others' marriages because, having fewer network members, there was less chance of there being problems. However, as some of our respondents' comments indicate, these perceptions reflect not so much accurate observations of others' marriages, as attitudes of mind. This leads us to suggest that network structure, rather than simply influencing actual perceptions, may sometimes act as a mediating factor in the way people *think about* both themselves and their significant others. Nevertheless it is possible that those whose marriages had already broken down may, as a consequence, have become more aware of others' difficulties. In the following extract a woman who was in the process of being divorced made just this point.

> Mrs Epsom, aged 48, executive director of small family firm, close-knit kinship network:
> 'Well, funnily enough until this happened to me I was pretty introvert, you know. I didn't talk about these sort of things. I realize *now* that everybody seems to talk about it but I don't think I was aware of what was going on . . . Now it would appear that friends talk to each other . . . My sister tells me all her friends — she has a very wide circle of friends — they all talk about their marriages very very freely.'

However, it may also be argued that had not this respondent belonged to a close-knit network, she might never have arrived at an increased awareness of others' marriages. In effect the perceptual change need not only be attributed to the break-up of her marriage.

There is a further general point worth making here about the effect of structure on respondents' awareness of marital problems, which concerns the flow of communication or gossip. The more relationships a respondent has, the greater his or her chances of acquiring knowledge or gossip about others, since each network member has his or her own social network and so on. Moreover, the more differentiated the network, the greater the proliferation of the sources of information. Sociologists have long drawn attention to the functions of gossip in maintaining conformity to social norms, but have paid less attention to its function in legitimating deviant social practices or changing social norms.[5] It is possible that where respondents have differentiated networks they have greater access to knowledge about people like themselves who have problematic marriages, and this may serve to make their problems seem normal or common occurrences, even if it does not make them desirable or normative.

It should not be supposed that those who acknowledged others' marital and sexual difficulties regarded them as obvious or easily discernible. The comments respondents' made about marriage in general attested to the ways in which people privately live out their marriages and present an overall 'brave face' to the world. The paradox between assumptions about the typicality of marriage in our society (in terms of prevalence) and the uniqueness of the lived experience, is hinted at in the following extract.

> Mrs Ripon, aged 40, shop assistant, truncated network:
> 'I feel different. I don't *think* I am, I just think this is how I feel

because of the situation. I think it's because you have to live a certain lie . . . You kind of put on a brave face . . . I've always felt I did put a brave face on the matter . . . It makes you feel a bit odd . . . You don't walk about with your heart on your sleeve all day long. No one does.'

The social pressures and taboos constraining people from acknowledging problems defined in *sexual* terms are considerable. We found little evidence of awareness of others' sexual problems, and very little acknowledgement of respondents' own sexual problems to other people. We did, however find a deviant case. This case serves to highlight the norm in the sense of the exception proving the rule. It concerns a man suffering from sexual impotence. He belonged to a close-knit kinship network which was also linked by ties of occupation, neighbourhood, and leisure activities. There was considerable evidence in the interview, which we will not detail here, that this respondent was somewhat of a sociometric star[6] in his particular network. His sexual problem started shortly after he began an affair, which he kept secret from his wife. His girlfriend was very sympathetic to his problem and urged him to seek help. He described how he began to tell his friends and workmates about his sexual problem (they also, incidentally, knew about his affair) and how they in turn began to admit to having experienced similar problems themselves. It is clear that this man recognized that acknowledging this kind of problem risked loss of face and that such acknowledgement was, for most people, an admission of failure. It seems that almost *because* of the potential stigma, he was prepared to risk disclosing his problem, as if being seen to survive it without loss of face would make the disclosure worthwhile. In so doing he was not so much using his prestigious position in his network to protect himself, as using it as a means of obtaining even greater 'glory'.

'I was sort of surprised at them sort of saying it, admitting it sort of thing.'
'Why do you say that?'
'You would never find a man admitting a sexual problem would you? They find it sort of lessens their manhood. When I was speaking to them about it, a young fellow like myself, having this sort of problem, one of the older ones said "Well, I've had it." And after that one or two others admitted it and then another two or three, sort of thing . . . *Most* people I spoke to had never been to see anyone about it. A lot of them said they admired my guts for going . . .'

'You got a sympathetic reaction. Did you get any unsympathetic reactions?'
'No not at all, not at all. They were all sort of admiring me for doing what I was doing, being a young fellow.'

It is interesting that there is some correspondence between respondents' perceptions of others' marriages and the types of networks to which they themselves belonged. We shall now go on to explore the ways in which they perceived and defined their own marriages and problems.

Definitions of problems

As we shall describe in greater detail in a later chapter, whether and how respondents defined their marriage troubles had implications for how and when they approached agencies. We found two main ways in which the problems were presented to agencies. In eleven of the twenty-eight marriages, one partner approached an agency, such as a general practitioner, with some kind of health problem. This we call an 'individual' focus since these respondents primarily located the problems in themselves; in these cases it was the agency that subsequently defined a marital problem. In the other seventeen marriages one partner went with a marital problem to an agency like the Marriage Guidance Council. It is the case that the majority of those who approached agencies with an individual focus, or had spouses who did so, had truncated networks (16/21) amongst whom there were six couples. In contrast, those with differentiated friendship networks or close-knit kinship networks approached agencies with a marital focus, or they had a spouse who did so (13/17 and 7/10).

Although communication was generally strained between all the couples in the study, some respondents acknowledged problems in their marriages while others did not. In exploring the question why problems were accommodated to in particular ways, it appears that network structures may play some part. Although a full explanation is not clear, it seems possible that avoidance of marital conflict, or avoiding acknowledging problematic areas in the marriage, was a more likely strategy amongst the truncated group, most of whom we have described as having mutual, pseudo-mutual, or uninvolved relationships. It is possible that close contact with a range of intimate and significant others, especially outside the immediate family, may influence and modify thoughts and definitions about the *self*, as well as having an impact upon respondents' perceptions of others, and that the absence of such contact may reinforce an incipient avoidance of their problems. The following example concerns a couple where the husband had contained the marital problem for a number of years before finally acknowledging its existence.

Mr Flint described his marriage troubles in terms of his wife's persistent 'infidelity'. He said that in the past he had feared making an issue of it because of the risk of losing his wife. It was only when his wife had a third affair and was actively considering leaving him that this husband defined the marriage as problematic and took some action which turned out to be too late to save his marriage. His network was highly truncated; he had no friends and the only relative he saw was his mother. He worked in a very small office, where his wife also worked (a situation he had brought about to enable him to keep an eye on her); he himself had worked there for many years. Most of his leisure time he spent on his own studying.

Mr Flint, aged 44, clerical worker, truncated network:
'This problem I had with my wife had been going on for years. I've had about twelve or thirteen years of it, prior to this last [affair]. In that time I didn't ask anybody for help. In fact nobody knew about it. Even though my wife's parents live next door, they didn't know one word about it and my wife is pretty close to her parents and I know them well enough. But we never put our problems on anybody else. We kept them to ourselves and we tried to work them out ourselves and I suppose we did a patch-up job over the years.'

We cannot say whether talking to others might have affected his definition of the situation, but the fact that he did not, seems likely at least to have sustained the consistency of his viewpoint. He went on to describe why he had not regarded his wife's earlier 'transgressions' as problematic:

'I realize now that we didn't talk over our personal problems the way we should have done. We didn't get to the bottom of it, thrash them out completely as we should have done . . . I knew that from my point of view that I was afraid I might lose her. I didn't want to express to her completely how I felt because even then I thought she might flare up and out.'

Whilst for some respondents a truncated network structure appeared to sustain fears that, by broaching the issues they might lose their spouses altogether, for others a truncated network appeared to

Figure 6(1) Mr and Mrs Rugby

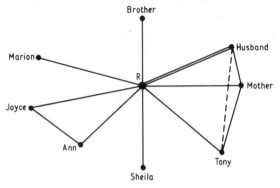

(Mrs Rugby) Differentiated friendship network

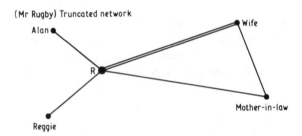

(Mr Rugby) Truncated network

Note: First names refer to friends.

reinforce patterns of avoidance *per se*. Where each partner in a marriage had a different network type it is interesting to note the different reactions of each to their problems. Mr and Mrs Rugby, for example, belonged to different network types: Mrs Rugby had a differentiated friendship network and her husband had a truncated network (see *Figure 6(1)*). Mrs Rugby disclosed the marital problems to her friends, and received some considerable emotional and practical support from them in the course of taking decisions and action in connection with the marriage which ultimately led to a temporary separation. Mr Rugby turned to no one until he had to find somewhere to live.

Mrs Rugby, aged 40, school and play-group worker, talked about her husband:
'My husband is the sort of person that doesn't talk to anybody. I think had he done so in the past I don't think he would ever have

got in the state he was in. He thinks if you've got a problem then you shoulder it and master it and don't ever talk to anybody. I mean that was another thing we rowed about, me going and telling everybody our problems. He believes that you should go out of the front door and smile and let the world think "There goes England's happiest couple!" [Laughing] when in fact it's not!'

We have argued earlier that such attitudes to disclosure are shaped by gender socialization and gender-defined marital experience. Nonetheless, we think that the disclosure behaviour of Mr Rugby and others like him is likely to be reinforced by the structure of their networks. As the diagram of Mr Rugby's network indicates, it offered few opportunities for support. Both his parents were dead and his only close relative was a half-brother who did not live nearby and with whom he was rarely in contact. In this case it was the wife who was instrumental (they had been to a Marriage Guidance Council some years previously) in bringing the marital problem to the fore against considerable resistance from the husband. However, it was only after the problem had taken a very serious turn — the husband became violent, which eventually led the wife to take out a court injunction against him — that any kind of resolution began to take place.

Thus we would argue that avoiding the definition of marital problems may sustain the marriage but it often seemed to do so at the expense of the health of at least one of the partners.[7] On the other hand, defining a marital problem is inherently a risky business, since it jeopardizes the relationship, often putting it under public scrutiny, and may ultimately lead to the break-up of the marriage. We would suggest that the structure of sets of intimate relationships surrounding respondents' marriages are likely to determine, to some extent at least, how they perceived and acted out their marital relationships and the problems that these came up against.

In this chapter we have examined respondents' networks in relation to types of investment in marriage and also in terms of how far respondents perceived both their own marriages and those of their significant others as problematic. In the next chapter we examine the relevance and use of networks in relation to the critical events and problems, including marital ones, that respondents had encountered.

Notes

1 One of the few studies concerns the application of network ideas to coronary heart disease (Finlayson and McEwen 1977).

2 Our working definition of a confidant aimed to include those persons to whom respondents seem to have disclosed in a relatively complete way, including some degree of revelation of how they felt. In doing so respondents appear to have sought or to have derived a certain amount of expressive support as well as (in some cases) instrumental help.

3 Wynne *et al.* (1967) use the term in a somewhat similar way in a study of the family relationships of schizophrenics.

4 Of the twenty-one respondents in the truncated group there were seven couples.

5 An exception is a study concerning the search for abortionists by Lee (1969).

6 The term 'sociometric star' is used in research on small experimental groups. Zelditch (1960) notes the tendency for a task leader and a sociometric star to emerge as part of a general pattern of differentiation within the small group. 'The sociometric star, although the term originally derives from attitudes taken toward ego by alter, also tends to show a certain pattern of behaviours and attitudes: namely the *expression* of emotions, supportive behaviour to others, the desire to please and be liked, and a more generalized liking for other members' (Zelditch 1960: 347).

7 We did not investigate the state of respondents' psychological and physical health though we systematically asked about health problems (see Chapter 5). There appears to be some evidence in our data to suggest that members of the truncated group had been particularly prone to severe 'conditions' such as depression, and some respondents in this group had had recourse to bouts of heavy drinking and to suicide attempts.

7

Informal consulting
and social networks

In the last chapter we considered respondents' current and recent social contacts — the persons with whom they interacted on a regular and intimate basis. Our conceptualization of respondents' social contacts as forming networks emphasized their structural aspect. We investigated network size, membership, and connectedness and categorized respondents' networks according to three types: the truncated, the differentiated friendship, and the close-knit kinship.

We originally decided to investigate respondents' social networks on the hypothesis that they might help to explain the significance of those persons to whom respondents turned for emotional and social support in times of trouble and adversity. In this chapter we shall examine how far the type of social network to which respondents belonged influenced their consulting and confiding behaviour, and also the character of the response or 'help' they sought and received from members of their networks. However, an issue which we raised in the last chapter needs to be considered at the same time, namely the relevance of social networks for those whose ways of dealing with their troubles precluded turning to others, whatever the potential resources available to them. Here it should be remembered that most of the men in our study group were in any case negatively orientated towards disclosing personal problems. Thus, with this in mind, we propose to look at whether respondents turned to others over the critical events and problems they encountered, including troubles in their marriages, as well as to whom they turned.

We elicited from respondents the critical events and problems which they had experienced during their adult lives, with special emphasis on the eighteen months before they approached an agency. The reader may like to turn to *Table 5(1)* in order to inspect the incidence of these events and those which *we* rated as likely to have had a fairly severe impact on respondents, given their circumstances at the time. We later asked them to select from among all these the three major events or problems which had made the greatest impact upon them *at the time they occurred*, and to tell us whether they had turned to anyone at the time and, if so, to whom. We also asked, as a separate set of questions, whether respondents had turned to or confided in anyone over their marital difficulties and, if so, to whom.

The kinds of events and problems

The events and problems respondents selected as having made the greatest impact on them were substantially the same as those we had selected as *likely* to have produced considerable effect. Over two-thirds of those occurred in the eighteen months before respondents approached agencies. (These are considered in greater detail in Chapter 5.) The other third which respondents selected differs from the rest only in that they had occurred earlier in their adult lives.

Virtually all of these events and problems had made a very marked *negative* impact upon respondents. We have grouped them into three categories. The first group refers to actual losses, through death, of respondents' parents, siblings, and grandparents. The second group refers to other kinds of loss, namely roles, persons (other than by death), and also objects and ideas which respondents had either given up or failed to acquire or achieve. The third group is characterized by danger and the *threat* of loss, to respondents themselves, their spouses, parents or siblings. It is interesting that these groups of events and problems are similar both in type and focus to those which Brown and Harris (1978) suggest are most likely to provoke depressive and anxiety states. Moreover, the underlying significance of these events and problems (for respondents) seems broadly to make sense in terms of Brown and Harris's notions of loss and danger. They suggest that depression arises from a profound sense of loss and that anxiety is linked to a sense of danger or threat.

> 'In general feelings of depression will follow from something which has happened and about which little or nothing can be done, while anxiety accompanies a situation of uncertainty. In the context of a loss, anxiety would be expected where something can still be done to restore the situation. In these terms a severe event may give rise to a number of emotions: disappointment on learning of a husband's unfaithfulness may go with concern that he may leave home.'
>
> (Brown and Harris 1978: 229)

As to the substantive aspect of these events and problems, the largest group concern respondents' marriages. Not surprisingly, of those who were currently in their second marriages, almost all mentioned the break-up of their first marriages, and those who had experienced separations and overt difficulties in their current marriages mentioned these likewise.

We were primarily interested here in whether or not respondents turned to others, and if so, to whom they had turned and confided when they had experienced these events and problems. In replying to those questions respondents vividly conveyed their feelings by the language they used to describe the events and problems. One woman described herself as 'devastated' by the sudden knowledge of a previously undisclosed friendship that her husband had formed with a woman over a six-year period. Most revealingly, she described this knowledge as threatening not only her current but also her *past* view and feelings about her marriage.

'The news that he had been seeing another woman affected me incredibly at the time . . . My world literally stopped, physically and mentally stopped. All the good things that seemingly had happened between us were just wiped out.'

Thus, in Brown and Harris's terms the significance of this event not only threatened the stability of her marriage, spelling danger and uncertainty in the present and future, but it also provoked a sense of loss and disappointment about the past.

Patterns of consulting

Before discussing the characteristics of respondents' consulting behaviour we want to point out that consulting, as we have defined it here, refers to all kinds of disclosures that respondents made to significant others over these events and problems. In practice, consulting incorporated a wide range of behaviour. At one end of the spectrum respondents had clearly *confided* very fully in particular persons and had given a relatively complete account of their feelings. Many of these respondents sought and/or received expressive (as well as instrumental) support from these persons and we shall henceforward refer to them as 'confidants'. In the centre of the spectrum are those who disclosed their troubles in a restricted or partial fashion, both in respect of actual details and of feelings. Some of those whose disclosures were limited in terms of information given and affect expressed, had explicitly sought practical help or information, while others had sought emotional help but usually to a much lesser extent. At the far end of the spectrum are those who said they had never disclosed their feelings and had disclosed either minimal information or none at all. Those respondents in the latter group we have termed 'non-consulters'.

In the following discussion concerning consulting behaviour we shall distinguish between, on the one hand, the three major events and problems which respondents selected and which we refer to as 'general events' (even though they include a high proportion of events connected with the break-up of their marriages) and, on the other, the current marital difficulties (whether or not respondents had themselves actually defined them as problems).

General events

When we consider the selected general events, it appears that the majority of respondents had consulted or turned to at least one person over at least one event. It is of course possible that questioning respondents about each individual event led to some inflation of the numbers of persons mentioned. However, as we suggested above, it is clear from the nature of the reported exchanges between consulters and consulted that consulting subsumed a wide range of behaviour, much of it being fairly superficial and 'en passant'. Nonetheless, one group of male respondents, almost all of whom had truncated networks, said they had not consulted anyone at all over any of these general events (7/21).

When we examine the extent to which respondents consulted confidants over general events, a rather sharper and more differentiated picture emerges. We gave the term 'general confidant' to those persons whom respondents consulted in an open, unrestricted, and 'in depth' fashion over more than one general event. It appears that the differentiated friendship group were almost twice as likely to have had at least one such general confidant compared with the truncated group. In the truncated group those who had general confidants confided in their wives and in almost no other person. The close-knit friendship group differed again, having had proportionately fewer general confidants than the differentiated friendship group but more than the truncated group,[1] together with the unique feature of having a great many persons who were 'in the know' about their troubles and difficulties.

Turning now to the question of the *kinds of persons* respondents consulted and confided in, it appears that the truncated group were far more likely to have consulted or confided in their spouses than in any other category of persons. In the differentiated friendship group friends were more frequently consulted or confided in, and in the close-knit kinship group family members and other closely related relatives were the most frequently mentioned category.[2]

Marital difficulties

In spite of the exclusive and privatized quality of marital relationships in general, the rates of consulting over marital difficulties in our study were not significantly lower than for general events, especially in the close-knit kinship group and in the differentiated friendship group. This may well reflect the fact that there were fairly high proportions of marriage break-ups amongst the general events. On the other hand, it is clear from respondents' reports that they were much more likely to have turned to others *after* the break-up rather than during or before, and it was persons turned to afterwards who were mentioned. At any rate, there does not appear to be any great falling off in the *number* of persons consulted over ongoing marital difficulties (taking 'marital difficulties' as equivalent to one general event) except in the truncated group where very few persons were consulted. This latter finding is hardly surprising, since the majority of persons consulted by the truncated group over general events were in fact their spouses; moreover, many respondents in this network group had resisted defining their marriages as problematic, preferring, consciously or unconsciously, to deny or avoid the problems.

But if we restrict consulting over marital difficulties to confiding, it becomes clear how *little* respondents confided over their marital problems, except for one group, the differentiated friendship group. For this group confidants were almost as frequent for marital difficulties as for general events.[3] Moreover, in the truncated group marital confidants, like general confidants, tended to be spouses and it seemed that even where there had been attempts to communicate fully over the marital problems these had generally reached an impasse. For some respondents failure in the past to resolve the problems with their spouses had reinforced their lack of consulting in the present. We also believe there to be some significance in the finding that those few persons who were confidants of the close-knit kinship group for marital difficulties were friends and not kin; where respondents in this group had friends as confidants, these persons were less likely to be enmeshed in the kin network and thus respondents could more safely entrust their confidences to them.

To sum up at this point, the great majority of the study group reported that they had turned to (however superficially) at least one person over all events including marital difficulties.[4] However, if we consider the nature of their reported interchanges and the extent of their disclosures, it emerges that many people frequently gave very restricted accounts to significant others, particularly about their feelings. When we re-defined consulting behaviour in terms of confiding, it emerged that just under one-half of the people in the study had no confidant at all (neither marital or general),[5] and that those who had no confidants were rather more likely to have truncated social networks. In addition, since respondents in this latter group were more likely to turn to spouses rather than to other categories of persons, their range of confidants appears to have been especially restricted. The close-knit kinship group emerges as having more confidants than the truncated group and fewer than the differentiated friendship group but with many of their network members (kin) being 'in the know' about their problems. The differentiated friendship group were in many respects in the 'best' position in that they had the widest choice of persons to turn to (categories of persons as well as absolute numbers) and none of the attendant risks of the close-knit kinship group of potential over-involvement or interference by network members.

We shall now describe and illustrate our material on consulting and confiding over critical events and problems in the following sections:

1 respondents as non-consulters;
2 the persons respondents chose not to consult;
3 respondents as consulters; and
4 the persons whom respondents chose to consult.

1 Respondents as non-consulters

Those who consulted no one at all in their adversity, or who consulted less often without revealing their feelings, were concentrated in the truncated group, and they were on the whole men.[6] We have already noted that this group had the highest proportion of people with no confidant and that few of them had acknowledged their marriage difficulties to others, and sometimes not even to their spouses. It was clear that a few men had hinted to their friends or workmates that their marriages were in trouble, but had regarded any discussion as unnecessary.

Mr Rugby, aged 37, fitter, truncated network:
'Comment was not invited and none was given.'

An examination of respondents' accounts of why they had consulted and confided rarely or not at all reveal a number of themes. One of these relates to a group of men who appear to have almost *never* consulted. For this group non-consulting was a central and stable characteristic of their general self-definitions as well as of their more specific attitudes and practices.[7] Mr York (aged 43, civil engineer, truncated network) put it this way:

'It is not a feature of me when encountering a problem, well an emotional problem anyway, to require the assistance of others to solve it.'

Some respondents who consulted rarely, rationalized what seemed to be an ingrained reluctance to disclose in terms of the 'embarrassing nature of the problem', especially over marital difficulties. However, in the case of non-consulting husbands, reluctance to disclose was also linked with a fear that others' knowledge of their problems might rebound badly on their own identities and self-esteem, rather than from the fear of embarrassing other people.

As with attitudes to disclosure the few women non-consulters generally described their reluctance to disclose in terms of a fear of hurting or upsetting others. In this sense women non-consulters bore a greater similarity to women consulters than they did to men non-consulters. Several women consulters described how they had met with negative reactions in the past, especially when they had confided personal problems to their parents, which thereafter served to reinforce their fear of disclosing, at least to their parents. In one rather extreme case, a woman spoke of her parents' reaction when, as a teenager, she had had an illegitimate baby, and which had made her reluctant to confide in her parents again:

'I went straight to my own home after the hospital and it was just never mentioned at all. If I tried to they would just look at the walls and pretend I hadn't!'

Some respondents described how their fears had been realized when they had disclosed problems which others construed as potentially threatening to the 'calm' of their own lives. In such cases it is often difficult for us (and for respondents likewise) to assess whether the source of their embarrassment lay in themselves or in others. One of the men in the study who had, it seemed, always been reluctant to confide in others, described the reactions of his neighbours and relatives when they learnt that his wife had left him. It seems to us that there is some likelihood that this man was projecting at least part of his own discomfort and feelings of shame on to others.

Mr Flint, aged 44, clerk, truncated network:
'I haven't turned to anybody but everybody knows. Of course everybody in the street knows. At Christmas time I popped in and saw the neighbours and the conversation eventually got round to Jill. I get the impression that everyone is embarrassed about it and they don't know what to say. They don't want to know about it. They seem afraid you are going to ask for something.'
'*What gives you that impression?*'
'Well, you can see it in their faces. You can see it in their answers. They tend to turn away from it when the conversation gets round to Jill. They were anxious to edge away from it . . . It's been the same with her parents and family and my own family . . . they can't offer anything to say or help. They keep away.'

Thus, for some respondents, not to consult others seemed to be an integral part of their strategies for dealing with their problems. Several respondents stressed the necessity of avoiding or trying not to dwell upon the unpleasant implications or possible consequences of a disturbing event. It is a necessary part of the confiding process that the threat of loss to the self (usually associated with a critical event or problem) is in some way recognized. The following comment was made by a man, a father of two young children, who was made uncomfortably aware of his own mortality by a sequence of unexpected deaths of several youngish acquaintances, all of whom died leaving young families.

Mr Wells, aged 39, small shopkeeper, differentiated friendship network:
'Christ! what they've left behind. I try not to dwell on it because we've all got to go sometime.'

Intimations of mortality seemed often to inhibit respondents from consulting or confiding over deaths, since to talk to anyone about them seemed to increase the threat of these events, heightening fears about their own vulnerability.

The language which many non-consulters used to describe themselves is striking and evocative and suggestive of a depersonalized approach to people. They referred to themselves using such vocabulary as 'cold fish', 'loner', and to the result of their own inhibited attempts at communication as 'a stone wall'. One man used the distancing pronoun 'one' instead of the personal pronoun 'I', and others talked about themselves as 'clamming up' and 'shutting people out'. These self-descriptions portray dispositions unconducive to revelation and trust.

Some respondents in this group may not always have been non-consulters, and their current inclination to keep their problems to themselves can perhaps be accounted for by the absence of choice of appropriate confidants in their current networks. As we noted in the last chapter, the deficit of parents and siblings was rather greater in the truncated group than in the other two groups. Moreover, in view of the absence of friends and extended kin in the truncated group, the impact of these deficits is likely to have had a disproportionately greater effect. The absence of people to turn to was sometimes mentioned by respondents as the main reason for not consulting others but this reason was also given along with other explanations, such as the inappropriateness of talking to others about a particular issue. For example, some respondents suggested, with probable realism, that there was little chance of evoking any sympathy or practical help from their families over their *particular* problems. One man, in trying to convey the present lack of help, indicated that none had been forthcoming in the past. He compared his current isolation and lack of support since his wife's departure, with the time when, as a young man and early in his marriage, he had had his leg amputated with little forewarning.

Mr Flint, aged 44, clerk, truncated network:
'I had to face up to it myself and get on with it myself. The new leg was thrown at you and from then on it was up to you. There was no help available in adjusting yourself to a new life. I don't know who you could turn to for help.'

Some respondents were reluctant to disclose the existence and the extent of difficulties in what were their *second* marriages. Those in truncated networks seemed anxious not to disclose their problems to their close relatives and few friends. One such woman described the considerable help she had received from friends when her first marriage had broken up. She now had almost no close friends, having lost touch with those who had formerly helped her.

Mrs Luton, aged 28, secretary, truncated network:
'I haven't got any girlfriends who are close enough or that I see for a long enough time. And they've all got their own problems . . . To say that I don't get on with my husband seems such a poor and insignificant problem, sounds stupid. Not only that, having made a mess of *one* marriage it sounds rather bad to go on beefing about saying *this* one's not working out very well.'

Thus, many respondents whom we have rather loosely categorized as non-consulters gave accounts of their non-consulting behaviour which frequently displayed some sort of 'fit' with their micro-social situations, defined in terms of their relationships with kin and friends.

2 The persons respondents chose not to consult

Both consulters and non-consulters alike said there were specific people whom they had deliberately not consulted in the past and did not intend to consult in the future. Altogether twenty of the twenty-six wives and sixteen of the twenty-two husbands interviewed, when considering to whom they had turned, made spontaneous mention of at least one person in their families (and much less commonly their friends) to whom they certainly did *not* wish to turn.

In keeping with their overall greater reluctance to consult, those in the truncated group tended to mention proportionately more people whom they would not consult. When we consider that their networks were in any case smaller, it is clear that the restrictions which they imposed upon themselves reduced their options still further.

In our study respondents expressed greatest reservations about consulting *spouses* and *parents* over particular events. It is interesting that they selected the two relationships which, for most people in our society, are the closest relationships which they are ever likely to have. This is not to say that respondents had never consulted their parents or their spouses but, particularly over events and problems related to their marriages, many found it hard or inappropriate to turn to them. Such unwillingness to confide marital problems to others reflects the high normative value respondents placed on loyalty to their spouses. Those who had actually tried to talk to their parents about their marriages found the experience had shattered any illusion of their being able to offer respondents much support or advice.[8] As one man said after his first marriage broke up:

> 'The only people I couldn't talk to were my parents. My mother took it very bad, because my wife and my mother were very close. She was quite shocked. My father, I couldn't talk to him because when I tried he would lose his temper.'

This is interesting, since a study of divorced people revealed that parents formed a major source of available help (Mitchell 1981). Since respondents in Mitchell's study were interviewed after their marriages had broken up, it is likely that any help asked for came at the end stage of marital breakdown. On the basis of our evidence it seems likely that although ultimately support may come from parents turning to them for help at an earlier stage was likely to be fraught with tension. In our study husbands were rather more likely than wives to mention their spouses, and wives, though not husbands, frequently mentioned their mothers as persons whom they would choose *not* to consult.

We shall now consider some reasons respondents gave for not consulting particular persons, which may also throw light on some of the necessary conditions for making consulting and confiding a satisfactory experience.

The deterrent of past reactions

One of the most common (and predictable) explanations given by respondents for not consulting their *spouses*, relates to the poor quality of relationships with them and to a lack of communication in the past, especially when they had previously tried to discuss their marriages: 'He just clams up'; 'It just doesn't sink in with her'; 'It always ends in a row.' Several wives described their current reluctance to consult their husbands because of past rebuffs, lack of interest and understanding.

> Mrs Hove, aged 25, secretary, differentiated friendship network: 'In the past if we'd had a disagreement or a row . . . he'd always say to me "Well, I'm sorry but you know what I am. I'm not going to change. If you don't like it, do the other thing." And I always heard those words . . . but there was no way that I would . . . we could never sort of sit down and find an answer, it was always − *he* wouldn't talk, *he* wouldn't discuss it. He would always get very very cross . . . or he'd just slam the door and go out. And I was left

thinking "I wish I hadn't said that." And I'd take it all back inside me again . . . and try and sort of shut it off. So that next morning I'd be all bright and breezy again and that would be fine. He'd be all bright and breezy again. That's great on the surface . . . But underneath it all we never really solved these sort of situations.'

Another woman described how over the years she had been 'put down' by her husband and every time she had tried to raise the subject:

'When I tried to talk he always gave me the attitude I was just a little kid and shouldn't worry about things.'

Wives complained that when they had broached the subject: 'He didn't understand'; 'He wasn't interested.' It is not surprising that, for some marriages at least, a situation often arose between couples where, as one woman put it:

'Things aren't always said now.'

Shielding

Wives explained their reluctance to consult significant others (especially parents) in a more positive idiom, in terms of 'shielding them for their own good'. The notion of 'shielding' was used by respondents to refer to strategies adopted in order to protect significant others from knowledge which they thought might damage them or affect the closeness of their relationships with them. Respondents talked about shielding parents from the 'shock', 'distress', and 'worry'. Many respondents disclosed their marital problems to their parents only when it became virtually impossible to conceal them any longer, as when one partner had left the household.

Mr Flint, aged 44, clerk, truncated network:
'I didn't want to tell her because I know she would worry too much. She is a terrible worrier. She is very old-fashioned and those sort of things would shock her. So I kept it from her right until the last moment. In fact Jill had even gone before I told my mother.'

Some respondents gave instances where they had successfully avoided *ever* disclosing certain events to particular persons, when they had feared that the knowledge of the seriousness of the events might irrevocably damage their relationships with them. One woman described how she had successfully concealed a teenage abortion from the grandmother who had brought her up. Paradoxically, her grandmother had been the one person in her life from whom she had wished for, and indeed received, any comfort. She said she had worried that if her grandmother ever found out about the abortion:

> 'I thought she wouldn't love me so much and that was very precious to me.'

Some respondents sought to shield others from their own distress. One woman described how she had concealed her worry from her husband about his ill-health:

> 'I didn't want to alarm or worry him by letting him see *I* was worried about him.'

Another woman attempted to conceal from her daughter the gravity of the father's disappearance. The father had suddenly disappeared in the middle of a family party at which the twenty-year-old daughter was present, and he had later telephoned to say that he was never returning. In spite of the daughter having been present and having understood what had happened, the mother continued to talk to her, but not to other people, as if her husband had simply gone away temporarily on business.

> Mrs Epsom, aged 48, executive director of small family firm, close-knit kinship network:
> 'I tried to protect her, I said to her "Don't worry, Daddy has had to go away." She sort of looked at me a bit peculiar and didn't say anything.'

Interestingly it was only in the interview that this woman first conceded that her daughter had known the truth all along. Her wish to protect her daughter, and thereby herself, from the threatening implications of the event, had somehow overridden her cognizance of the daughter's awareness of the situation. It is of course true that protecting close others from knowledge that is likely to upset them is also a strategy for protecting the self, and that is especially so when a sense of self is dependent upon preserving an idealized and static quality in relationships.

In some respondents' relationships with significant others, shielding was clearly reciprocal, whilst in others it had an asymmetrical character. The latter was especially true of women whose networks consisted largely of dependants. A fifty-year-old woman in the study, Mrs Bath, described herself as having to be 'the tower of strength for all the family'; her network consisted largely of her children, including some grown-up daughters who were themselves starting families, and several elderly dependants, including a sick husband. Mrs Bath saw herself as a person who shielded others in times of trouble, and as a consequence of this she felt she could not express her own feelings of anger and distress. She had recently experienced several critical events and problems, including the serious and worsening ill-health of her husband; the couple also had long-standing difficulties in their marriage. The stalwart role, in which Mrs Bath had both cast herself and had been cast by her family, was increasingly under strain and she had begun to regret the lack of anyone to turn to for support. Since those who were her 'nearest and dearest' were also the persons whom she felt she had to shield from knowledge that might 'affect' them, she had in reality few people to whom she could turn. Moreover, the rare occasion when she had given vent to her feelings had reinforced her resolution 'not to give way'.

Mrs Bath, aged 56, housewife, truncated network:
'Well I led off the deep end instead of being a tower of strength. . . . I pulled myself together and sorted myself out and thought "Well, that's no good. It doesn't do anybody any good." But sometimes I feel that it's a bit difficult that I can't relax sufficiently to lead off the deep end without it affecting him so much that he can't cope. Therefore, it's a luxury I cannot afford at the moment.'

Just as mothers talked about shielding their children and dependants, so some wives talked about shielding their *husbands*, especially from disclosures which might publicly reflect badly upon the *ego*. One wife said she wished she could have shared with someone her concern about her husband's mismanagement of their finances. However, she felt that, had she done so, she would have been disloyal to him.

Mrs Crewe, aged 23, cashier, truncated network:
'I wouldn't have talked about the nitty gritty of things with them [friends], not anything to do with the basics, because people ask questions and they probably would have thought little of Joe. I don't think it's fair to discuss somebody's feelings.'

This fear of disloyalty was echoed by another wife who, although she felt desperately in need of help over her marriage, yet could turn to no one informally.

Mrs Derby, aged 40, nurse, close-knit kinship network:
'I didn't see who I could turn to without letting down my other half. It felt like carrying tales or gossiping behind his back.'

This attitude seems to reflect a widely held inhibition about talking about marital relationships which arises from their exclusivity and privacy. But it also reflects the unequal and deferential position of wives who are thereby bound by loyalty to their husbands.

There was, significantly, a marked absence of comments by husbands about 'shielding others'. We would suggest that the notion of shielding only arises as part of people's vocabularies where the necessary conditions exist together with a shared acceptance of the desirability of disclosing and turning to others. The notion of shielding, we therefore conclude, is located within a *gender-specific* vocabulary since, as we have described earlier, disclosure to others was both generally accepted as being desirable and commonly practised by the women in our study and not the men. The majority of men were negatively orientated towards self-disclosure and, for some, non-disclosure was in actuality a stable and salient part of their self-identities. Thus shielding constitutes part of a rationale whereby respondents (mostly women) distinguished between the close and significant others they chose to consult and those they did not.

3 Respondents as consulters

As we suggested earlier, consulters were more likely to be found in the differentiated friendship and the close-knit kinship groups than in the truncated group. Those who confided (that is to say those who had confidants) tended to be mainly concentrated in the differentiated friendship group. We shall now go on to describe the character of consulting and confiding in the two groups where it was more common.

The close-knit kinship group

Consulters in the close-knit kinship group exhibited a particular type of consulting behaviour, being unlikely in practice to select a particular person in whom to confide. The members of their networks, linked mainly by ties of kinship, were often already 'in the know' and respondents were unlikely to confide in them individually; respondents in this group consulted within a climate of potentially open public knowledge. Furthermore, the events and difficulties experienced by respondents in this group tended or threatened to implicate their networks as whole entities (because of their interconnected structure). Thus in those cases where the kinship network had become involved in the marital difficulties, turning to kin was rarely seen by respondents as useful. Even where network members were not involved in the marital difficulties, respondents excluded them on the grounds that they were likely to be partisan by virtue of kinship loyalties. Several respondents who had previously found their kin unhelpful for the above reasons, appeared resolved no longer to rely on them, at least for emotional help. A young housewife talked about her relatives' response to the news that her husband had taken an overdose after she had, not for the first time, run away from him.

> Mrs Hull, aged 21, housewife, close-knit kinship network:
> 'Everybody I told, or who knew, were relatives and they took the attitude that a lot of it was "put on" . . .'
> *'And how did you feel about that?'*
> 'I just couldn't understand why nobody liked him, though at the time I hated him . . .'
> *'These were* your *relatives?'*
> 'Yes, even his relatives up to a point were on my side and his father and stepmother were sort of saying it's *his* fault . . . Everybody was giving me advice but the trouble was it wasn't what I wanted them to say. Nobody would say "Go back and try again." My mum and the relations, none of them got on with him very well. So it was always "Oh try and get a new life and start again. Find somebody else."'

When asked about her preferences for turning to other people, she later commented:

> 'I think a stranger helps . . . They can listen to both sides. They don't sort of just listen to one side and go deaf to the other. They are not in the actual situation and the actual triangle of the problem. So they can look at it from all angles.'

The consistency of her relatives' reactions appears to have left Mrs Hull little space in which to feel resolute about her own feelings and decisions, and ultimately she turned for help beyond the confines of her immediate social network.

Although the kind of emotional support provided by such close-knit networks was felt by many respondents in this group to be unsatisfactory, it is important not to overlook the practical and instrumental help, such as the provision and exchange of goods, services, and information, which such networks tend to provide. Several studies have found that kin provide instrumental and practical help whilst friends offer a more expressive type of support (see Horwitz 1977). It is of course possible that the greater value that respondents seemed to place upon emotional help and understanding reflects a bias in our questioning. But it seems to us just as likely that practical help was not necessarily appropriate or sufficient for many of the critical events and problems which respondents had experienced. As we have described earlier, many events and problems involved elements of loss and danger which threatened most of all central and salient aspects of respondents' identities.

Nonetheless, it is significant, if somewhat predictable, that the close-knit kinship group had received more instrumental or practical help (usually from kin) than the other two groups, and that the truncated group had been given very little instrumental support. More men than women mentioned the importance of practical help, which was sometimes seen as a necessary prerequisite before any other kind of less tangible support could be envisaged and accepted.

Mrs Derby (aged 40, nurse, close-knit kinship network) talked about an event which had severely disrupted the life of the family:

'I'm basically the sort of person who keeps things to myself. I didn't see what there was to *gain* by talking to other people about it. If they didn't voluntarily phone or enquire . . . The only help *I* got was in talking things over . . . I expected some kind of support like "If you can find a part-time job, of course I'll have the kids."'

We are not suggesting that emotional support is not necessarily forthcoming in networks of close-knit structure but simply that the network, because of its interwoven structure is itself likely to be constrained by respondents' marriage difficulties. As a consequence, any concern or support may be rejected or shied away from because it is likely to be partisan and to implicate other sectors of the network.

The differentiated friendship group

In this group consulters and those who had confidants were mostly women. Unlike many respondents in the close-knit kinship group who, particularly over their marital problems, felt pried upon and sometimes trapped by kin involvement and concern, women in the differentiated friendship group were able to exert greater control when they consulted and confided. This was because they were generally in situations where, because of network structure, they could select persons they considered suitable to confide in without the risk of the whole network knowing or becoming involved. For this group, therefore, consulting and confiding over a particular event or problem was an *encapsulated* experience with fewer unintended consequences. These respondents had a wider range of choice of confidants and consultants, including both friends and kin, and they also had greater freedom of manoeuvre in turning to them.

In this network group, a greater proportion mentioned the importance of emotional help than in the other two groups. It is possible that this is a general characteristic of the women in the study. Nonetheless, it is clear that the women in the differentiated friendship group, compared with the other two groups, were more likely actually to *find* the emotional support they sought.[9] We would suggest that precisely because of network structure, the differentiated friendship group were generally not at risk of their confidences being disclosed to others in their networks. As one woman put it: 'You've got to pick and choose who you talk to.' A differentiated network structure provides a protective and facilitative environment in which to disclose confidences.

It should not be supposed that the expressive and emotional support respondents received was in their eyes particularly active or effective. At the very least it consisted of the feeling of someone always 'being there', a sympathetic ear or the opportunity to 'off-load' in a relatively uninhibited way, without fear of censure or of confidences being passed on. At most it produced a feeling of relief and reassurance.

Mr Ascot, aged 32, surveyor, differentiated friendship network:
'Some one to talk to who would listen patiently and sympathetically. They made the right noises.'

Mrs Hove, aged 25, secretary, differentiated friendship network:
'Letting everything out and knowing they would listen. I could say what I liked when I liked . . . didn't matter if they understood or not.'

Mrs Ascot, aged 32, media consultant, differentiated friendship network:
'They knew how much it meant to me . . . They would know just how low it would make me feel.'

In contrast with these sentiments are those of the men who received emotional support but who did not regard it as useful, because the actual situation or problem had not been improved.

Mr Wells, 39, small shopkeeper, differentiated friendship network:
'He's like a brother to me and you could discuss whatever you like

but it wasn't helpful talking to him. It's *results* that count. A bloody social worker can give you a load of shit and no flat. And *that* is the answer − the flat.'

Thus consulting behaviour, although more common in the differentiated friendship and close-knit kinship groups than the truncated group, assumed rather different characteristics and significance in each of these three groups.

4 The persons respondents chose to consult

We suggested earlier that in adversity the truncated group had more often consulted spouses than other categories of persons, and that the close-knit kinship group generally consulted their kin and the differentiated friendship group their friends. The differentiated friendship group were more likely to have confidants than the other network groups.

The persons in whom respondents chose to consult and confide were also, in a majority of cases, those whom they ranked as being *affectively* significant. For, in addition to asking respondents with whom they interacted on a regular basis, and to whom they had turned over the specific events and problems they had experienced, we also asked them to list, in order of importance to them, the people to whom they felt closest or most attached. There are some slight but perhaps significant differences in the extent to which respondents in the different network groups consulted those who were affectively significant. Those in truncated networks consulted persons 75 per cent of whom respondents ranked as affectively significant compared with 65 per cent and 62 per cent in the close-knit kinship and differentiated friendship groups respectively.

Predictably, those consulted who were also affectively significant, were more likely to be kin (either by blood or by marriage) in the truncated and close-knit kinship groups than in the differentiated friendship group.[10] Moreover, friends accounted for most of those who were not mentioned as being affectively significant in the differentiated friendship group.[11] Thus ties of affective or emotional attachment appear to be important criteria on which respondents selected confidants and consultants. Even so, it is clear from respondents' accounts of where they had satisfactorily consulted and confided in significant others that feelings of attachment and closeness often depended upon *structural* characteristics of their chosen confidants; they felt close to, and able to confide in, particular *kinds* of persons because of particular aspects of their background, situation or experience.

Choice of similars

Most significantly it was women, especially those with differentiated friendship networks, who turned to other women of similar age and life cycle stage, and, specifically over their marital problems, they turned to those who had been through similar experiences.

Respondents attached considerable importance to those instances where their women confidants had undergone difficulties in their own marriages. Caplan (1974: 13), in a description of the role of informal care-givers, refers to a genre which he calls 'specialists'. They are 'people known to have suffered some misfortune or to have undergone a particularly trying experience and to have worked out ways of achieving a successful adjustment and adaptation'. However, it seems equally significant to us that it was with other such similarly placed *women* (and never men) that women respondents identified in their adversity. Moreover, the sympathy and understanding which they received was valued precisely because the experience from which the understanding of their predicaments had sprung was a *shared* experience. Nonetheless, as will become clear in our next instance, the bonds which linked the women who confided in each other were invariably rendered non-threatening to the 'offending' or 'offended' husbands.

> Mrs Frome, aged 31, housewife, differentiated friendship network: 'She's been a very close friend for many years. We've been through good times and bad times together . . . She for a short time left her own husband . . . I knew she would understand. Also she knows us both and likes us both. Notice it was mostly people who liked us that I went . . . She's in much the same sort of position herself, never knowing where the next penny is coming from. She knows how bad it is.'

Mrs Rugby described how her three closest friends had been supportive over her marriage troubles, especially when she decided to take out an injunction against her husband for violence, which banned him from the house for a month. She continued to turn to them after she had taken her husband back. It emerged that her friends had experienced similar problems in their own marriages.

Mrs Rugby, aged 40, school and play-group worker, differentiated friendship network:
'I still talk to Joyce. She would 'phone up and ask if everything was all right and how Chris [husband] is and if he'd like to go round and have a chat . . . she said "Don't forget if anything arises . . . If things get a bit heavy you can always come round here or send him or get Jean [daughter] out of the way" . . . She's a very good person, so is Marion as well. You can go over there anytime . . . Joyce has a similar situation when she left her husband for a while . . . I think she knows a lot, I wouldn't say *more* than Marion, because Marion has had an injunction and it didn't work out . . . They are not the sort of people who condemn . . . They are the type to say "The best of luck if you can make a go of it."'

Another woman described how similarity of life situation between herself and the friend, who was her chief confidant, provided a basis for the *reciprocal* exchange of confidences, which she felt was essential for the honest and open disclosure of her marital problems.

Mrs Ascot, aged 32, media consultant, differentiated friendship network:
'I didn't have this "pretend" relationship with Susan and pretend that everything is going very smoothly — I know things aren't altogether smooth in her life and she's soldiering on the best she can with her difficulties and I feel I can be the same with her.'

Not all of Mrs Ascot's friends were reciprocally confiding to her and she comments on the importance of this for a satisfactory confiding relationship.

'I am able to talk to Susan more honestly than I am to Caroline for example.'
'*Why?*'
'Caroline is actually a counsellor — general counsellor — I am very fond of her but I do find she adopts the role of a counsellor a bit when I tell her my problems and she doesn't tell me hers. I feel its rather an unequal relationship. She sits and listens and sheds light and drops useful hints but sometimes I wish she would tell me *her* problems. Then it would make me feel more confident it was a friendship. I feel it is a friendship but it is rather one-sided.'

Choice of dissimilars

While some confided in similars, others chose people who were different from them in some key way. Some respondents selected people whom they wished to emulate or become more like. This seemed to occur when respondents were about to embark on a change of role or status which would in turn require a change in their identities. Mrs Hove felt that her marriage was inhibiting her 'growth' as a person and decided to separate from her husband. She chose as a confidant a woman who was unlikely to dissuade her from her decision and who herself had a very different kind of marriage from her own.

> Mrs Hove, aged 25, secretary, differentiated friendship network:
> *'What was it about Janet?'*
> 'Because on the surface she's a very unemotional person and she's been not in any way *continually* involved with me; I'm not a long-standing friend that she's grown up with. We talk together and get on very well. We enjoy the same things and she's quite a hard, cool sort of person who will look on the situation quite objectively — give you her answer quite frankly, openly and honestly. Not sort of pat me on the back and say "There, there! How terrible it all is! I know how you feel!" She will look at me quite coldly and tell me . . . Her marriage is quite different — she's always thought that if you don't like it, don't stick with it — she'd say. I'd say "Why? Oh! All the vows we made eh?" and she'd say, "Yes, but you're both very different and it's like hitting your head against a brick wall."'

Mrs Dover, who believed that she had made a positive and liberating move away from an unsatisfactory marriage, chose to confide in a single girl who represented the attitudes and perspective she herself now wished to adopt.

> Mrs Dover, 24, computer operator, differentiated friendship network:
> 'I'm thinking for myself now and therefore talking to someone who is single and who *has* thought for herself, she gives me another angle, another way of looking at things.'

Others chose people whose situations were rather different from their own but whose values and attitudes made them feel secure in their transition from one status to another. Mrs Poole was trying to work out long-standing sexual problems which centred around a child-like dependence on her husband, which he had been chiefly instrumental in encouraging and maintaining from the beginning of the relationship. She had endeavoured to break away from this situation by building her own independent circle of friends and had taken a lover in order to discover more about her own sexuality. It became very important to her that she was approved of in her new project. She chose as one of her chief confidants a man who was sexually deviant and unattached.

> Mrs Poole (aged 29, dancer, differentiated friendship network) said of him and another friend:
> 'They didn't disapprove. They approved. They just said: "Be jolly careful!" We used to have therapy dinners — we called them therapy dinners . . . We'd all get together in my home or his house and we'd all bring something to eat . . . and that would go on till three in the morning. We'd discuss everything in detail. They were very into that sort of thing . . .'
> *'So you talked about your affair?'*
> 'Yes, the whole thing. They wholeheartedly approved.'

Choice of mother surrogates

In some instances respondents, again all women, selected as confidants women who were considerably older than themselves. Some respondents seemed to relate to these persons as if to parental figures, and sometimes they even described them in these terms. Mrs Ascot confided in her domestic help, especially over health worries and about her children.

> Mrs Ascot, aged 32, media consultant, differentiated friendship network:
> 'I tell Mrs Pitt a lot of things. My cleaning lady, she's a sort of mother figure to me — more of a substitute — my own mother has reached a sort of frail point in time. She's very loyal to me and very sensible. She's a practicable sort of woman, she gets me out of lots of worries on a physical-practical basis and in terms of the children's health, she's a very comforting sort of person.'

Two respondents described their relationships with Marriage Guidance counsellors in these terms.

> Mrs Wells, aged 29, shop assistant, differentiated friendship network:
> 'She's elderly and I suppose in a way I look upon her like, not exactly as a mum . . . but somebody that I've felt I've always needed but never had.'

For Mrs Wells, the relationship with her counsellor had an idealized quality, embodying the sort of relationship which she had wished for but had never had with her own mother. In another instance, a woman made a confidant of her doctor's receptionist. The receptionist was closely involved in this respondent's medical problems and the respondent, Mrs Neath, was in almost daily contact with her for informal advice and support. Moreover, Mrs Neath placed her first in her list of affectively significant others. It also emerged in the interview that she did not feel particularly close to her own mother and, like many other respondents, was unable to discuss her marital difficulties with her.

Mrs Neath, aged 37, housewife, differentiated friendship network: 'She's sort of a motherly figure for me when I need a . . . because my own mother is not so sort of motherly. I don't see *her* as much so *she* doesn't know my problems as Ann does.'

For other respondents the significance of older women confidants was less apparent. Such confidants had something in common with what Caplan has called 'generalists': 'people who are widely recognized in their neighbourhood to have wisdom in matters of human relations' (Caplan 1974: 12). Such characteristics are often combined with others; for example, in the next instance the respondent's confidant had also experienced problems in her own marriage.

Mrs Tenby, aged 47, housewife, differentiated friendship network: 'She is someone who can understand people, a warm-hearted human being who is always understanding and has compassion for people, who loves to help people . . . and always says the things when she is not agreeing with me.'

Respondents did not always choose such confidants because of like-minded views, nor for the ways in which they had resolved problems in their own marriages.

Mrs Rugby (aged 40, school and play-group worker) turned to an older woman when her first marriage broke up:
'I turned to her, but then she was like a mother because she was years older than me. But I worked with her and she knew me. She'd known me since the age of sixteen when I first started work. She came to my wedding . . . she said "Never try to hang on to something that isn't there . . . you've got to be a woman and face up to life and carry on" . . . She was a very old-fashioned type of person. Her views were obviously when you got married you got married for life, but, as she said, you can't have stable views in a vastly changing world. The thing was that she had a very stormy marriage herself but she never broke her marriage up you know.'

Thus we have suggested that feelings of closeness or bonds of emotional attachment were important in respondents' decisions to turn to particular persons. But we have also shown that particular structural and relational characteristics, such as social background, current situation, and past experience also play a significant part in the process of selecting confidants. We have shown how some respondents selected similars, especially women who, like them, had been through marital difficulties, while others chose dissimilars, people whom they would like to become like or who approved of them. Finally, we suggested that some women sought a parental type of relationship in which to confide such as a mother surrogate. This last type of confiding relationship would seem to be especially important, since many respondents found it inappropriate or unsatisfactory to turn to their real parents, especially over marital difficulties.

Notes

1 The proportion of respondents in each network group who had at least one general confidant are: close-knit kinship group 5/10; truncated group 8/21; differentiated friendship group 11/17.

2 Table 7(1) *Number of times particular categories of persons were consulted (over general and marital events)*

Events	Spouse	Kin	Friends	Others
Truncated				
general	39	27	36	4
marital	14	3	8	3
Total (expressed as a proportion of the 41 events consulted over)	53/41	30/41	44/41	7/41
Close-knit kinship				
general	10	32	21	6
marital	4	9	11	3
Total (expressed as a proportion of the 27 events consulted over)	14/27	41/27	32/27	9/27
Differentiated friendship				
general	18	13	53	
marital	9	5	22	
Total (expressed as a proportion of the 34 events consulted over)	27/34	18/34	75/34	

In the truncated group 41/85 (48 per cent) events were consulted over; in the close-knit kinship group 27/41 (66 per cent) events were consulted over; and in the differentiated friendship group 34/60 (57 per cent) events were consulted over.

3 Table 7(2) *Proportions of respondents in each network group who had at least one confidant*

	Marital confidants	General confidants
Close-knit kinship group	3/10	5/10
Differentiated friendship group	10/17	11/17
Truncated group	5/21	8/21

4 The average number of *persons* consulted (not necessarily confided in) for the whole study group is 3.8, which approximates to the average for the differentiated friendship group. The averages for the other two network groups fall either side of this figure. (Truncated group = 2.7: close-knit kinship group = 4.9). The figures for the average number of *times* respondents consulted over all events and difficulties reflect the above differences. (Truncated group = 3.7; differentiated friendship = 5.2; close-knit kinship = 7.1.)

5 21/48 respondents had no marital or general confidant, eleven of whom were in the truncated group, and five each in the differentiated and close-knit groups respectively.

6 Komarovsky (1967) found that two-thirds of wives had at least one person, apart from their husbands, in whom they confided, compared with only one-fifth of husbands.

7 Komarovsky talks about 'the trained incapacity to share' when describing the communication pattern of husbands (1967: 156).

8 In a study of young newly-weds (the Marriage Research Centre, Central Middlesex Hospital) more than a quarter of respondents said that if they were ever to have any serious problems in their marriages they expected to turn *only* to family and, of these, some women said they would turn to their mothers with whom their relationships were extremely close.

9 The differentiated friendship group received most expressive or emotional support in that they mentioned more expressive items of support, such as people being empathetic, reassuring, understanding, being 'always there'. Likewise this group mentioned more characteristics of *persons* consulted, which they had found conducive to the process of confiding and consulting, such as a balanced common-sense viewpoint, trustworthiness, and other enabling characteristics. Overall, where respondents consulted, the differentiated friendship group had more positive experiences (in respect of turning to particular persons) than the other two groups. Differentiated friendship group 65.5 per cent; close-knit kinship group 49 per cent; truncated group 45 per cent.

10 In the close-knit kinship group 85 per cent of affectively significant others were kin, in the truncated group 77 per cent, but only 57 per cent in the differentiated friendship group. (It should be noted that a high proportion of so-called kin in the truncated group were in fact spouses.)

11 Of the 38 per cent who were consulted but not regarded as affectively significant in the differentiated friendship network (19/50) the vast majority of these were friends and not kin.

8

Formal help-seeking: social networks, approaches, and pathways

Social networks

The last chapter focused on social networks as a context in which respondents consulted and confided in informal others over critical events and problems. Before examining and describing respondents' approaches and pathways to agencies, we shall first consider some ways in which the action of seeking help from agencies appears to be influenced by network structure.

In general there seems to be an association between network type and certain aspects of formal help-seeking, although it is somewhat confounded by gender differences: over half of all the husbands in fact had truncated networks, whereas over two-thirds of wives had differentiated friendship or close-knit kinship networks. But it can also be argued that social networks act as intervening variables which mediate gender socialization and formal help-seeking action.

The first connection between network structure and formal help-seeking concerns the ways in which problems were presented to agencies. Those who belonged to truncated networks were likely to have presented problems (or had partners who did so) which had an individual focus such as health problems. In contrast, those with other network types were likely to present at an agency (or had a partner who did) with explicit marital or sexual problems.[1] Secondly, the kind of agency which was first approached by respondents appears also to have been influenced by network structure. Those with truncated networks were generally more likely to have approached a general practitioner or other medical agency in the first instance than those with differentiated friendship networks, for the majority of the latter went to a Marriage Guidance Council. This is not surprising since the kind of agency first approached reflects the way in which the problems were defined and interpreted by respondents. The third main connection between network structure and formal help-seeking concerns which partner instigated the approach to the agency in the first place. In fact, those who instigated the approach tended to belong to differentiated and close-knit networks, and those who took no such initiative to truncated networks. Here again, however, gender differences were also highly significant, with wives being much more likely to be instigators of formal help-seeking than husbands.

In the last chapter we considered the extent to which respondents consulted informal others over a wide range of events and problems, including marital ones. We found that almost half of the study group did not have a confidant, and that where any respondents did consult significant others, it was often only to a limited extent and in a highly restricted fashion. Although, on the whole, very few respondents received suggestions from members of their social networks about consulting professionals or going to agencies, there is some evidence to suggest that respondents with differentiated friendship networks were particularly likely to have become aware of the existence of Marriage Guidance through various sources. Three such wives with differentiated friendship networks, who approached Marriage Guidance in connection with their current marital difficulties, had been told about it by their mothers-in-law. Surprisingly, no respondents in this group discussed approaching agencies with their friends and only two respondents (married to one another) mentioned friends with any counselling experience. This couple, both of whom had differentiated friendship networks, had two friends, one of whom had been a client of Marriage Guidance and the other was herself some kind of counsellor: however, despite their friends' contact with counselling they did not discuss their decision to go to Marriage Guidance with either of them.

A further six couples with differentiated friendship networks said that they had heard about Marriage Guidance through external sources; most often this was from the media, either from magazines or through radio phone-in programmes. In the final section of our interview schedule we sought to explore the extent to which all respondents were interested in and listened to radio phone-in programmes, read problem pages in magazines, and looked at sex manuals, and it is perhaps worth noting that respondents with differentiated friendship networks appear to have taken greater interest in these. On the whole they showed more knowledge of media material concerned with such subjects as personal relationships and sexuality than the members of the other network types.

Although respondents in *all* network groups appear only rarely to have received any advice or suggestions from members of their networks in connection with seeking formal help, the respondents in the differentiated group were the most likely to have discussed their marital problems and had confided, particularly in those of their women friends who themselves had experienced similar problems and situations. However, the reactions they received, although supportive, were generally non-directive; friends tended to encourage them to make up their own minds about their situations and supported them in the decisions they themselves eventually came to. One woman (Mrs Rugby, aged 40, school and play-group worker) talked about　the response of her friends when she decided to take her husband back after the expiry of a court injunction banning him from the house:

> 'Well, they said they thought I had done the right thing at the time. But obviously the decision about whether or not to have him back was my own and nobody could tell you. They just turned round and said "Well you've just got to do what you feel is best. We can't tell you what to do. We can't turn round and say that you must do such and such and everything will be all right." Nobody can say that to you. They were just *there*, you know.'

In only one marriage in the study was there evidence of informal others playing a highly active role in facilitating the search for formal help. In this one instance a respondent used her social network (which was, interestingly, of the truncated variety) as a means of gaining both access to and influence over formal agencies.

Over the previous two years this respondent and her husband had experienced several major adverse events and were encountering a number of problems. The genesis of some of these lay outside their control, as when serious illnesses or family deaths befell them; others, however, seem to have been, at least in part, of their own making. The pattern of the wife's consulting behaviour over the various problems and difficulties was very striking. Although most of the people she chose to consult were from within her social network, nevertheless it did seem as if they were selected and used for very defined reasons, such as their having some specific familial or formal connection with a particular agency or organization which she considered would prove highly beneficial to herself and her husband. She plainly used her network in order to gain some useful information, or to facilitate some formal approach she ultimately wished to make.

She tended to speak of her friends in this very fashion: someone 'who knows the ins and outs'; someone who occupied a convenient professional position; someone with a relative in a relevant medical specialty. Most significantly perhaps, looked at in terms of her marriage, this respondent, on her own initiative and without consulting her husband, involved herself in his problems at work and elsewhere. The agencies which ultimately became involved in this couple's problems were drawn quite deeply into the marital struggle and were frequently played off by the couple against each other. We have termed this kind of consulting and help-seeking 'the spider's web' syndrome because of its manipulative quality, which rendered those brought in to help quite powerless. The woman respondent who had constructed this nexus of involvement, and whose husband had largely colluded with her, possessed a considerable degree of insight into her actions; she said reflectively of one person who had unwittingly become involved in their situation: 'I really wondered if we were using her . . . I think we probably did.' The social networks of this couple were both truncated, which was perhaps not surprising, since the manipulative strategies employed by the wife seem often to have alienated their kin and friends. Moreover, in the absence of many kin or friends to turn to, the wife had enmeshed a few acquaintances in her quest for outside professional help. This was the only case we found where a respondent had consciously utilized her social network in the search for formal help, and it is interesting that it was such a specific style of utilization.

In Chapter 6 we suggested that social networks provided a context in which particular types of marriages could be understood. In addition, we have suggested that social networks may provide part of the explanation both for the kinds of problems for which respondents initially wanted help and the types of help sought. However, as far as the impact of informal others (network members) on respondents' decisions to seek formal help was concerned, they do not appear to have had any obvious instrumental impact. Nevertheless, social networks provide the *context* or backcloth against which formal help is sought and provided.

In the last chapter we discussed patterns of consulting and confiding in relation to network type. For example, we noted the importance of the close-knit kinship network as a source of material and practical help. We suggested that the highly interconnected structure of this latter type of network (with its members bound by reciprocal ties and obligations) was in itself conducive to the exchange of goods and services. We also noted that any emotional help or support provided by such networks was likely to be over-involved and frequently unsatisfactory where marital difficulties were concerned. Moreover, since the agencies with which respondents in this study came into contact did not offer (nor even pretend to offer) any practical or material help, their help-seeking actions must largely be interpreted as a search for expressive or emotional help, such as may be found in the 'talking' therapies. Thus, we would argue that for members of close-knit kinship networks, approaching an agency assumed a special kind of social significance or meaning, since it represented a possible *alternative* to the over-involved or biased concern which they had previously experienced from their relatives, in connection with their marital difficulties.

For the differentiated friendship group, the social significance or meaning of approaching an agency was somewhat different. Although respondents in this group rarely received positive suggestions or feedback from network members concerning formal help-seeking, they appear to have consulted and confided in them to some extent about their problems and, in return, had received their support, which was usually of an emotional kind. For respondents of this network type, therefore, approaching an agency may be construed as an *additional* help-seeking strategy, but one essentially similar in character to the way in which they had already turned to their network members.

In contrast yet again, those in truncated networks who consulted agencies did so in the context of a *deficit* of persons in their social networks. Therefore, it may be argued that they were substantially lacking in varied experience of consulting and confiding, and hence may have failed to acquire an adequate model of such relationships, which in turn was likely to have had implications for their subsequent involvement in formal therapeutic encounters.

It is our contention, therefore, that approaching an agency assumes a characteristic significance in the case of each client, since it occurs in the context of a particular set and structure of social relationships which confer meaning upon it. Moreover, once agencies become involved with clients, it also seems possible that agencies' influence upon clients may be differentially received and acted upon according to the type of network to which clients belong. Moreover, the specific interventions of agencies are likely in turn to have some impact upon clients' social network since even though people become clients they still remain active participants in their social networks.

One way of estimating the potential influence of an agency upon a client, especially concerning marital or family problems, is to consider its relative strength in relation to the more immediate influence which networks members may bring to bear. The position of the agency *vis-à-vis* the client's social network emerges best when the network is considered visually (see *Figures 8(1)*, *8(2)*, *8(3)*). Where a client and her partner belong to truncated networks, the agency

Figure 8(1) The truncated networks of Mr Ryde and Mr Flint

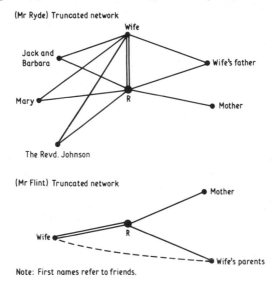

Figure 8(2) The differentiated friendship network of Mrs Ascot

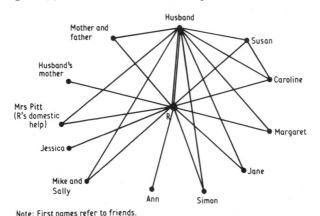

Figure 8(3) The close-knit kinship network of Mr Cowes

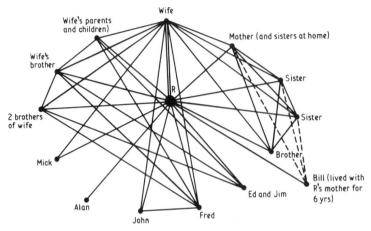

Note: First names refer to friends.

intervenes in a situation where the spouses are somewhat socially isolated, and where other social contact is typically limited to parents or to one or two friends. In the case of clients with close-knit kinship networks, the agency has to compete with the whole network, whose influence is likely to have considerable strength and pervasiveness. In relation to clients with differentiated friendship networks, the agency is likely yet again to have a rather different influence. Since clients with this network type are already accustomed to greater latitude, choice, and control in whom they consult and confide informally, they are in a strong position to weigh up and reflect upon the interventions of the agency in relation to other possible influences and considerations. Explanation of the relationship between the course of counselling and therapy, and the social networks of clients may well prove a fruitful approach to pursue in further research.

Approaches to agencies

One of our initial conceptualizations of this study was that the process of becoming a client could most usefully be understood as consisting of a number of analytical stages. In Chapter 4 we suggested that although people may well have become aware quite early on in their marriages of unsatisfactory aspects (the 'symptom-experience' stage), initially they accommodated to these difficulties in a variety of ways which often included locating an external source of attribution. It was not until a later stage, when the marriage had been *defined* as problematic (either by respondents or by an agency) rather than simply *experienced* as such, that people began to look back to the earlier years and reconstruct their marital past. Once they had recognized and defined their marriages as problematic, respondents began to re-interpret those elements which they had previously regarded and explained in particular ways as signs or omens prefiguring the marital problems which had eventually been defined.

We have also already suggested that it seemed as if those respondents who defined their marriages as problematic and made an approach to an agency for help did so only after one partner had taken unequivocal action which put the marriage itself in grave jeopardy. In contrast, in those cases where it was an agency and not the respondent that defined the marriage as problematic, we discovered that although the approach to the agency had almost always been prompted by some critical event or problem these were not necessarily directly or obviously related to the marriage.

We now move on to examine the next stage in the process of becoming a client, and we shall consider which partner initially approached the agencies and how the problems were presented. We shall additionally examine the implications that this and other aspects of respondents' current and past help-seeking behaviour might have in shaping their pathways through the agencies.

The literature

Little is actually known about clients who consult for marital problems, such as whether they consult agencies. A survey by Chester (1971) of female divorce petitioners revealed that the majority of respondents experienced a deterioration in health prior to and during separation, and that approximately three-quarters of them claimed to have visited a general practitioner in consequence. In view of the general absence of such information, we are forced to rely on data concerning help-seeking for personal, psychological, and non-medical problems, and in considering this research, it is important to distinguish the perceptions of problems from the standpoint of the client from those elicited from the practitioner. We will first consider the evidence from the clients' point of view.

Studies of general practitioners' patients in the United Kingdom indicate that patients say that they would consult their doctors about personal problems *rather than* other professional agencies or informal others (Cartwright 1967; Acheson and Fitten 1979). However, the findings of these and other studies also indicate that the majority of patients were in practice disinclined to consult their doctors about non-medical matters (Cartwright 1967; Arber and Sawyer 1979; Cartwright and Anderson 1979). One study (Cartwright and O'Brien 1976) found that social classes III, IV and V were twice as likely as social classes I and II to say that they would *not* consult their doctors about a serious personal problem.[2] Another study (Arber and Sawyer 1979) notes that the minority of patients who say they would consult their doctors for non-medical problems do not expect counselling as such; the researchers suggest it is possible that this depended upon the quality of their relationships with their doctors. One of the problems with this evidence is that it is derived from interviews with people about the subject of doctors, which is likely to bias reporting towards greater rather than fewer mentions of doctors, and second it is largely based on hypothetical questions. A common and consistent finding about help-seeking for medical problems in Britain is that *women* (aged between fifteen and fifty-four) are more likely than men to present at doctors' surgeries (OPCS 1974).[3]

This sex difference needs to be treated a little cautiously, however, because it is likely to mask a complexity of phenomena. Such phenomena include, for instance, large numbers of women seeking help connected with fertility, and those taking sick children and elderly relatives to the doctor. In addition, the fact that women rarely adopt the 'sick role', in the sense of ceasing to engage in the full range of normal activities, should also be borne in mind (Koos 1954). American studies suggesting that women are more likely than men to consult for physical and psychological symptoms need to be treated with similar caution (Nathanson 1975; Mechanic 1978).[4] Nonetheless, the available American evidence on help-seeking for psychological problems, although both theoretically and methodologically problematic and making interpretation thus somewhat difficult, indicates that gender is a consistently crucial variable at several stages in the help-seeking process: first, at the symptom experience stage (Suchman 1965); second, at the stage of discussing symptoms with others (Suchman 1965; Horwitz 1977); and third, at the stage where the decision to seek help is made (Greenley and Mechanic 1976).[5]

On the professional side, there is little evidence about the incidence of either client-defined or practitioner-defined marital problems. Although one study by Shepherd *et al.* (1966) indicates that general practitioners rated marital problems as amongst the most common factors implicated in the psychiatric illness of their patients, there is no indication of how far patients themselves were aware, or in agreement with, the doctors' perceptions of their marriages. Nor indeed is it clear in the study what the implications were, if any, of doctors' judgements concerning patients' marriages on their methods of treatment. Nonetheless, the context in which the researchers themselves locate this finding is, we believe, illuminating and relevant to our discussion. 'Taking into account the overall excess of female psychiatric cases it would be a justifiable exaggeration to say that, in the eyes of the general practitioners, psychiatry in general practice consists largely of the psycho-social problems of women' (Shepherd *et al.* 1966: 149). The question why women patients were more likely to be defined as psychiatric cases is therefore raised, which in turn leads us to ask the further question why it was that general practitioners attributed psychiatric illness to marital difficulties amongst their female, but not amongst their male, patients.

In a recent study of social work and clients with marital problems, Mattinson and Sinclair (1979) note that, at the client intake stage, the number of cases categorized by social workers as having overt marital problems was very small indeed. 'Clients neither referred themselves nor were referred with an overt request to deal with the marital problem for its own sake' (p. 26). However, once clients had been allocated to caseworkers, it appears that a very large increase took place in the proportion of clients regarded by workers as having marital problems.

Who approached the agencies?

It is important for the reader to grasp at the outset our distinction between current and past help-seeking episodes. In disentangling respondents' pathways to and through agencies, we grouped help-seeking actions which flowed one from the other as one sequence or episode. These help-seeking actions consisted of initiatives taken by respondents, as well as referrals by agencies. Where there was a lapse of many months between help-seeking actions we regarded such actions as part of respondents' *past* help-seeking behaviour. A careful investigation of who made the decision to make the *first* contact with the agency, in respondents' current help-seeking episodes, revealed that wives were much more likely to have made the decision to establish contact, whatever the initial presentation of the problem. In nineteen of the twenty-eight couples in our group it was the wife who decided to approach the agency; in two couples it was a joint decision; and in only seven couples was the husband the decision-maker. Moreover, even where the problem directly concerned the husband's state of health, wives dominated the decision-making. In the following quotation, a woman described her part in her husband's decision to go to the doctor, which eventually led to a later consultation for sexual difficulties.

'A year or so after that I noticed . . . as if his blood pressure was up again. It wasn't as if I was looking for trouble but I could sense he was worked up about things . . . I said "I really think you should go back to hospital" to see what was causing it.'

In the next quotation a woman describes her own unsuccessful attempts to get her husband to go to the doctor in the immediate period before he made a suicide attempt, after which the husband himself decided he was in need of help. Up to that time the husband had defined his depressed wife as being the only one requiring help. The wife said:

'I was pretty shocked when he took an overdose and ended up in hospital and from that point when we both felt we needed to seek help together, things have been an awful lot easier . . . It was when we actually came to going and getting it, it was then that I actually believed that he really would seek help. Before that it seemed to be a bit of something that I wanted and he didn't really. I don't know whether that was the case at the time but it seemed to be that he didn't really want to go outside . . . and having sort of hit the bottom it wasn't so bad, that it wasn't *degrading* or something like that.'

The findings concerning which partner made the first contact with the agency reveal a similarity with the patterns of decision-making. In the twenty-eight marriages investigated, twenty wives, but only eight husbands, made the initial approach to the agency. However, many spouses (though not all) later became clients themselves. Several wives spontaneously commented on their own greater propensity (that is compared with their husbands) to involve agencies and outsiders generally. One wife said:

'I've always been led to believe that marriage is between two people, though it is usually *me* that brings people into the problem, never to my husband's knowledge usually.'

Whereas a husband said:

> 'I like to keep a lot of things to myself — personal problems — I try to sort them out between us. I don't like to, or I never have previously brought anybody into it. I never spoke about things really, my mates or anything whereas the wife does, you know.'

It is worth referring to a particular case in which both partners were experiencing minor stress symptoms and where each had visited their general practitioners in swift succession. However, it was only after the *wife* had visited the doctor that the doctor took up the question of their marital difficulties. Furthermore, in the three cases where husbands eventually visited the surgery at the doctor's explicit request, their wives, before they themselves visited the doctor, had tried without success to persuade their husbands to attend.

The initial presentation of problems

Let us consider how people presented their problems at the first agency which they contacted in their current help-seeking episodes. In seventeen marriages respondents presented, in the first instance, with sexual problems, such as the onset of impotence, or with other problems connected with the continuation of their marital relationships, such as one partner threatening to leave. In eleven marriages one of the partners attended the surgery with a symptom located in herself as an individual, or (in one instance) in a child. In these marriages it was largely women who presented with individual problems, which the agencies, usually general practitioners, ultimately redefined or perceived in conjunction with difficulties in marriage.

The following quotations illustrate how agencies took up the individual problems with which respondents presented. One woman who had been married two years, described how she had been attending the doctor for severe stomach pains and for which she was referred by the general practitioner to a hospital outpatient clinic. After no organic condition was diagnosed the general practitioner began to question her about the marriage.

> Mrs Crewe, aged 23, cashier, truncated network:
> '. . . He asked me if I had any emotional problems or problems in the family and I said that my husband and I were experiencing difficulties in communication and with sexual intercourse in particular, and he asked more personal questions into that . . . after I

told him I felt relieved, but also anxious as to what my husband was going to say to me that I'd actually told someone about the difficulties. At that stage nobody else had sort of had a word out of me about it . . .'

When asked whether she had ever thought of going to the doctor herself about the marital and sexual difficulties, she said:

'I never actually got to the point of thinking "I'm going to the doctor tomorrow" . . . As the problem got worse it was sort of something I couldn't bring myself to talk about to anybody, and I thought "Perhaps in the end I'm going to go to the doctor," but I never actually got to that decision. I never got that far.'

In the next case the respondent had given up her job in order to study for a professional examination and had become lethargic and lacking in confidence.

Mrs Leeds, aged 32, unemployed library assistant, truncated network:
'Mainly I went to see the doctor because I thought I was about to get into a state. Having gone into three jobs I didn't feel I was getting anywhere . . . I was beginning to lose confidence in myself and I was sure it was worrying Roger [husband] and causing problems there . . . But I thought it was just me and once somebody had given me a kick in the right place, then everything would be all right again . . . I felt I was being silly going to the doctor and saying [laugh] "I think I've got something wrong; I don't know what it is quite." So I said to Roger "If you push me, then I'll go" . . . In the end, I just sort of went. And it wasn't until we *both* went to see the GP [the husband attended at the general practitioner's request] that the GP said: "Well, it seems as if Roger's got a problem as well." Then I thought "Well we'd better do something about it definitely and I'd better stop putting it off."'

We suggested earlier that approaching an agency with a health, or other kind of individual problem, did not appear to be solely a function of the distribution of critical events and problems. Crises and difficulties, including health problems, were common throughout the *whole* study group, and in particular in the eighteen-month period before agencies were approached. The difference between those who presented with a marital focus and those presented with an individual focus lies chiefly in the meanings respondents imposed upon their situations and their symptoms, and not simply upon how seriously they regarded them. In fact, both groups construed the moment at which they approached agencies as a point of desperation, and often as a last resort. A young working-class housewife and mother of two young children had left her husband on several occasions. She had been back and forth to the doctor who had suggested Marriage Guidance for both of them but the husband had refused to go. The general practitioner then referred her to a hospital psychiatrist on her own, who in turn referred her to a social worker whom she didn't like and whom she refused to go on seeing. The last time she had run away from home her husband became ill and took a drug overdose. She decided to try to persuade him once again to go with her to the Marriage Guidance Council.

> Mrs Hull, aged 21, housewife, close-knit kinship network:
> 'It was the last straw; it was the only thing I had left.'

Another woman talked about the first occasion she went to the Marriage Guidance Council.

> Mrs Wells, aged 29, shop assistant, differentiated friendship network:
> 'It was a sort of desperation. It was either me walking out . . . and I thought "Well, I must give it [the marriage] one last go."'

Respondents talked in a similar vein about how they felt when they approached agencies with individual problems. In the next quotation the respondent clearly regarded her marriage as being in trouble. However, she only revealed the problems to the doctor after considerable close questioning.

> Mrs Luton, aged 28, secretary, truncated network:
> *'And you went into the surgery and said what you'd come for?'*
> 'Yes. I said "Well, I've got this mole and also I feel permanently tired . . . and all this sort of thing and it's getting me down. And he said "Why don't you come to see me about your real problems and not look for excuses." And I said that these things really had worried me and he said "Well they're just minor things. You wanted an excuse" sort of attitude.'

She went on to talk about how she felt at the time:

> 'It was at the stage where I was going to go or he was going to go. We were going to have to do something because one of us would have had a nervous breakdown . . . or would have had an affair.'

Another respondent said about approaching an agency with individual problems:

'It was only really in a desperate measure − of ending up in a state
where something absolutely had to be done somehow, somewhere.'

It is important to emphasize that, in our study, of those who initially presented with individual problems, at least one of the partners
had accepted the agencies' definitions of marital problems, although
they did not always accept their actual interventions. Thus, in these
cases people's subsequent help-seeking careers depended upon: (a)
the way in which the agencies responded to the presentations of their
problems, and (b) their own responses to the agencies' interventions.

On the first point, we have no basis on which to estimate how common it is for general practitioners in general to pay much attention to
patients' marriages. However, it seems to us highly likely that the
general practitioners in our study were an atypical group. First, they
were unusual in the sense that they had access in their area to a small
hospital-based service offering specialist marital help. Moreover,
since this service was located in one of their local hospitals and was run
by a consultant psychiatrist, they were offered the ready opportunity
for referring within the medical 'fraternity'. Second, it emerged that a
change of general practitioner had taken place in eight of the nineteen marriages where one partner approached a general practitioner
with an individual symptom or a marital or sexual problem. In three
instances respondents had encountered a locum when they had
expected to see their own doctors, and the locum had clearly taken a
fresh view of the patient's situation and had approached the management of the patient in a radically different way. In the other five cases,
the respondents had been allocated to new doctors within the past
year or so, either because their old doctor had died or because they
had moved house.

The significance of these changes is not clear in every case. In two it
seems probable that the arrival of a relatively young doctor had led to
changes in the treatment and diagnosis of the patient which departed
from the orthodox 'medical model'. In addition to those with locums
and new general practitioners (8/19) another four respondents had
women doctors, whom they described as being extremely sympathetic
to their problems. In two further instances, it appears that the general
practitioners had referred their patients because they felt unable to
deal with marital difficulties themselves. In one of these cases the
general practitioner was said to have commented that, although

sympathetic, he felt unable to help the patient because of his own marital problems. Interestingly, this doctor had himself been a client of the same therapist at the hospital marital service to whom he suggested referring these patients, something which he told the couple concerned and which, in their eyes, added weight to his recommendation.

One further point about this group of general practitioners is worth mentioning, which suggests the possibility of their also being atypical in their patients' eyes: this concerns the great surprise which respondents said they had felt when they found their doctors showing interest in their marital or sexual problems. Plainly they had not thought that the general practitioner would concern himself with these aspects of their lives.

Mrs Bude, aged 30, secretary, close-knit kinship network:
'I was most surprised because I have never seen a doctor that has shown so much . . . I wouldn't say concern but you felt you weren't just on a conveyor belt, just in and out, write you a prescription and out you go, which is what it has become so much now. He said to me "I think this goes deeper than just your going off sex and I'd like to see you again" and "Would you come after surgery hours?" which I did.'

Except for one case, the women in our study appear to have welcomed rather than to have resented doctors who probed into their marriages. In the case of the exception, the woman concerned regarded neither her doctor nor any other person (apart from her husband) as being able to help or change the situation in any way.

Further overall implications arising from the interventions of the general practitioners and the responses of the different groups of clients will be explored in the next chapter. We shall now go on here to investigate the consequences of the differing initial presentations to agencies in terms of the agencies approached, and their implications for respondents' subsequent careers as clients.

Pathways through the agencies

Current help-seeking

We have delineated three routes or pathways through agencies in respondents' current help-seeking episodes.

The first route is exclusively medical. Most respondents following this route first approached their general practitioners and were subsequently referred to other medical agencies, with the culminating referral being to the hospital unit for marital therapy. This we have called the *Medical Route* and includes respondents from fourteen marriages. The second route consists of self-referrals to the Marriage Guidance Council and is termed the *Marriage Guidance Route* (eight marriages). The third route consists of initial approaches to medical agencies, followed by referrals or approaches to non-medical agencies, notably to the Marriage Guidance Council. We have termed this route the *Mixed Medical Route* (six marriages).

There are a number of ways in which these routes differ from one another, as the terms we have used to describe them suggest. One of the main differences between the medical routes and the other two routes is that those who consulted general practitioners, especially for sexual and health problems, were likely to have been first referred by them to one or more hospital departments, in short, to other doctors. For example, a man with a sexual problem was first referred by his general practitioner to a hospital where drug treatment proved unsuccessful. The man went back to his general practitioner, who referred him to another hospital where the treatment was equally unsuccessful. However, this last hospital suggested that the general practitioner should refer the man to the hospital marital unit. It is interesting that where general practitioners did refer to this marital service, they had already tried the more usual medical channels, with no successful results. The use of orthodox medical channels for their patients is, of course, hardly surprising, since our respondents initially presented with physical or psychological symptoms which the general practitioners accordingly tried to treat in medical ways. It was only when the possibilities within orthodox medicine had been exhausted that the general practitioners appear to have turned to the hospital marital service. However, even though this particular service happens to be run by a consultant psychiatrist and operates according to the conventional medical referral system, referral to this service by the general practitioners and hospital doctors may well have been regarded by them as a 'last resort'. Nevertheless, it is still a service which was indubitably regarded by them as residing within an over-riding *medical* framework. This pattern is in accord with other evidence, which suggests that if general practitioners refer at all, they are unlikely to refer outside the medical network. In the 1960s Shepherd *et al.* (1966) found that, although general practitioners attributed the course or cause of psychiatric illness to social factors in about 50 per cent of cases, they almost never referred to or liaised with social agencies such as social workers. Even though this pattern is undoubtedly changing, referral rates to medical and non-medical agencies are still relatively low and do not appear to vary according to the rates of health, or social problems (Morrell, Gage, and Robinson 1971; Fry 1979).

In contrast, those who took themselves directly to Marriage Guidance Councils were never referred on and, by definition, had not come into contact with medical agencies in connection with their marital problems. Where general practitioners had recommended that their patients should go to Marriage Guidance, these respondents had sometimes approached additional agencies themselves. Moreover, where Marriage Guidance was suggested by general practitioners it was not usually followed by a formal referral; patients were left to make the contact themselves.

One effect of referral within a *medical* context, therefore, seems to have been that it deterred people from themselves initiating contact with other kinds of agencies. (There is, by definition, an absence of contact with agencies other than medical ones amongst those on medical routes.) This is fairly predictable, in that the action of putting oneself in the hands of a system or network of professional others, over which one can exert very little control (Friedson 1961; Bloor and Horobin 1975; Byrne and Long 1976), may detract from individual initiative or render it redundant.

The process of referral was therefore a prominent feature of those following the medical route, and served to make their help-seeking pathways more complex. One of the characteristics of a complex, as distinct from a simple, help-seeking pathway was the disproportionately greater time involved. Respondents who referred themselves to Marriage Guidance Councils usually went straight there, once they had obtained an appointment, although a few clients commented on the long waiting periods they encountered, which was anything up to four months. By comparison with Marriage Guidance pathways, the duration of those following medical or mixed-medical routes was generally much greater. Where general practitioners redefined patients' problems and first referred them to outpatient departments and only eventually referred them to the hospital marital service, half of the help-seeking routes exceeded a year, which is a long time when people are experiencing serious difficulties.

A further factor which differentiates medical pathways from other routes concerns the role of the spouse. Where the initial problem was presented in individual terms to the agency, the process of referring the patient for that problem often served to reinforce its definition in those terms, and to perpetuate the exclusion of the spouse. Moreover, the longer this process continued, the more difficult it may have been for either of the parties to alter course. Furthermore, since each partner in a marriage is an *individual patient* of a general practitioner, the general practitioner must relate to each person largely in those terms. Thus, if general practitioners become concerned about their patients' marriages, they are likely to become implicated in tripartite negotiations: between themselves and their patients; between themselves and the spouses; and to become involved in the marital dyads themselves.

We suggested in Chapter 4 that husbands frequently played a crucial part in locating and sustaining 'the problem' in the wife, the classic example being 'It's all the wife's depression.' It is our contention here that where general practitioners, for whatever reasons, refrained from entering into complex and often long drawn-out negotiations with each partner over their marriages (which the process of redefinition usually involved), they may have unwittingly sustained and reinforced the initial presentation of the problem and the couples' accommodation to it. Thus wives, defined as sick either by their husbands or by themselves, may have become confirmed in that status through the agency of the general practitioner. Evidence from respondents' *past* help-seeking behaviour testified to the process by which the presenting problem was reinforced in this way. We think that this is likely to be a common outcome of doctors' management of their female patients.

In one case a woman had been treated for depression by her general practitioner from the beginning of her marriage four years previously. Even so, a major sexual problem − her husband's impotence throughout their relationship − had never come up as an issue on the many occasions when she had seen her doctor. However, one day the woman encountered a locum instead of her usual general practitioner, who suggested to her, and later to her own doctor, that she and her husband should go to a marriage counsellor.

In several cases the considerable difficulty and length of the time taken for the doctor even just to persuade the patient's husband to attend the surgery was evident. In the following comment a husband indicated his great reluctance to attend the surgery when his wife, who had been going to the doctor for severe stomach pains, told him that the doctor wanted to see him.

Mr Crewe, aged 31, sales clerk, truncated network:
'Did you find it difficult to go?'
'It was a bit of an upheaval . . . I knew that he knew roughly what
the trouble was, or might be the trouble, so I had the feeling
"You're one up on me, you know". He knew something about me.'

Mrs Crewe (aged 23, cashier, truncated network) talked about per-
suading her husband to go to the doctor:

'The doctor had advised me to say to John [husband] that it was
important that he tried to discuss the matter with me or with him,
in order that I got over this stomach trouble because he [the doctor]
felt certain they [the marriage and the symptoms] were connected.
I didn't get a very good reaction from my husband at that time and
he felt the doctor was interfering . . . I think I went back in about
two weeks to see the doctor again. He'd asked to see me . . . Again
he asked me how we were getting on and I said things weren't any
better . . . and he gave some advice . . . and he also advised me to
try to persuade my husband to come to see him, either together, or
on his own . . . He certainly wasn't pushing him to come along and
he suggested that I didn't either . . . I think I might have expected
the doctor to — for me to insist he came along, I'm not quite sure
. . . I think I visited the doctor three or four times at two weekly
intervals before John [husband] actually came along . . . Eventually he not so much threatened but said that I should suggest to my
husband that if he didn't come along and see him that things would
only get worse and it could mean we would part.'

It is clear that the role of the general practitioner can be crucial in
determining the future course of an individual's help-seeking career.
However, in addition to the difficulties doctors may encounter in
communicating and negotiating with patients' spouses, other factors
reinforce the *status quo*, so that, for example, the problem would continue to be located in the wife. Since the majority of initial help-
seekers in our study were women, the relationship between women
patients and their doctors assumes a particular significance. If it is
accepted that the balance of power in marriage resides in the man,
and in the doctor–patient relationship in the doctor, then the relationship of the woman patient to her doctor (where the doctor is a man)
replicates the balance of power in her marriage. At least one study has
indicated that women are more likely than men to lack or to lose confidence in encounters with their doctors (Sawyer 1979). In circumstances where women were undergoing considerable difficulties in

their marriages and themselves felt, or had been told by their husbands, that it was all 'their own fault', the diagnosis of male doctors, which appear to have supported these definitions, actually increased the oppression that women were experiencing.

We do not wish to suggest that women patients, either consciously or unconsciously, were suppressing their 'real' reasons for going to their doctors. Their physical and psychological symptoms were indeed 'real' to them and they regarded them as appropriate matters to discuss with their doctors. Moreover, we have argued that people only defined their *marriages* as problematic and sought help after one partner had unequivocally threatened the relationship or put it in jeopardy. Thus individualistic explanations, such as patients' resistance to or denial of their problems, which are frequently given by therapists,[6] would seem to take no account of perspectives and situations pertaining to the status of patients and clients, and are often inappropriate to understanding clients' expectations of practitioners in their encounters with them. One study of doctor–patient relationships (Barrett and Roberts 1978) found that women were more anxious than men about going to the doctor, a tension which was associated not with the fear of serious illness but with the fear of what the doctor would think of them if their complaints turned out to be only trivial.

It is possible that general practitioners interpret patients' anxiety in the doctor–patient encounter as evidence of neurosis, or even as reflecting marital problems. There is, moreover, some evidence that actual social and personal problems account for general practitioners' complaints about the burden of 'trivial ailments' (Cartwright 1967; Mechanic 1975). General practitioners may also believe that their initial impressions have been confirmed if these patients do indeed admit under questioning to marital or psychological problems. Doctors may, therefore, wrongly interpret patients' behaviour in their encounters with them in terms of their problems, rather than in terms of the doctor–patient relationship itself. The argument that general practitioners act upon stereotypical views of women (Stimson 1976)[7] is one explanation for the observation that they interpret the symptoms of women patients differently from those of men patients. However, it does not fully explain why some doctors may reinforce the initial definition of the problem, in terms for instance of a woman patient's neurosis, whilst others may go beyond the presenting symptoms and investigate women's marital or sexual difficulties. The explanation for the differing responses of general practitioners is likely to lie in the changes taking place in medical socialization and education. But it is highly probable that only a tiny proportion of those marriages in serious difficulty which come within the orbit of doctors are dealt with by them as marital problems. In the majority of such cases it may simply not be on the agenda to do so, especially since the established diagnostic and aetiological models in medicine have scarcely paid even lip-service to psycho-social explanations of illness. Moreover, those medical practitioners who do take up people's marital problems must counter the dominant notions about appropriate presenting problems amongst their patients, as well as in their own professional communities. They must also compete against more prestigious branches of medicine for control over their patients. However, these issues, although fascinating, constitute a topic for further research and are not our concern here.

We have so far established that gender is important, not only in determining the outcome of competing definitions of the situation in the marital relationship, but also in influencing who becomes a client and for what. In addition, gender affects the ways in which *medical* agencies react to their clients and the problems they present to them. Thus those who embark on medical pathways to help encounter relationships which are defined by male professional dominance at two levels: at the level of the doctor–patient relationship and at the ideological level of medical beliefs and explanations about patients and their problems.

In contrast with those on medical pathways, those who approach marriage counsellors are in voluntaristic relationships. Clients are not tied to counsellors in the way that patients are to their doctors. If clients decide they do not want their counsellors' services they need never go again and can make a fresh approach to another similar agency without difficulty. The patient, by contrast, is tied to his or her family doctor and must take cognizance of the fact that he or she is a gatekeeper to a wide range of important services. A second important difference between medical practitioners and marriage counsellors is that the latter are predominantly voluntary workers and not paid professionals as such. The 'competence gap' is therefore smaller between counsellors and their clients than it is between doctors and their patients. Thus counsellor–client relationships are likely to be less constrained by the dynamics of power. Thirdly, in contrast to doctors, marriage counsellors are still, at the present time, more likely to be women than men.[8] There is, therefore, a higher congruence of gender between counsellors and those clients who initiate help-seeking than between patients and their doctors. In short, the modal client—counsellor relationship is characterized by a lack of obligation and by elements of equality and similarity. These characteristics contrast with those of the modal doctor—patient relationship, which is marked by ties of obligation and gender difference and considerable disparity in power and competence.

However, in making these overall comparisons, we do not wish to over-emphasize the elements of similarity between clients and counsellors at the expense of the differences which also exist between them. We are thinking particularly of class and status differences; marriage counsellors are predominently middle class and are frequently married to professional men, whereas their clients are drawn from all social classes (Heisler 1975).[9]

Even though counsellors may be in a somewhat different position *vis-à-vis* their clients, compared with doctors and their patients, they are equally likely to become caught up in the power struggle of the marital dyad, and perhaps are even more at risk of this. Although the practice is changing, it is still common for Marriage Guidance counsellors to see individual spouses on their own in those cases where the other spouse is unwilling to attend.[10]

This practice differs from that obtaining in other organizations practising marital therapy, such as the hospital marital service, where it is exceptional for only one partner to be seen. In our study there are examples where one partner (usually the husband) attended Marriage Guidance much less frequently and also less willingly than the other. There was some evidence in these cases of the husband trying to use the counselling relationship to sustain the *status quo* in the marriage. Thus, the counsellor, lacking the authority of, for example, the doctor, and being therefore unable to exert much pressure on the husband to attend may, simply by seeing the wife on her own, be unwittingly drawn into supporting the husband's position. This was illustrated by certain husbands who were especially favourably disposed towards their wives continuing to attend Marriage Guidance:

> Mr Neath, aged 41, draughtsman, truncated network:
> 'It makes *her* feel so much better.'

Mr Wells (aged 39, small shopkeeper, differentiated friendship network) described how he had 'sent' his wife back to Marriage Guidance many times.

> 'And when she feels she is doing all the work, I'll go along and make a show.'

Figure 8(4) Examples of respondents' current help-seeking routes

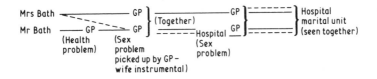

Key : – – – – – – recommended course of action
         ───────── went to agency

1   *Medical route* – initial presentation = a health problem

Mrs Bath ────────── GP } ──────────GP } – – – – – } Hospital
Mr Bath ──── GP ──── GP } (Together)   GP } – – – – – } marital unit
         (Health   (Sex   Hospital   } (seen together)
         problem)   problem   (Sex
                       picked up by GP – problem)
                       wife instrumental)

2   *Marriage guidance route* – initial presentation = a marital problem

Mrs Frome ────────── MG } Seen together
Mr Frome ─────────── MG } and separately

3   *Mixed medical route* – initial presentation = a marital problem

Mrs Tenby ────────── Solicitor Wife ──────GP────── MG } Seen
Mr Tenby   Husband   Husband ────── MG } separately

This man made a token guest appearance in the ratio of one visit to ten of his wife's. He described his own involvement with Marriage Guidance thus:

'The reason I go on Marriage Guidance is that the counsellor is a good help to my wife. She can say things I've spent years trying to convince her of . . . When I did it, it was like talking to a brick wall. When it is reiterated through the counsellor, my wife starts listening and now she realizes that what I've been saying all along is right.'

The attitude of this man illustrates how the interests of a husband structured the marital relationship, and reflects his concern with maintaining the *status quo*; he in fact wanted his wife to be a more efficient and organized housekeeper and also, by working for him, to help him to build up his small business. Irrespective of whether or not the counsellor saw herself as colluding in this situation, it was clear to us that the husband was attempting to strengthen his own position by appropriating the power of counselling practice and knowledge, and his consistent failure to attend sessions was part of his strategy.

Medical pathways to help therefore differ from those whose help-seeking involves contact with non-medical agencies in a number of ways. In order to illustrate the differences, an example of each of the three types of help-seeking routes are presented visually. It is also interesting to note that the differences in current help-seeking patterns are also to some extent apparent in respondents' earlier help-seeking behaviour.

Past help-seeking

A quarter of those who first contacted their general practitioners in their current help-seeking episodes, particularly over sexual or marital problems were also likely to have consulted them on previous occasions for these or similar problems. In a few cases the general practitioner had offered to refer the patients elsewhere. Thus where people had previously been referred for marital or sexual difficulties, their help-seeking careers exhibited further complexity.

Moreover, those respondents who had previously consulted either Marriage Guidance counsellors or psychiatrists (6/28 marriages) described their experiences as largely unsatisfactory. That they nevertheless later returned to their general practitioners for re-referral suggests the importance of general practitioners as gatekeepers to services. In addition, the fact that respondents' earlier unsatisfactory experiences did not deter them from 'trying again', perhaps reflects the long term and chronic seriousness of their problems.

In contrast with others who followed medical or mixed-medical current help-seeking pathways, those who referred themselves direct to Marriage Guidance, with one exception, had neither contemplated nor sought help in relation to their marriages at any time previously. It seems likely that the marriages in this group, which were amongst those at greatest risk of breaking up, have certain features which render them distinct from those that followed medical or mixed-medical routes to help. Unfortunately, since the Marriage Guidance self-referral group consists of such a small number of cases, it is difficult to draw overall comparisons, but some observations can be made.

If the difference between those who went direct to Marriage Guidance and those who followed medical pathways to help lies mainly in the *meanings* they attributed to their situations and symptoms, as we have argued earlier, then differences in the amount of previous contact with medical agencies are not very relevant to this argument.

In fact, in the eighteen months preceding help-seeking episodes contact with general practitioners and with hospitals was fairly high for all respondents, whatever their pathways to formal help.[11] Respondents had contacted medical agencies for a wide range of somatic, psychosomatic and psychological problems. Many of these health problems, described more fully in Chapter 5, were fairly serious matters and included such things as a road accident, a suspected case of tuberculosis and pneumonia. Thus going to an agency for one type of problem did not necessarily determine where people went for another kind of problem. We cannot of course hypothesize about the consequences for the self-referral Marriage Guidance group, had agencies intervened at an earlier stage of the difficulties.

Respondents who went to Marriage Guidance directly, had not on the whole approached agencies for symptoms associated with their distress about their *marriages*, although it was obvious to us that some had quite debilitating symptoms, such as a deeply depressed mood. Thus it may be that their previous consultations for health problems had lacked any ambiguity and had, therefore, offered no openings for doctors to probe into their marriages. We conclude, therefore, that most respondents had sought some kind of formal help at some point in the *past*, but that what they specifically sought help for, and the context in which they defined their problems as requiring help, are the central and significant issues.

There is some evidence, however, that those who had long-term psychological problems became locked into medical help-seeking pathways. (This was especially true in two marriages.) There also appears to have been a slightly greater amount of contact with psychiatry amongst those referred by general practitioners for marital help to the hospital marital unit compared with the rest of the research group. How far this explains why general practitioners had offered to refer these patients to this particular service, especially since it was run by a consultant psychiatrist, we do not know. Even so, in almost every such case, respondents were highly critical of their past experiences of psychiatrists. It is, therefore, possible that this group were rather exceptional but, since we have no idea of the extent to which previous psychiatric contact may have deterred *other* patients from being referred to the hospital service, we cannot say in what ways.

In general, it emerges that current help-seekers were likely to have been help-seekers in the past. A few had sought help (or attempted to do so) for marital or sexual problems, whilst many had been in contact with medical agencies for quite serious physical or psycho-logical problems. There was also a small but possibly significant association between previous contact with psychiatry and subsequent referral by general practitioners for marital therapy to the hospital unit.

We will conclude this section with a reference to an exceptional and quite *deviant* case, which is instructive in its rarity. It concerns a man who described his past decision about, and experience of seeking help for, psychological problems, as a pointer towards subsequently recognizing problems in his marriage and deciding to do something about them.

> Mr Ascot, aged 32, surveyor, differentiated friendship network:
> *'What influenced your decision to go to Marriage Guidance?'*
> 'What influenced my decision, what I feel you are getting at is —
> Well, five years ago I had a lot of psychological trouble. I went to group psychotherapy in a hospital . . . It was a turning point in my life, when I realized I was going down the plug hole of life and that I needed some help. It was a big moment for me to realize that I had a problem. Now, although that vastly improved me . . . and our marriage improved consequently, it never got as right as I hoped it would . . . Anyway the point about it is that it seeded in my mind, that when you've got problems the right thing to do is to recognize the problem and go out and seek help about it . . . A lot of people don't realize that they have got a problem or that it is a problem they can resolve. They haven't got a marital problem; they think there is something wrong with the *other* person. It ends up in screaming rows . . . it gets out of focus between you . . . I suppose all that went before me with my psychological problems and it gave me the lead how to deal with the marital ones, you see.'

This example of a decision to seek formal help is perhaps nearest to the counselling model of how people do and should approach agencies[12] but was quite atypical of the group of help-seekers we have studied. It is perhaps therefore instructive of the way in which reality rarely conforms to the ideal.

Notes

1 In the truncated group 9/14 marriages presented with a medical problem with 10/13 and 5/17 marriages doing so in the other two network groups. Because *both* partners in a marriage did not always belong to the same type of network some marriages are counted twice in these figures.

2 Cartwright and O'Brien (1976) found that working-class patients were more likely to *say* that they would discuss a personal problem with a general practitioner but in actual consultations the researchers observed that they were no more likely than other social classes to do so.

3 The morbidity statistics from the Second National Study of General Practitioners (OPCS 1974) suggest big differences in the rates per thousand of those who consulted a general practitioner in a two-week period, especially those aged 15—44. The numbers of consultations per thousand were 83 for men and 144 for women.

4 Nathanson (1975) extensively examined the evidence and concludes that women have higher rates than men for almost all indices of morbidity and medical utilization in the United States and that this is so even when women's conditions associated with reproduction are excluded.

5 Greenley and Mechanic (1976) suggest that women are disproportionately represented in populations treated by psychiatrists. Horwitz (1977) found that although men were equally as likely as women to consult physicians women had a higher utilization rate of other types of professionals such as marriage counsellors and social welfare agencies.

6 This is based on the authors' personal communication and observations made in various therapeutic settings.

7 Stimson (1976) in his small-scale study notes that four in nine doctors mentioned that the patients who caused the most 'trouble' had psychological problems and were, in most instances, women.

8 According to NMGC only one in four or five counsellors is a man and there has been little change in this ratio in recent years.

9 Heisler (1975) compares the NMGC data with the Census (1971) and concludes that NMGC clients considered in relation to husbands' occupations form a representative cross-section of the population.

10 The NMGC Annual Report 1979 shows a growth in the number of conjoint interviews. However, it is unclear whether this growth relates to a change in practice by counsellors or to an increase in the number of couples who wanted to attend together.

11 Of those respondents who took the medical route 6/26 had consulted a general practitioner, visited a hospital outpatient clinic or had been an inpatient for a relatively serious 'condition' (see *Table 5(1)* where only serious problems are included). Medical contacts in respondents' *current* help-seeking are excluded from this figure. In the mixed-medical and Marriage Guidance routes the corresponding figures are 6/8 and 7/14 respectively. If current medical contacts are included the rates even up considerably.

12 For example *Marriage Matters* (WPMG 1979) suggests that people once they have reached the point of recognizing a problem in their marriages must next solve the uncertainty about the choice of an agency to help them and of 'overcoming their anxiety' about 'crossing the threshold' of that agency.

9

The agencies: perceptions, expectations, and initial impact

Studies concerning patients' expectations of, and satisfaction with, medical practitioners have generally painted a picture of stable and generalized dispositions; surveys of general practitioners' patients indicating high levels of satisfaction with doctors in our society are a particular case in point (Bevan and Draper 1967; Cartwright 1967; Marsh and Kaim-Caudle 1976). In general, the range of subtlety and variability in patients' attitudes towards doctors over treatment of specific health conditions is rarely revealed. While it is no doubt true that what appears to matter to patients about doctors is to some extent inevitably an artifact of whatever the researchers are studying, it would still seem meaningful to explore patient and client perceptions and expectations in relation to specific types of illness-career and modes of help-seeking.

Our respondents in no way constituted a homogenous group of patients or clients, whether considered in terms of the symptoms or problems they initially presented, or in respect of the agencies they approached over them. All our respondents acknowledged to us the existence of serious difficulties in their marriages, and yet the ways in which agencies such as general practitioners became involved with the problems were strikingly different: in some cases the involvement appeared extremely haphazard in nature, whereas, at the other extreme, it was a sequence of specific decisions which led to the choice of a specialist agency such as Marriage Guidance.

In this chapter we propose to examine in some detail the range of perceptions, expectations, and initial reactions of our respondents to the various agencies with which they came into contact over their marital and sexual problems. Although we recognize the limitations imposed by having been unable to obtain respondents' expectations before they actually approached any agencies at all, nevertheless, in the vast majority of cases, we were able to interview them shortly after they had embarked on marital counselling and therapy.

The range of agencies available

We were interested, first of all, to discover what respondents knew about the range of formal help available for marital and sexual difficulties, so we asked at the beginning of the interview where they considered people in general would go with such problems. We found, possibly due to the positioning of the question and perhaps also because we had obtained our study group through recent contact with agencies, that respondents seemed orientated towards mentioning agencies rather than informal sources of help. Not all respondents gave replies to these questions[1] and some clearly found it hard to think beyond their own individual experiences, which they frequently regarded as atypical, to more general possibilities.

Table 9(1) *Agencies people go to for marital problems*

	% of mentions	Number of times mentioned
General practitioner	26.3	25
Marriage Guidance	22.1	21
Kin and friends	17.8	17
Nowhere	9.9	9
Others (media, CAB, other medical agencies, churches, solicitors, etc.)	21.0	20
Don't know	3.3	3
Total	100.4	95

Some respondents mentioned agencies, the usefulness of which they themselves had discounted, whilst others thought that most people in general would not approach an agency at all, even though they themselves had done so. Mrs Ascot (aged 32, media consultant) gave a very thoughtful account:

'I think most of them don't go anywhere at all. I think most people soldier on on their own. I think it's a difficult subject to turn to anybody for help. If they've got a sex problem the best place to start with is your doctor, but I doubt that many people actually do because I don't think doctors are very approachable for this sort of thing. I wouldn't have gone to mine. I suppose women who go to family planning clinics might ask the doctor there sometimes. They seem a bit more sympathetic and if it were a particularly sexual problem they might help.'

Several respondents said rather emphatically that they felt there were no obvious places to go with sexual problems.

Mrs Deal, aged 34, clerical worker:
'I think people with sexual problems probably don't go anywhere . . . There are no places to go. Society is supposedly tolerant of sexual problems but it is not in fact.'

Some respondents suggested there was a stigma attached to seeking help for problems of this nature, which acted as a strong deterrent.

Mrs Bude (aged 30, secretary) considered this a difficulty:
'I think people are a bit frightened of seeking help . . . I think it's a lot to admit that you do need help of this kind. It's not where you can go to a doctor and say "I've got a cut on my hand, I need it healed." It's something that's in your mind . . . you've got to confess how you feel and ask for help.'

The general practitioner was one of the most frequently mentioned sources of help, which is not surprising given that thirteen of the twenty-eight couples in the study had recently acknowledged the existence of marital difficulties, either at their own or their doctors' instigation. Several respondents mentioned family doctors as a possible source of help but modified their replies with negative comments such as:

'Your GP, and when you go, you get no help there.'

The most significant and commendatory of respondents' perceptions of their general practitioners concerns their perceived role as gatekeepers to other services. As one person said:

'I think usually to their doctor first and then he usually puts them on to somebody.'

Other comments suggest that the doctor was seen as appropriate if the patient's problem was sexual but not marital. In the next quotation the respondent rather graphically equated sexuality with other bodily functions which he regarded as the province of the doctor:

'With sexual problems they'd probably go to a doctor, someone who knows the ins and outs of the body and where your sexual block is.'

On the other hand, some women respondents expressed entirely the opposite view, suggesting that most people would find it embarrassing to reveal sexual problems to their general practitioners:

'I can't imagine going to the doctor's with *that* sort of problem.'

The Marriage Guidance Councils were mentioned as frequently as doctors by respondents as a source of help, although many mentioned it in a rather curt, even dismissive way, even where they themselves had become clients. Several respondents, some of whom were Marriage Guidance clients themselves, suggested that other people would only go there if they were really desperate and as a last resort.

Mrs Frome, aged 31, housewife:
'The general thing seems to be that you either don't talk about it at all to anybody and retreat into a bottle or a packet of cigarettes or you talk to a friend or relation, and in the last resort, provided they get to see they are that desperate, they might as well go to Marriage Guidance.'

All other sources of formal help, such as solicitors, the churches, welfare services, and the media, were mentioned by small numbers of respondents only. Samaritans were not mentioned here, although they had in fact been approached by two respondents and had been warmly recommended by them. Interestingly, many of those (mostly the husbands) who had not instigated formal help-seeking, mentioned specific agencies as 'doors' on which it was *theoretically* possible to 'knock',[2] which suggests that knowledge of services alone is insufficient in provoking formal help-seeking.

The previous chapter (Chapter 8) ended with an instance where an individual's approach to an agency for marital help had been very positive. Mr Ascot, a member of the professional class, had found his experience of psychotherapy very helpful, and when he subsequently acknowledged the existence of serious difficulties in his marriage he and his wife both went to a Marriage Guidance Council. Mr Ascot was unique in our study group in a number of ways: first, here was a husband rather than a wife taking the initiative about going to an agency; second, his pathway to help was based upon the recognition of the *value* of defining problems and seeking formal help; third, he was unusual in that, *because* of his past help-seeking experience, he had formed some relatively clear expectations of Marriage Guidance before he went there.

Such relatively defined expectations of marital help were on the

whole absent from our study group, most of whom had little idea at all
of what to expect. Expectations about Marriage Guidance and
general practitioners were, interestingly, rather different as the
examples of Mr Hove and Mr Crewe below illustrate. Even so both respondents described a general sense of uncertainty.

> Mr Hove (aged 35, partner in a small firm) said of Marriage
> Guidance:
> 'I didn't really know what to expect. I really had no idea – no
> experience to go on.'

Mr Crewe (aged 31, sales clerk) was requested by his family doctor to
visit the surgery with his wife to discuss sexual difficulties, and was
subsequently referred to the hospital unit for marital therapy.

> 'I didn't know what to expect. I wasn't frightened of going. I knew
> there would be *some* course of action but I didn't know what form it
> would take . . . tablets etc. I didn't dream he would send me to [the
> hospital service].'

We have tried to reconstruct respondents' expectations prior to their
going to the agency, but we have had to derive these from the retrospective accounts they gave in their interviews. In order to reduce the
degree of retrospection, we endeavoured to interview respondents after
only the first or second visit to the agency. However, because of difficulties of access, particularly to Marriage Guidance clients, certain
respondents could only be interviewed at a later date than we had
hoped. Nevertheless, although it was not always easy, we have endeavoured to distinguish between prior expectations and those which
were *post hoc*. But it was evident that many respondents only became
clear about their expectations, or rather their hopes, *after* they had
actually visited the agency and experienced its impact. We shall now
discuss respondents' expectations of the different agencies they
approached, and also the impact made upon them by their initial visits.

Expectations of general practitioners

There is little evidence to suggest that people in general expect their
general practitioners to be particularly helpful over marital difficulties, nor that they in fact go to their doctors with the express
purpose of disclosing their problems and getting formal help or
advice. Research has tended rather to suggest that where the medical
component is predominant the doctor may be seen as the appropriate
person to consult (Arber and Sawyer 1979).

Medicine itself appears unclear about the 'proper' role of general practitioners here. The Office of Health Economics (1974, 1975) for example has maintained that the general practitioner's role should not extend into 'pastoral' work, except in so far as social factors are implicated in a *diagnosis*. The British Medical Association (1970), on the other hand, argued that social and clinical aspects are highly interrelated and that general practitioners have an important part to play in both areas. But as Balint (1968) has pointed out, there is little in medical training which would lead anyone to expect that general practitioners are especially competent in the areas of marital relationships and sexuality.

It does, however, seem to be the case that a high proportion of respondents in our study had had some recent contact with medical agencies, over a wide range of problems often associated with marital conflict (Dominian 1980b). Moreover, research on battered women has found that considerable proportions of women experiencing persistent battering from husbands and other male intimates have received treatment from medical services (Dobash and Dobash 1980). Concerning the five cases of violence to wives in our study, only two of the four doctors approached by the women for treatment of their injuries, had openly acknowledged to the patients that the battering had taken place, and only one had offered any help. Five of the women went to the police for help and one fled to a Women's Refuge.

In a study of marital violence in the United States (Stark 1981) it was found that one in five women who used the emergency medical services (the equivalent of hospital casualty departments in this country) had been battered, and that they were rarely offered help, such as referral to social agencies, in the initial stages. The authors of this latter piece of research suggest that medicine's failure to recognize wife battering is systemic. Moreover, they suggest that failure to identify battering as a cause of injury constitutes one of the ways in which medicine can mystify and control people's lives. In short, their thesis is that medicine, by failing to diagnose the provoking agents of widespread forms of injury, has thereby significantly contributed to sustaining patriarchal dominance in American society.

A large proportion of our respondents approached their general practitioners at what we (restrospectively) considered the start of their help-seeking pathways (16/28). However, in the main they did not disclose their marital difficulties until they were encouraged to do so by the doctors. We shall first consider respondents' expectations of their doctors as appropriate persons to consult for marital problems. The following expectations were derived both from respondents who had acknowledged their difficulties to their doctors and from those who had not done so at all.

Eight respondents, almost all of whom went to Marriage Guidance Councils, spontaneously volunteered that they would under *no* circumstances go to their doctors with their marital problems, and the reasons they gave indicate that they considered doctors to lack competence in this area. Some suggested, realistically, that their doctors' competence lay mainly in the area of physical disease, or as one man (Mr Clare, aged 46, junior manager) put it, somewhat curtly:

'You go to your GP and get pills: you think it's physical . . . and when you go to the doctor there's always the magic pill.'

One wife, whose husband went to a Marriage Guidance Council after she left him, said she had never considered going to her doctor.

Mrs Hove, aged 25, secretary:
'This I felt was a human problem, an affair of the mind and the heart and not of the body, and why should he be any better or more fitted to discuss it with me or help me than my mother or someone else.'

Another wife expressed a similar view:

Mrs Cowes, aged 22, housewife:
'Our doctor is a friendly doctor, but . . . he would be more on the medical side. He wouldn't have anything to do with anything like *that*.'

There was a handful of people who perceived their family doctors as appropriate individuals to turn to at times of marital distress, although they did not refer to them as having any specific competence in this area.

One woman (Mrs Epsom, aged 48, executive director of small family business) whose husband had precipitately walked out on her and her family said:

'He was the *only* person I could think of.'

Mrs Epsom had searched for someone she felt she knew and could trust, outside her kinship network, since most of the members of her family were themselves very distressed by the episode. As it happened, Mrs Epsom's family doctor did not attempt to deal with the situation himself but referred her to a woman doctor in the practice who was reported to have said: 'Quite honestly I don't have the time to deal with this sort of thing.' She in turn suggested Mrs Epsom go to the Marriage Guidance Council, which is what happened.

A second type of expectation expressed by respondents, and again a somewhat negative one, concerned what respondents felt to be their doctors' lack of detailed personal information about their patients. The expectation of the doctor as an impersonal and substitutable professional is reflected in such comments as that from Mr Corby (aged 47, fireman):

> 'She doesn't really know us . . . there are four of them in the same practice and sometimes when you go it's a different person each time . . . I don't think they can know us quite well enough . . . our background or anything like that.'

A third expectation which relates to respondents' perceptions of doctors, both as impersonal professionals and as experts on disease, concerns the fear of being thought 'silly' by the doctor, especially where they were unable to give a clear description of their problems. It was significantly women who expressed such fears but even so they were still more likely than their husbands to go to the doctor.

> Mrs Leeds, aged 32, unemployed library assistant:
> 'I felt silly going to the doctor and saying "There's something wrong and I don't know what it is quite . . . lack of energy, not wanting to work" . . . I was relieved . . . mainly that it was not just my imagination, and something can be done about it.'

The fourth expectation (and the only one with any positive aspects), concerns the role of the general practitioner as a gatekeeper to other services. The few respondents who considered it appropriate to consult their doctors about their marital or sexual problems, and who in fact did so, did not necessarily expect the doctors to deal with them themselves, but hoped for a referral. As one wife put it: 'I thought he might be in a position to recommend somebody.'

Overall, respondents' expectations of their general practitioners were not very great in terms of the doctors helping them with their marital and sexual difficulties. The minimal quality of this is additionally highlighted when we consider respondents' reactions to being referred elsewhere for these problems. At the same time, whenever a doctor spontaneously raised the subject of marital problems or encouraged respondents to talk about these matters, our respondents described themselves as having been extremely surprised and often grateful.

The experience of being referred by general practitioners

We reported in the previous chapter (Chapter 8) that those doctors who suggested that a couple might benefit from marital help were frequently new to their patients, and some were in fact acting as locums for the regular general practitioners. It thus appears that a recommendation or referral for marital therapy was most frequently given in surgery encounters where the doctor had only had a brief acquaintance with the patient. These patients appeared to benefit from the newness of the doctor, whose fresh perspective on the situation was able to reveal different aspects of their problems from those seen by their usual doctors. It is interesting that we had no example where a patient's doctor acted towards the marital problems in an effective 'pastoral' capacity arising from a life-long doctor—patient relationship. Conversely, we had parallel examples of unsatisfactory outcome, as with the woman (instanced in the previous chapter) whose elderly general practitioner had referred her to several hospitals for treatment of various abdominal symptoms; none of the treatments had been successful. This general practitioner had recently died, and the new (and younger) doctor with whom she then registered viewed her case very differently, and offered to refer her and her husband to the hospital marital service, an offer which they gladly accepted.

Another woman appeared grateful to the doctor who, having been unable to find any physiological basis for her symptoms, took the initiative and questioned her about her sexual life. He too eventually offered to refer her and her husband to the hospital service for marital therapy.

Mrs Crewe, aged 24, cashier:
'I was quite pleased with the reaction I got from him. It wasn't a dismissive reaction as I thought might have happened when they found nothing wrong. Some doctors are just not interested on that side.'

The comments of these and other respondents suggest that it was not simply the personal approach of the doctor in the first instance but also the fact and feeling of being given adequate time which was valued by them. In fact, several respondents were given out of hours appointments by their general practitioners, and appreciated this.

Mrs Rugby, for instance, had made repeated visits to her doctor in connection with the health of her child, her elderly mother, and herself over a period of a year. She said she had been offered an out of hours appointment on more than one occasion. However, Mrs Rugby initially rejected the doctor's offer of marital help, having decided to take out a court injunction against her husband for being violent. Nevertheless, some months later, when the injunction was about to expire, Mrs Rugby decided to take her husband back. It was at this point that the doctor again offered to refer them both for marital help; this time Mrs Rugby and her husband agreed to a referral.

'She's the sort of doctor that she does have the time to sort of listen. Not like some of them she doesn't sit yards away . . . She's a doctor an' a half if you know what I mean. She seems to be interested in you, whereas the average doctor couldn't care less . . . She seems to be a different sort of doctor, whether it's because she's a woman, I don't know. But she seems to take much more time with her patients . . . she's quite able to sit and talk to you. Even if she's got a surgery full of people, she'll still give you ten minutes and even if she hasn't the time she'll say "Come back tomorrow night" . . . It was a consolation really that you didn't feel nobody cared . . . She even gave me her phone number.'

As already mentioned, doctors in the study did not, on the whole, formally refer their patients to Marriage Guidance Councils, but simply suggested that they might go there, leaving them to make their own appointments. Moreover, the general practitioners do not appear to have compensated for not having made formal referrals (spending time writing letters and so forth) by giving their patients any detailed information or recommendations about Marriage Guidance. In the case of Mrs Epsom (mentioned earlier) her own doctor passed her on, somewhat dismissively, to another doctor in the practice who, perhaps significantly, was a woman. She in turn suggested the Marriage Guidance Council because she was too busy to see Mrs Epsom. It would thus seem that suggestions by doctors to their patients about going to Marriage Guidance Councils were made in a somewhat casual manner, and may not have appeared to patients to carry a great deal of conviction. It is more likely that the few people who finally went to Marriage Guidance Councils at their doctors' suggestions did so in the context of their doctors' unhelpfulness and because of their own desperation.

In contrast, referrals to the hospital service were conducted within the traditional medical framework, whereby the general practitioner wrote a letter formally entrusting patients to the care of one of its doctors, both of whom were psychiatrists with formal titles within the medical hierarchy.[3] Moreover, the general practitioners almost always wrote to these doctors and thereby delegated to them a measure of medical responsibility, rather than to the non-medical therapists who also worked there. Thus, general practitioners referred their patients within their own professional community, to doctors who were frequently known to them by name and almost always by rank. It therefore seems likely that these referrals were made with greater conviction than were their suggestions to patients about going to Marriage Guidance Councils, with which they had no formal contact and whose workers were mostly voluntary and of lower status than themselves. The little evidence available on this issue suggests that Marriage Guidance clients are less likely to turn up for their appointments when they have been sent by professionals, like general practitioners, than when they have made the approach themselves (Timms and Blampied 1980). In the following comment, the wife described how their general practitioner had *personally* recommended one of the psychiatrists who worked for the hospital service and that this recommendation had tipped the balance in favour of her husband seeking help.

Mrs Luton, aged 28, secretary:
'I think having the recommendation of somebody that the doctor trusted helped. I think if he had said "Just go along to your local Marriage Guidance Council and make an appointment" my husband would never have done it.'

Although general practitioners may have referred their patients with greater conviction when they referred them to other doctors, they did not necessarily prepare them for the types of treatment they might receive from them. For example, the men in the study who had been referred to one or more hospitals for sexual problems, such as secondary impotence, said they had expected 'miracle cures'; additionally, none of them appears to have been apprised of the possibility of psychological determinants of their conditions by their general practitioners before their arrival at the hospital marital service. Thus it seems to us fairly clear that general practitioners played very little part in shaping respondents' expectations of any specialist marital or sexual help, whether this was given by Marriage Guidance or by medically based specialist clinics.

It may be equally well argued that the general practitioners made more convincing efforts when referring their patients to the hospital marital service than to Marriage Guidance because they felt that their patients might have perceived the hospital service as somewhat stigmatizing, in view of its known association with psychiatry. As we have suggested earlier, it was probably a measure of respondents' sheer desperation and frustration that they were willing to receive help with a psychiatric orientation, since those who had had previous contacts with psychiatric services described them as bewildering and unsatisfactory. However, since we cannot say whether or not the general practitioners were *aware* of their patients' earlier dissatisfaction, it is not possible to estimate its subsequent impact on any referrals.

We shall now briefly consider the reactions of our respondents to the doctors' offers of referral to the hospital service and to their previous contacts with psychiatrists. The reader may thus gain some idea of the obstacles respondents may have overcome in accepting and proceeding with a referral to the hospital service.

Perceptions of psychiatry

Even those respondents who had had no prior experience of psychiatry exhibited a fear of being labelled mentally ill. For example, a woman who was referred to the service with her husband, because of a long history of abdominal symptoms, expressed her apprehension of mental disturbance.

Mrs Bude, aged 30, secretary:
'I was a little bit apprehensive, a little bit scared because I thought "Don't tell me there's something *mentally* wrong with me."'

Nine of the twenty-three respondents (thirteen marriages) who were referred to the hospital service had had some previous contact with psychiatry, some in the distant past and some in their current help-seeking episodes. Most of these respondents had made only one visit previously to psychiatric outpatient departments, and the majority of them seemed to regard their encounters as cursory and impersonal.

Mrs Corby, aged 31, waitress:
'I thought it would have taken him much longer . . . He seemed to assess the situation very quickly . . . He said halfway through "Well, we know what's wrong with you. You don't want to be loved." And I said, "Oh! don't I?" And he was unable to do anything further.'

A similar kind of experience was reported by a wife who had been referred some time ago to a psychiatrist for a sexual problem, and who later went to Marriage Guidance. She complained:

> 'He didn't tell us anything we didn't already know . . . We didn't have much confidence in him . . . He tried to say I had a guilt complex [over sexual episodes in her childhood] . . . We just had to wait and everything would come out all right . . . They seem to think you can be cured by talking about it but I know I can't . . . It's like talking to a book and the book talking back. It didn't do much good . . . He didn't seem as if he *really* cared.'

Several respondents felt impatient with the attention that the psychiatrists had paid to their past, and unhappy with the emphasis on the patient doing most of the talking. One woman in the study had been referred to a psychiatrist for marriage difficulties many years previously, and even after several sessions had failed to obtain anything helpful.

> Mrs Ripon, aged 40, shop assistant:
> 'They didn't do anything at all. They were just listening and being very patient . . . I wanted to give it time . . . I didn't want to be hasty and think "Oh this is no good. I shan't do this." So I went along with it but it wasn't doing any good. It was doing good in the sense someone was listening . . . so I had a lot of relief but I wasn't getting any help with what was *really* wrong. Once you have been listened to two or three times. You know what I mean? So I led her to believe that things had looked up and it had been a great help and we didn't need it any more. In any case the clinic was closing and it was going out to X Mental Hospital and I was frightened of the thought of going there.'

Respondents' impatience with talking, and especially with talking about the past, needs to be viewed in the context of their encounters with psychiatrists, which in many cases did indeed appear from respondents' accounts to have been fairly cursory, impersonal, and highly controlled. These characteristics, in conjunction with respondents' fear of the stigma attached to psychiatric treatment, served effectively to make them feel negatively disposed towards it. One respondent (Mrs Wells, aged 29, shop assistant), who had been referred to a psychiatrist some years previously for a sexual problem, and who later approached Marriage Guidance of her own accord, had clearly received peremptory treatment.

'He gave me some nerve tablets . . . He said "There's no point in your coming." He more or less gave me the Bum's Rush. He said "There are people who do need my help." So I said it was true and he wasn't doing me no good so − I mean when I went there was a woman who thought she was a tree and I thought "Blimey, I might end up like that!" '

Even those few who had been in receipt of sustained psychiatric treatment in the past were not very positive. Their major criticism was that they had been treated without proper cognizance of the situations which had caused their symptoms in the first place, and that they were expected to return to more or less identical situations once their treatment was over. One couple had suggested to a hospital psychiatrist, who was treating the husband after an overdose, that their psychological problems might be handled in conjunction with one another. The wife was angry, though not surprised, when this suggestion met with a swift rebuff.

'I've had sessions of being treated before and it was always me in isolation and then it's thrown me back into a situation that I couldn't cope with again.'

Mr Ascot, whom we have mentioned more than once, was the exception in that his experience of psychiatry had been a very positive one. In the past he had had a long period of group psychotherapy (as a day patient within a psychiatric hospital) and had come to some understanding of what the process involved. Furthermore, his experience of psychotherapy had led him to approach a Marriage Guidance Council with his marital problems, and had also helped to give him some fairly clear and positive idea of what to expect from that agency.

Mr Ascot, aged 32, surveyor:
'I didn't expect any startling revelations to come up first time, that it could be a long slow process and that what does happen eventually . . . is the change that you yourself make. I mean I went to psychotherapy, as most people do, expecting to be cured by the doctor but of course that is not the case at all. I mean the process really is to make you *aware* of your own false perceptions of yourself and then to give you the means by which to alter yourself into a more favourable, stable − and this is what I expected from Marriage Guidance . . . As psychotherapy tends to slowly give you a deeper insight into yourself so Marriage Guidance might give you a deeper insight into your marriage.'

The hospital marital service

It seems clear that few respondents who were referred to this service had any clear notion of what kind of help to expect, though almost all knew the name of the doctor who was its director and most were aware of his psychiatric connection. However, because of our own associations with the service, we did not question people explicitly about their initial experience of it. Such comments as were made to us suggested a general sense of relief that some action was taking place, undoubtedly reflecting the high degree of desperation respondents were experiencing at the time. Some of the following comments are characteristic.

Mr Bude, aged 34, technical college lecturer:
'We were at a stage then that we had tried everything else and we had nothing to lose by giving it a try.'

Mrs Derby, aged 40, nurse:
'I felt either I needed professional help or I would have a nervous breakdown or walk in front of a bus.'

It is interesting that only one respondent (Mrs Bath, aged 56, housewife) seems to have felt really hopeful when her general practitioner suggested the referral to the hospital service. She described herself as being particularly pleased, since she had always felt that the marital problems were a complex mixture of problems which were to some extent psychological, but which also related to her husband's physical health. However, it was also clear that she thought that the psychiatrist in charge might be able to be helpful to her, in view of the religious affiliation which both she and the psychiatrist had in common. She felt pleased about the referral:

'I felt − oh yes! I came home to the girls [her daughters] and said "Better than I dared to hope." I was sort of filled with feeling that this is the turning point . . . At long last we were going to sort things out.'

To sum up at this point, we suggest that where the general practitioners referred patients to the hospital service for marital therapy they emphasized the informal, if not always the formal, aspects of the medical nexus. This was just as well, since most respondents had to overcome what they perceived to be the stigma of an association with psychiatry. We concluded that most respondents were, in fact, driven to approach the service quite as much by their own desperation as by their doctors' recommendations. On the other hand, general practitioners appear to have suggested Marriage Guidance much less frequently, and where they did so it seemed to have been in a much more cursory fashion. Only five of the twenty-eight couples had received from their doctors a suggestion about Marriage Guidance at any time, and even fewer had actually been there as a consequence. On the whole, it appears that where respondents went to their family doctors they expected very little from them in respect of help with marital problems, and were surprised if and when the doctors raised these matters with them. Moreover, respondents appeared to be grateful, if not particularly hopeful, when their general practitioners offered to refer them to the hospital marital service. But, whichever agency doctors suggested, the patients were given little or no idea of the kind of help they could reasonably expect, and this often left them in a state of anxious uncertainty.

Expectations of Marriage Guidance

As we have already indicated, the majority of those who approached Marriage Guidance had marriages which were already under serious threat and, for some, separations and break-ups had already taken place. Thus, many came to Marriage Guidance with little hope, and without any great expectation that the counsellor would be able to achieve any effect within the marriage. It was therefore not surprising that many perceived Marriage Guidance to be 'a service for marriages that are breaking-up', as one husband described it. Interestingly, this appears to be a common perception, even among those whose marriages were not in trouble.[4] Moreover, some people suggested that an approach to an agency was in itself an indication that a marriage was at breaking point. Very few suggested that they came feeling that they had a realistic chance of achieving a positive change in their relationships. Even those who had not themselves approached Marriage Guidance described it as 'a last resort' and 'a final option'.

Generally respondents do not appear to have had much idea of what the counselling situation would involve, perhaps because they were entirely taken up with very painful feelings about their own predicaments. We noted earlier that, where general practitioners had suggested Marriage Guidance, they do not appear to have enlightened their patients about what they might expect. Five respondents said they had heard Marriage Guidance mentioned on the radio or in women's magazines. One wife said she had written to a newspaper agony columnist hoping to be told that she ought to leave her husband, but instead had received a reply advising her to go to a Marriage Guidance Council. Moreover, she interpreted this response as a recommendation not to give up on her marriage, and suggested that this was a hidden bias in much of the media advice. Three people said the suggestion had come from their mothers-in-law. Only one couple mentioned friends who had any connection with counselling. Another wife (Mrs Hull, aged 21, housewife), who had run away from her husband to a women's refuge, said she felt there was something worth fighting for in her marriage because, unlike most of the women in the refuge, she had not been battered. While she was there she heard one of the women mention Marriage Guidance, and even though it was a disparaging remark, she was determined to pursue that possibility.

'They said they'd tried it but it was no good, but I thought there was no harm in trying . . . so . . . I went to the Citizens' Advice Bureau and asked where it was . . . and I phoned up.'

Most people had acquired little information about Marriage Guidance beyond its title and whereabouts. Research undertaken by the National Marriage Guidance Council has recently confirmed the lack of any clear expectations on the part of clients, presenting a picture of very diffuse expectations, and a considerable uncertainty about the role of counsellors and the nature of the counselling process. The research involved asking former clients in a particular geographical area what they had expected at their first appointment with the counsellor:

'The answers to this question were very various and they seem to reflect a very confused picture, with a large proportion saying that they hadn't known what to expect, others hoping that a defaulting spouse might be traced. Others spoke of hoping to understand their problems, or get advice on specific topics, such as sexual dysfunction. Others wanted to talk to someone neutral.'

(Heisler 1980: 117)

Expectations of Marriage Guidance *before* respondents went there appear to have been relatively undefined, and this was also true of those who had not approached Marriage Guidance. One man (Mr Flint, aged 44, clerical worker), whose wife had just left him, had almost no opportunity to discuss personal problems informally with others, and showed a strong reluctance to self-disclosure. He said about his approach to Marriage Guidance:

'I don't know what I expected. I mean I had just read about it . . . . I knew it obviously existed in the same way that, although I haven't got a car I know the Automobile Association exists. I mean, it's just general knowledge you acquire over the years. So I knew there was an office locally, and for me it seemed the *final* opportunity to do something about my marriage.'

Most people were able to describe what they expected of Marriage Guidance in the context of some experience of it. Bearing in mind therefore, that respondents' expectations are likely to have been influenced by their contact with the agency, we will now consider their expectations of agencies within the context of their initial experience of Marriage Guidance.

One of the most striking themes which emerged here concerns the strong expectation, on the part of many respondents, that the counsellor would act as an independent and unbiased commentator on their marriages. As we have indicated in the last chapter, the need to turn to an 'outsider', as the counsellors were often described, was partly created by the nature of respondents' social networks. For example, in the case of respondents with close-knit kinship networks, the network members were likely to become implicated in respondents' problems and situations and an 'outsider' had a special kind of significance. One woman, with a close-knit kinship network, said she had hoped for (and expected) someone who could 'see with a clear view rather than the family interfering.' Another woman who wished to be married no longer and, in addition, was waiting to train for a new career, wanted to talk to someone who was not associated with her past. She appears to have made use of her differentiated friendship network in much the same way as she later utilized the services of the counsellor.

Mrs Dover, aged 24, computer operator:
'I wanted to talk to someone who wasn't involved, somebody outside who didn't know me before I was married and didn't know me now. When you think about things you get into a trap and you just go round and round . . . I just wanted someone to bounce ideas off, somebody who might be able to get on a different train of thought.'

Some respondents had clearly expected a good deal more from Marriage Guidance than they received (at least at the initial stage of counselling) even though they had no very clear idea about what the counselling situation and process might involve. Several mentioned, somewhat critically, that they had gone there hoping for more directive help and even for advice, but certainly not just to be listened to.

Such retrospective expectations and complaints were, on the whole, more likely to come from men than from women clients in the study. For example, Mr Flint (aged 44, clerical worker) said:

> 'I expected to get some advice. As I understood it, that's what they were in the business of — advice. But having been there I've got my doubts now.'

The expectation of advice expressed by some clients may partly have arisen because of the agency's title, which is one of the most obvious ways through which the Marriage Guidance Councils present themselves to the world. However, since counsellors consider their work to be what their national organization has described as 'essentially a listening process' (Tyndall 1972: 3), this could well prove a disappointing irritant for certain clients, whose expectations of guidance, even if not advice, may not be unreasonable. As Keithley points out: 'The very name 'Marriage Guidance' implies the giving of positive advice, and as such it may not convey very accurately the nature of the help many of today's counsellors are prepared to give' (Keithley 1977: 379). However, behind the expectation of advice lay hidden a number of unexpressed wishes and needs. Some people had clearly expected, rather unrealistically, that 'on the spot' solutions to their problems might emerge straight away. Some respondents, and these were husbands, went to Marriage Guidance in the firm belief that the counsellor would support and positively strengthen their own positions and points of view about the marriage. Other men said they had not expected 'miracles' but simply a more directive approach from the counsellors.

Thus, although respondents had no clear idea of what the counselling would involve before they went, once they had some initial experience of the agency, they held various notions of the kind of roles they wanted the counsellors to perform in relation to their marriages. At one extreme respondents seemed only to want to talk about themselves in the presence of an unbiased 'outsider', whilst others wanted a more directive approach from the counsellor. We shall return to these themes when we consider respondents' prescriptions for counselling in the next chapter. But most pertinent, perhaps, is the fact that our respondents, whatever their general expectations concerning counselling and counsellors, approached the agency frequently feeling hopeless and desperate, and regarding it as a 'last resort' or 'final option'. They were thus in a highly vulnerable and sensitive state.

Experience of Marriage Guidance

About half of the fourteen couples who were Marriage Guidance clients described their experiences as being very positive, with most of the others having mixed feelings and only three respondents expressing entirely negative views. The reader should note, however, that these clients had had, on the whole, more contact with this therapeutic agency than had the medical group at the time of interview. We shall consider respondents' comments from three aspects: first, with respect to their initial encounters with the agency as an organization; second, in terms of their reactions to the counselling situation and process; and third, their perceptions of individual counsellors.

The organization

Some of respondents' criticism was directed at the delay before counselling started; five respondents commented on this, and some suggested that when counselling finally began it was too late, because their spouses had already left or started divorce proceedings.[5]

Two respondents referred to the resentment they felt at the moral pressure to pay for the counselling. Although only two mentioned this aspect, it highlights the difficult position occupied by voluntary workers and organizations in this field. The voluntary method of payment suggests, on the one hand, the non-professional status of marriage counsellors, which perhaps helps people to relate to them more as equals and less deferentially than towards paid professionals, such as doctors. On the other hand, the obligation to pay is still there and tends to 'tarnish' a relationship when it is defined in terms of equality and informality.

Mr Hove, aged 35, partner in a small firm:
'The last thing she said to me was "Well, we are a voluntary organization and a donation would be nice." And I thought that that sort of tarnished it a little . . . Until that time I felt it was quite useful to open up completely to a stranger — she didn't ask my name . . . I don't think it was done in a nasty *way* . . . and I don't begrudge the *money* but.'

Only a few people commented (positively or negatively) about any other aspect of the organization. Mr Hove complained that when he telephoned his local Marriage Guidance Council, in a very distressed state, the reception

'was not all it might have been. I felt it was just a job to them and they weren't really interested.'

One woman (Mrs Ascot, aged 32, media consultant) was critical of the booklets on sex she found in the waiting-room:

> 'I felt it was reinforcing the many problems people have about sex. There was one bit I loathed. It said something to the effect that women should always keep themselves sweet and inviting. And I thought that this is the crux of many people's problems that it's all such a clean fastidious business . . . They don't come to terms with the reality of sex . . . This sort of *Women's Own* attitude to sex I abhor.'

The counselling

A major source of satisfaction in the counselling which several respondents said they derived from their first sessions was that they afforded the opportunity for the release of bottled-up feelings and, as one person put it, 'brought things out into the open' between them and their partners.

Mrs Hull, aged 21, housewife:
> 'We have found out how to say things which hurt which are coming out into the open, that should have come out years ago.'

She was, however, worried lest her husband might have found it 'a bit of a waste of time'. Mr Hull was basically a non-discloser, with a truncated social network. Nevertheless he spoke appreciatively:

> 'The way she brought everything out – the sort of medium. It was easier for someone else to do it than for you.'

A woman client described how counselling had enabled her to express her suppressed feelings after her husband had suddenly walked out and left her.

Mrs Epsom, aged 48, executive director of small family business:
> 'She helped me to be able to talk because when I first went to her I couldn't even talk and after that she sort of opened the floodgates . . . *Then* I was able to talk to [members of the family].'

Where there was criticism of the counselling situation and process it centred on the limitations of the client 'just talking', and the lack of direction from the counsellor. As we would predict, many men, being non-disclosers, found it very difficult to 'open up' in the counselling situation.

Mr Frome, aged 32, systems analyst:
'I find it very difficult to talk about myself and the counsellor had a
hell of a job trying to get anything out of me . . . The impression I
got was that she was trying to bully me because she thought I was
being deliberately obstructive and it was obviously getting her back
up. And because she was getting *her* back up I was getting *my* back
up . . . After we relaxed we started talking . . . but even *now* I still
find it hard to talk about myself.'

Most of those who were critical of counselling for being insuf-
ficiently directive were men and themselves lacked confidence since
they were unused to talking about intimate subjects. It is possible that
in seeking advice and direction from the counsellor, some of the men
may have been attempting, albeit unconsciously, to avoid the self-
exposure which a client-centred approach to counselling inevitably
invites. We shall refer again to respondents' dissatisfaction with lack
of advice in the next chapter where we consider respondents' counselling preferences.

Once again, Mr Ascot, who was a highly educated and articulate
professional man with a circle of friends aware of the therapeutic
professional world, had perhaps the most accurate perception of marriage counselling in terms of the *counsellors'* model. Not only did his
previous experience of psychotherapy alert and prepare him for counselling, it also provided him with a benchmark of comparison when he
went to Marriage Guidance.

Mr Ascot, aged 32, surveyor:
'The biggest difference [between Marriage Guidance and psycho-
therapy] is that psychotherapy involves a very passive role for the
psychiatrist. In fact, he very rarely says anything . . . Whereas the
Marriage Guidance counsellor in our experience is more dynamic.
I mean she takes an active role. She doesn't just sit there and listen
to us bicker, she tries to guide in a broad sense the way she would
like things to go, not too obtrusively but firmly . . . But I'm talking
about Marriage Guidance with relatively little experience . . . At
first she let us talk about what we wanted to talk about and now she
is increasingly getting us to the sort of areas . . . fruitful areas,
where she thinks our problems lie.'

Perceptions of the counsellor

Clients perceived their counsellors in both positive and negative ways.
Sometimes the counsellor was perceived as an *ally* of one partner and

not of the other. There is obviously a dynamic element to this perception, but there are also particular kinds of situations where this perception may become fixed, with the most obvious example of this being where only one of the marriage partners was seeing the counsellor. As we mentioned when we discussed informal patterns of consulting and confiding (Chapter 7) two wives had relationships with their counsellors which they described as having a strong 'parental' character, but one which was idealized rather than real. Two men, also already referred to (Chapter 8), said they had encouraged their wives to go to Marriage Guidance and even sent them in the hope that the counsellor would say 'things that I've spent years trying to convince her of'. Thus, even where wives formed firm relationships with their counsellors on their own, their husbands did not necessarily regard such alliances as threatening, and tended to assume (as they in fact commented) that if the wives felt better by going to Marriage Guidance, this would have positive reverberations for the marriages and for themselves. Another client (the wife of Mr Ascot mentioned above) felt that the counsellor might be critical of her because she did not subscribe to traditional roles of housewife and mother and, as a result of this, began to perceive her as being on the side of her husband.

Several women found the person-to-person aspect of counselling satisfying. Some described the counsellor as fulfilling the role of an interested friend, but without the emotional ties and social obligations of a real friendship. Mrs Epsom (whom we have mentioned earlier in this context) spoke with feeling about being able to relate to her counsellor in the way that she would perhaps like to have talked to her close kin, but to whom she was in fact unable to disclose.

> Mrs Epsom, aged 48, executive director of a small family business: 'I could talk with her in a way I couldn't talk to my mother or father or sister . . . She was absolutely marvellous. Although, she couldn't mend the marriage . . . she made me feel whole again.

A similar type of relationship was described by Mrs Neath, whose 'formal friend'[6] was the receptionist at her doctor's surgery with whom she had almost daily contact. (Interestingly, this receptionist was also a part-time counsellor in a voluntary capacity.)

Most respondents who had sought formal help of one kind or another felt desperate at the time. However, they do not appear to have held out any clear or great expectations of the agencies concerned. Those who went to their general practitioners did not expect them to offer very much help for marital difficulties. Those who had sought out specialist marital help such as Marriage Guidance appear to have been equally desperate, and to have lacked any clearly defined expectations of what counselling would involve. Clients of Marriage Guidance, for example, often described their search for formal help as a final course of action, and generally had not thought beyond this. We have noted that where people were referred for specialist marital help they were rarely given any idea of what to expect by their general practitioners and some were quite unprepared for the strong psychological orientation of the specialist marital agencies. Only women clients had some notice of the therapeutic emphasis on the client talking, and this was largely intuitive and derived from their own personal experience. Nevertheless, overall, respondents described the agencies' initial impact upon them in fairly positive terms.

Notes

1 This specific question was added after the first eight interviews were conducted.

2 The process of seeking help is thus described in *Marriage Matters* (WPMG 1979).

3 One psychiatrist was a senior consultant in the Department of Psychological Medicine in the hospital where the marital service is located and the other psychiatrist had the status of clinical assistant in the medical school of which the hospital is a part.

4 In a study of young newly-weds (conducted at the Marriage Research Centre, Central Middlesex Hospital) respondents were asked hypothetically whether they would consider going to Marriage Guidance with any serious marital difficulties they might at any time experience. Of those who commented, 22 per cent of the wives (14/64) and 17 per cent of the husbands (10/60) articulated their perception of Marriage Guidance as an agency of last resort or final option. A further 33 per cent of the wives (22/64) and 43 per cent of the husbands (26/60) were either unwilling to consider Marriage Guidance or were negatively disposed towards attending it. Respondents' reasons for their attitudes were not sought in the study.

5 Out of the fourteen marriages where spouses became clients of Marriage Guidance, seven had split up by the time that the first counselling session took place and in those seven only one partner became a client. The delays our respondents experienced may partly have arisen from the fact that some of them had approached the London Marriage Guidance Council where pressure for appointments is likely to be considerable.

6 A term given by Timms and Blampied (1980) in their study (of Marriage Guidance clients and counsellors) to marriage counsellors and used to epitomize their respondents' perceptions of them.

10

Prescriptions for counselling: assumptions, meanings, and approaches

We shall now look at what respondents considered to be the assumptions underlying marital counselling, and to examine their preferences for counselling approaches. In doing this we shall endeavour to suggest some of the possible meanings of these approaches for particular groups of clients. There are a number of points which we would like the reader to bear in mind. For the sake of simplicity, throughout this chapter we shall refer to those who work with people whose marriages are in trouble as counsellors (whether or not they describe themselves as such) and to the process itself as counselling. Our questions to respondents were worded to take account of the different agencies with which they had contact. It is also relevant here to remember that the majority of our respondents were interviewed by us as a matter of policy soon after the first counselling or therapy session.[1] This decision to pick up clients as early as possible in the counselling process was an important part of our research methodology. It was made partly in order to ascertain respondents' attitudes and perceptions of counselling at a point when we considered that the influence of their actual counselling experiences would be only minimal and, additionally, in order to maximize the ability of respondents to recall what had led them to that particular agency in the first place.

Assumptions underlying counselling

In this analysis we have distinguished between what respondents considered to be the basic assumptions about marriage, both those operative in counselling generally and within the organizations themselves, and what they themselves perceived and would have preferred in terms of specific approaches within the counsellor–client relationship.

It seemed to us that certain general assumptions underpin counselling which the counsellors themselves might not articulate or perceive. On the one hand, we expected that some counsellors and agencies might work within the value premise of the importance and desirability of preserving most marriages, whilst others might operate on the assumption that the happiness of each individual partner was paramount. In practice this issue turned out to be very difficult to explore, mainly because when we interviewed respondents, we found that the majority were committed at some level to keeping their marriages intact if at all possible, and thus were *already* allied to that assumption. This being the case, any inferences we have made concerning the assumptions underlying counselling are based on respondents' experiences of counselling agencies, in addition to their views about what they thought should generally happen in counselling.

It is perhaps useful to begin our consideration of respondents' views and feelings about counselling by reflecting upon the general self-presentations, both formal and informal, found in the most widely available marriage counselling service, the Marriage Guidance Councils, and also in agencies such as the hospital-based marital service. It is interesting to observe how the formal statements of principles and aims asserted by their central organization, the National Marriage Guidance Council, have changed since its inauguration in 1937. The original statements of intent of the NMGC persisted until 1961, advocating for example:

'That the right foundation for this unit [the family] is permanent monogamous marriage, which alone provides the satisfactory conditions for the birth and upbringing of children, for the expression of the function of sex, and for a secure relationship between men and women . . . That it is the public duty to do everything possible to prevent the tragedy of the broken home and the train of evils which it initiates . . . That parenthood normally brings to marriage, not only the fulfilment of its racial end, but also the achievement of one of its deepest satisfactions, and that everything should be done to promote fertile unions.'

(NMGC 1947–1961)

In 1961 these formal aims and principles were rephrased in a much less dogmatic way but many of the underlying values remained essentially unchanged. In 1967, however, these principles were formally discarded (although presumably many of the counsellors who had previously adhered to these values continued to do so and to work as counsellors), and a descriptive statement of the services and functions that the Councils aimed to provide was substituted (see NMGC 1961, 1969). The report by the working party on marriage guidance (WPMG 1979) described the current ideological commitment on the part of Marriage Guidance Councils thus: 'After many years of debate, a corporate profession of certain moral principles ceased to be required in 1967 though a general statement of belief still remains that the well-being of society is dependent on the stability of marriage' (WPMG 1979: 8). The Marriage Guidance Councils and their national body NMGC are no longer committed to saving marriages 'at any cost'.

It is however open to question whether the counsellors, and particularly the longer serving ones, regard the current ideological stance as merely a deviation from the past or whether they now consider themselves committed to a radically different value position. Moreover, even though the Councils offer their services to people in a wide range of marital statuses, there is little evidence to suggest that they very strongly advocate new approaches to take account of different marital statuses. Although divorce counselling is practised in some Councils it still does not appear to have become widespread. On the subject of the marital status of counsellors it is interesting to note that as recently as 1972 those coming forward for selection were, in the vast majority of cases, still in their first marriages themselves. Moreover, those candidates who were not in their first marriages appear much more likely than those who still were to have been rejected as potential counsellors (Heisler 1977). (We do not of course know how overt a factor this may have been, against other factors, in the decision not to accept them.)

Medically based agencies, such as the hospital marital service, are much less likely to make statements about values underlying their organization and practice; at least, these are not usually accessible to the patients who are referred there. Nonetheless, when individually pressed, the therapist is likely to make claims similar to those made by Marriage Guidance counsellors, namely, that he or she is not concerned with saving marriages 'at any cost' and that each case is 'treated' on its individual characteristics and according to the clients' wishes.

At the level of the counsellor—client relationship, it is difficult to gauge from respondents' reports about counselling the kinds of assumptions which underpin it. This is partly because the counsellor—client relationship, in Marriage Guidance Councils at least, has been inaccessible to direct observation, and has therefore been difficult to research. But, as we shall go on to suggest, this may also be a consequence of the counselling relationship itself and the approach which is adopted, at least as it is practised within the Marriage Guidance Councils.

When those who work as Marriage Guidance counsellors are questioned about the importance they themselves place upon the marital relationship, as distinct from the interest and happiness of the individual partner in the marriage, they frequently respond by stressing the characteristics and uniqueness of each case they counsel, which appears to preclude any more general assessment, either of their own practice or of counselling in general.[2] Additionally, because of the non-availability of their practice to outside observation, Marriage Guidance counsellors are in reality unlikely to compare their own ways of working with those of others and hence may be quite unaware of any intrinsic biases that they may possibly exert in their work. By contrast, patient–practitioner relationships in medical settings are more visible. In some therapeutic centres practitioners employ videos and one-way screens. In the hospital marital service (whose patients we examined) the 'diagnostic' interviews were often carried out with a group of other therapists viewing them simultaneously on a video-tape in an adjacent room. Thus therapists working in such settings have more opportunity to scrutinize others' practice and to reflect on their own. Nonetheless, it may be argued that, because these practitioners tend to regard their work as value-free and scientific, they are just as unlikely as Marriage Guidance counsellors to question or reflect upon the values which underpin their practice.

An examination of assumptions underlying counselling raises many questions. For example, to what extent do moral stances and beliefs in society reflect a concern with the stability and preservation of marriage and the family as against the interest and happiness of people as individuals? Moreover, if it is the case that many counsellors and clients take such values 'for granted', the exploration of the extent to which such values govern the direction and bias of counselling is likely to be a very difficult task. Our own project enabled us to examine these issues only in a limited way because we were concerned mainly with the perspectives of clients and not of counsellors. Nevertheless, as sociologists who were aware of the 'taken for granted' nature of assumptions about marriage and the family, we were very sensitive to the subtlety of the ways in which respondents described counselling and counsellors.

It was generally the case that clients took it for granted that the aim of the agencies that they approached was to try to keep their marriages intact. Furthermore, with only one exception, this coincided with clients' wishes concerning their own marriages, which is also perhaps one of the reasons they chose to attend that agency. Of those respondents who initiated the contact with that agency, only one person became a client with a clear understanding on the counsellor's part that the client wished to receive help in order to separate. This particular couple was unique in our study on other counts also, and it is perhaps worth briefly outlining the very positive features of their situation which led the wife to seek help for separation. First, they were the only couple we found where a positive rather than a negative event, in this instance a trip round the world, had put the marriage under threat. Moreover, this event was one which both partners described as an extremely positive experience, even though the wife had used the occasion to put an end to their marriage. We interviewed this respondent after she had made two visits to a Marriage Guidance Council, a number of sessions which she and her counsellor had both regarded as sufficient. Mrs Dover (aged 24, a computer operator) volunteered the following comment about her experience:

'I didn't go there to save my marriage. I went there because I had decided that I couldn't stay married and I needed help to handle the decision, I suppose, or handling myself, I'm not sure really. But I didn't go there because I wanted to save my marriage.'

In this case the sense of mastery which both the wife and the husband felt over their lives was reinforced externally by the presence of various opportunities and positive circumstances, and by an absence of major negative constraints upon their lives. Perhaps because of this the agency also responded positively in terms of facilitating the client's wish for divorce. It was clear to us that most of our other respondents who approached agencies with self-defined marital difficulties were very different from this couple. The other respondents differed from them in that their marriages had either broken up against their will or were under serious threat in what they felt were adverse situations, over which many of them considered they had little control. For all these reasons it would, therefore, seem that they would be only too willing to assume and hope that counselling, both in theory and in practice, was concerned with trying to 'mend marriages', or at least prevent them from breaking up irrevocably.

In those cases in the study where one partner had already left the matrimonial home by the time the first appointment with the counselling agency arrived (and was kept), counselling appeared to have ceased after one or two sessions, unless the client specifically requested further help. In cases where already separated clients had requested further help for themselves and were receiving it, there was no evidence to suggest that they had either realized that they could ask for, nor that they had been given, help for the separation or divorce as such. In one instance, although the client considered that he had indicated to the counsellor a wish for further sessions with her, it appeared that counselling finished fairly abruptly. Interestingly, this respondent believed that the break-up of the marriage had itself been the reason for the sudden termination of the counselling.

Overall, therefore, there appeared to be a *tacit* acceptance on the part of our respondents that, in most cases, counselling both was and should be governed (or at least underpinned) by the assumption that counsellors, where possible, would aim to repair and to preserve clients' marriages. Moreover, about a third of our respondents implied that their perceptions and experiences of counselling were entirely in accord with their wishes about their own marriages, which were to save them if at all possible. We found that when respondents talked about counsellors and counselling they tended to use 'directive' phrases such as 'putting the marriage back on the right track' or 'helping you to put the marriage right'. We picked up a very real sense that the notion of mending rather than ending marriages was for many the very essence of marital counselling and was regarded by them as so obvious that it scarcely needed alluding to, let alone emphasizing. Only one person articulated what she saw to be a pervasive adherence on the part of Marriage Guidance to maintaining existing marriages.

Mrs Wells, aged 29, shop assistant:
'Well, I think the counsellor's job is for . . . mainly I would think to give you or to give a person a better insight into the other one. But I also think, which I haven't found and which I think is wrong . . . I've never come across it . . . that if they think the marriage is finished and that the persons or couples have tried and still they haven't been any better off, I think they should say to the people: "Well I think you should get divorced." I've never heard that.'

However, although as many as a third of respondents implied that counselling was or should be geared towards saving marriages, we would wish to qualify this conclusion.

First, whilst most respondents we interviewed were on balance concerned that their marriages should continue, they did not necessarily share a belief that marriages in general should be saved at all costs, as their responses to general questions about marriage and divorce indicated.[3] The vast majority of respondents accepted the inevitability of divorce, but many considered that it should be avoided if at all possible where young children were involved.

Second, a high proportion of our respondents were interviewed at crisis points either in their marriages or in their separate individual lives. Such crises often involved a considerable degree of threat and, concomitant with the fear which this engendered, there also existed a wish, if not a real hope, that somehow the decision to seek help might bring about a positive and beneficial change in their marital relationships.

Third, as we have already noticed, a high proportion of our respondents were in their second marriages or relationships, which rendered them especially vulnerable to a fear of a second marriage breakdown. This meant that they were, or at least believed themselves to be, under pressure both from themselves and also from significant others (especially relatives) to 'make a go' of their current relationships. This being so, it was therefore in many ways not at all surprising to have found that these respondents readily concurred with the view that counselling not only was, but also should be, biased in the direction of trying to maintain existing marriages.

Counselling: meanings and preferred approaches

In addition to examining respondents' perceptions of the basic assumptions of counselling, we also sought to discover what they considered were the most effective ways in which counsellors might be of help. We compiled this evidence principally from the replies that our respondents gave to questions about the role of the marriage counsellor, supplemented by their own initial counselling experiences. Their perceptions concerning the most helpful approaches of counselling were many and various, but it seemed that they could be regarded as forming a kind of continuum. At one end of this continuum lay the replies of those who considered that the clients played the major part in the counselling relationship, and those respondents tended to consider the counselling relationship as essentially a vehicle of expression for the *client*, with this as its predominant role. In contrast, clustering at the other end of the continuum, were the replies of those respondents who emphasized the importance of the *counsellor*, and who considered that the counselling relationship was most effective when it enabled the counsellors to operate in terms of understanding the nature and causes of the marital difficulties, and to offer advice and solutions to them. Mrs Crewe (aged 23, clerical worker) a client of the hospital service for marital therapy, was one of those whose description of the goal of counselling placed the emphasis on the client doing the work.

> 'To try and get people to talk about their problems to each other and to really try and allay their fears that they have within the marriage. I think that's the main thing, for people to talk about it to each other. It probably means being the one in between [i.e. the counsellor] that can break the ice, whatever's formed.'

In contrast, Mr Corby, whose wife became a client whilst he did not, prescribed a more directive counselling approach; he depicted the counsellor as playing the prominent part in the counselling relationship, with the client accepting or rejecting what the counsellor proffered.

> Mr Corby, aged 36, fireman:
> 'Well, it seems very strange really. I don't know where they get their information from or where they get the advice from to give to anybody. Whether it's their own advice or whether it's something laid down, I don't know . . . No, they can only advise what they think best to do. Then it's up to the people concerned whether they go along those lines or try something else. The same as an instructor who teaches driving, you're the one who has got to do it to get through.'

These two quotations represent the extremes of the continuum of counselling prescriptions, and between them we could define a number of gradations, with respondents placing varying degrees of emphasis upon the counsellor and the client. By disregarding the more subtle nuances it is possible to group respondents' preferences (albeit somewhat roughly) into two categories, and we can then consider these broad preferences in relation to some of the factors which may influence them.

An overall breakdown of respondents' prescriptions by gender (*Table 10(1)*) indicates that, generally, women were more likely to favour a non-directive approach on the part of the counsellor. They used phrases which indicated the value they attached to clients being given a chance to 'ventilate' or 'off-load', to talk and express feelings

Table 10(1) *Respondents' prescriptions for counselling approaches by gender*

	Men	Women	Total
Directive approach	13	3	16
Non-directive approach	4	18	22
Uncertain as to kind of approach	1	0	1
Negatively disposed towards counselling	1	2	3
No response etc.	3	3	6
Total	22	26	48

freely, and perhaps even more significant, an opportunity to be listened to. Men, in contrast, indicated a preference for a quite different approach in the counselling—client relationship; they considered it more effective if the counsellor performed a directive role, and some went so far as to consider it a useless exercise if this were not the case.

It seemed to us that the preferences expressed for particular counselling approaches might well be related to the attitudes respondents held about disclosure of personal problems to others. *Table 10(2)* shows that there is evidence of such an association, but in view of our earlier findings on attitudes to disclosure, it would seem highly likely that this is mediated by the influences of gender.

However, if we consider the counselling preferences of men and women respondents in relation to patterns of help-seeking and conjugal roles, an interesting picture begins to emerge. We found that, as help-seekers, wives were much more likely than their husbands to decide to approach and to initiate contact with agencies. With regard to conjugal roles, there is a growing body of evidence for concluding that wives have less power than husbands within the marriage, and that they have access to lesser and fewer opportunities and resources in the wider society (see e.g. Stacey and Price 1981). In relating respondents' counselling prescriptions to the above factors, the meaning of counselling for the two sexes is therefore likely to emerge as significantly different.

Women clients tended to see and to seek counselling as an opportunity to share with others the problems in their marriages, and they seem also to have wished to work out these problems with minimal influence from the counsellors. This model of counselling is very suggestive of the way (already described) in which many women in our study disclosed and turned to their friends. Moreover, we found that

Table 10(2) *Respondents' prescriptions for counselling by attitude towards disclosure to others*

	Negative attitudes towards disclosure	Positive attitudes towards disclosure	Total
Directive	11	5	16
Non-directive	8	14	22
Other	7	3	10
Total	26	22	48

where respondents, mainly women, were able to draw upon their social networks for social support, problems in their marriages were more likely to come to a head. The fact that women were more ready than men to admit to problems in their marriages, and to do something about them, may reflect women's subordinate position both in marriage and in the wider society. Such subordinate status may have served to generate, on the part of women, a sensitivity to problems and an ideology which emphasized the value of disclosure. The meaning of counselling for men and women may therefore be structured in accordance with the types of social relationships and ideologies in which they are situated. By contrast, men commonly seem to have taken the view that the counsellor should make some kind of active intervention, such as giving advice, and should offer recipes for solving the problems. However, those men who took this view were in practice unlikely to have sought help of any kind, either formal or informal. It is therefore likely that men's desires for a directive counselling approach reflect the values of the *public* arena, which are oriented towards the achievement of measurable goals, and where men are pre-eminent. On the other hand, it might also be argued that a preference for a directive approach arises from men's superordinate position in marriage, and reflects a desire for the counsellor to take control, but in *their* interests.

Thus, in so far as counselling may hold a distinctive and different meaning for each gender, so may it also have a different impact on them. If this is in fact true, questions posed by agencies concerning which counselling approach to adopt may need to be considered in relation to the characteristics of their clientèle. As far as the Marriage Guidance Councils are concerned, their 'house style' of counselling would generally more often seem to match the expectations of the women rather than the men in our study. The current Chief Officer of the NMGC, Nicholas Tyndall, has described their counselling approach in the following terms: 'The counsellor's approach [to marital problems] is fundamentally client-centred. His task is not to diagnose nor to prescribe remedies, but rather to share with clients the troubles, doubts and tensions of their marriages. This is essentially a listening process' (Tyndall 1972: 3). In the light of a certain congruence between women's prescriptions and the 'official' description of what Marriage Guidance counsellors do, it was not surprising to discover that the women Marriage Guidance clients in our study were more committed to such counselling than were their husbands.

The approach adopted by marital therapists in medical settings was much more concerned with specifying and with the achievement of therapeutic goals, and considerable emphasis was placed upon the highly specialized knowledge and practice of the practitioners in this task. This latter approach, with its greater professional authority, provided a closer approximation to men's preferences. Interestingly, many men clients expressed a desire for advice and directive techniques generally, and in practice they were likely to be fairly critical and rather less committed to Marriage Guidance counselling than were women clients.

Returning for a moment to the question of whether an underlying bias in favour of maintaining marriages exists in counselling, it is clear that counsellors do not necessarily need to play an active part in order to contribute to such a bias. Given both that women have expectations of counselling as being mainly a listening relationship and that they are more likely to be help-seekers than men (and since Marriage Guidance seems to conform to these expectations) all this is almost certain to ensure that, in many cases, such assumptions are part of a hidden agenda which is neither activated nor questioned. Counsellors who play a more dominant part in counsellor–client relationships, such as those at the hospital marital service, have relatively more power in setting the agenda than Marriage Guidance counsellors and hence contribute to bias more deliberately by failing to make the values underlying their practice explicit.

We have isolated a number of elements or nuances in respondents' prescriptions for counselling. In so doing we are not proposing that one element alone characterizes each response; in many cases respondents' prescriptions embraced more than one (though usually an adjacent) element along the continuum we suggested earlier. We shall now go on briefly to describe and illustrate these different elements as they are revealed within respondents' vocabularies.

1 The client: talking and feeling

We have already mentioned the emphasis placed by some respondents on the counselling relationship as a medium in which clients should be able to 'off-load' both verbally and emotionally. We see this prescription as lying at one extreme of the prescriptive continuum. Furthermore, several respondents remarked on the importance of the counselling situation as an opportunity for talking and expressing 'bottled-up feelings' to the *other partner*. Many wives who indicated this said they felt that their husbands were normally very unreceptive when they expressed their feelings to them. We have described a number of instances where husbands had been unwilling to acknowledge that their wives had any basis at all for dissatisfaction within the marriages: to admit that a problem existed was to admit that they too had a part in the problem. For example, a young housewife with two small children kept leaving her husband for no reason that was apparent to him throughout the five years of their married life. She implied that one of the things that Marriage Guidance had done for her had been to give her permission to say in front of her husband how she felt about the marriage. However, although she found airing her feelings helpful, she also seemed to fear that this might be the only thing that happened and that counselling might simply make the marriage more bearable for her. Mrs Hull (aged 21, housewife) talked about the importance of Marriage Guidance:

'I think mainly to be somebody there to listen and not really to take sides.'

Describing her own experience of Marriage Guidance she said:

'The first time we went it was very upsetting . . . my husband wanted an answer from me, whether I am coming home or not, which I just didn't have. The second time we have found out how to say things which hurt that are coming out into the open, that should have been said years ago . . . I find it very helpful . . . I think he thinks it's a bit of a waste of time but as long as it's keeping *me* happy, it's helping and he's willing to go . . . in fact I'm a bit worried about stopping it.'

2 The client: understanding and insight

Many respondents mentioned the importance of counselling as an opportunity for gaining understanding of themselves and insight into the other partner, and for realizing what had gone wrong in the marriage, through their own explorations in the counselling situation. This latter notion has much in common with what Timms and Blampied (1980) described as the cognitive thrust. As Mrs Wells (aged 29, shop assistant) said:

'Well I think her (the counsellor's) job – mainly I would think was for them to give you – to give a person – a better insight into the other one.'

She described some of her expectations about Marriage Guidance in similar terms, suggesting that she required more than simply an opportunity to talk and indicating that she saw the counsellor as taking a fairly active role in enabling her to gain understanding.

'I went mainly not so much for somebody to talk to; more for somebody to, you know like help me, with sort of . . . my problems . . . and to understand and be able to give *me* an understanding of my husband.'

3 The counsellor: a neutral and third party

At this point on the continuum of respondents' preferences, the emphasis shifts from the client to the counsellor. Here the counsellor is required to play the role of 'third party' but in a non-advisory and non-judgemental manner. About a third of our respondents focused on the importance to them of the counsellor's *neutrality* and particularly on the counsellor's position as 'third party' in the counselling situation.

There are a number of different kinds of neutrality to which respondents referred. The first kind of neutrality related to the issue of confidentiality. This was regarded by many respondents as an essential condition for the disclosure of personal problems, and the fact that the counsellor was neutral in the sense of being *socially* unconnected to them in any way was very important to them. The following rather jokey comment by Mrs Ascot at the beginning of her interview illustrates this point.

Mrs Ascot, aged 32, media consultant:
'I wouldn't have gone to my doctor, for example. I would have felt that he would have been terribly interested and before I knew where I was, it would be all over the neighbourhood, you know.' (Laughs.)

A second kind of neutrality also emphasized by respondents concerned *emotional* detachment. Both in the processes of selecting a personal confidant and in seeking counselling, respondents stressed the importance of a clear unbiased view, uncoloured by strong feelings, either of emotional attachment to one or other party or arising out of their own particular situations.

Mrs Clare, aged 43, clerical worker:
'It's somebody who is not emotionally attached that could really help you sort your own feelings out, because the one person who should be able to can't, and really somebody else is bound to be partisan one way or another or affected by their own situation. Presumably if one is professional, you can be detached.'

Mrs Luton, aged 28, secretary:
'I think if you really did have a serious problem, I think you would need somebody who was trained to help and to advise and to maybe mask their true feelings of horror or whatever.'

A third kind of neutrality to which respondents referred concerned the kind of neutral *action* that a third party can perform as a negotiator between two persons or groups. This is the middle ground occupied by the 'go-between' or intermediary. Intermediaries can of course have varying functions; some stand in judgement over the parties with whom they deal and some do not. Several respondents commented that counsellors should try to 'bridge the gap' between the partners and be 'equally fair to both parties', but at the same time many noted that it was *not* necessarily part of their role to give them advice. It was the *task* of the intermediary that the following speaker was describing as well as the characteristics of the person or role *per se*.

Mr Hull, aged 41, fitter:
'Well, the thing is [the counsellors] don't get involved and they don't take sides. How shall I put it? They sit there and keep the flow going and if it begins to slow up, they inject more fluid. It [Marriage Guidance] is like a flow of liquid going backwards and forwards and it needs motion. So they put the motion in by asking you questions or they pick up on something that is being said to keep it going. So that the two people who it is really concerning can begin to feel and pick out wherever this is needed in the marriage.'

4 The counsellor: getting to the root of the problem

Where respondents noted the importance of arriving at some interpretative explanation being given for their marital problems within the counselling situation, they sometimes assigned greater importance to the counsellor than to themselves in uncovering 'the root' of the problem and 'shedding new light on it'.

> Mrs Epsom, aged 48, executive director of small family business: 'They come up with logical answers where the average person would be swimming in deep water . . . they have the answers. For example, if she asks me a question and I answer it, she would say to me "I don't think that's right," and so she says "Let's go a bit deeper." She says you *think* that's the answer . . . until she makes you understand yourself.'

The fact that some respondents thought there was a *single* cause of their problems, the knowledge of which was usually only accessible to the counsellor or expert, needs partly to be understood in terms of the way in which the dominant belief systems of science and medicine about diagnosis and aetiology are transmitted and become part of lay beliefs. Male respondents especially attested the belief that the explanatory frameworks for their marital problems ought to be those of the counsellors. Such prescriptions had a particular congruence with the goals and practice of practitioners in medical settings. However, the fact that several husbands had abrogated all responsibility for searching for explanations of their marriage troubles, and that most had shown a marked reluctance to approach agencies, suggests perhaps that they did not even wish, consciously or unconsciously, to recognize the existence of problems in the first place.

It is interesting to note that even where respondents preferred and experienced 'diagnostic' counselling approaches, such as those which operated in the hospital-based marital service, they often reworked the explanations given to them so that these fitted with the ways in which they themselves *wished* to see things. Where respondents came to disagree with the diagnosis or explanation given to them by counsellors, they often continued to search for an explanation in the belief that there was a 'right one'. Mrs Ascot described how she initially approached Marriage Guidance in the belief that 'they would be able to illuminate the problem'. As the counselling progressed, however, she had begun to question both the explanations given to her by the counsellor and the basis of her expertise.

Mrs Ascot aged 32, media consultant:
'But I haven't really discussed with her exactly what kind of training she's had . . . and why it is that she is going to be able to help us, what is it she's going to be able to do, what are we asking from her . . . Sometimes, at the moment I feel what we are looking for from her is a referee, which isn't perhaps what I feel we *should* be looking to. I don't want someone to say "Well you are right here and you are wrong there." I suppose what we want is somebody to say "Well maybe this is the root of the problem and maybe this is the area you tackle." I suppose I started off going to Marriage Guidance thinking there is a problem which I couldn't see. I've looked for it and searched for it and I couldn't see it and maybe somebody else could eliminate it. Now I'm beginning to think that maybe she's going to say "You should never have been married in the first place" and "The differences are not reconcilable." In which case, I think maybe I would have been better never to go and never to find that out, because I don't really want to know that, you know.'

5 The counsellor: a normalizing approach

A rather minor theme, but nonetheless an important one, was detected in respondents' vocabularies, which we have termed the 'normalizing approach'. Some respondents felt quite strongly that counsellors should try to make clients feel that they were normal and that their problems were not unique to them.

Mrs Deal, aged 34, clerical worker:
'Yes, I think the most important thing is to make them [clients] realize that they are not the only people who are going through these problems.'

An interestingly different perspective on the concept of 'normal' is reflected by the instance where another respondent, a client of the hospital service for marital therapy, indicated that he and his wife felt reassured by the counsellor telling them 'that our problem is normal and one of the commonest on record'. However, although the client may have inferred from this the same meaning of 'normal' as Mrs Deal intended, in her quotation above, it is important to understand that the context of the two meanings is very different. In the second case, it was evident to us that the counsellor, who was also a psychiatrist, had meant that this was a common type of case encountered in his *clinical* practice. The clients themselves interpreted what he said rather differently; they understood that he meant that their problems were not unlike the problems most people run into at some point in their lives. However, it is improbable that a particular medical 'case' is as common in general experience as it is in clinical practice. Thus what may be termed the client's desire for normalization may only *appear* to have something in common with the professional's notion of it and certainly has different implications. Such incongruity of meanings is unlikely to arise in relationships between clients and Marriage Guidance counsellors, since the latter would not be generalizing from a medicalized model which distinguishes between pathology and normality. On the other hand, clients' expectations of counselling as a normalizing process are likely to be counter-balanced by some of their other expectations and perceptions of agencies. We have already suggested that Marriage Guidance was considered by many respondents as a place or at a point of 'last resort'. Some respondents in our study said they had felt very hesitant about approaching an agency, mainly because they thought it was necessary to have a 'very serious problem' before doing so. Others regarded the very fact of approaching an agency as automatically putting their problems into the 'serious' category. Since most people approached an agency only when they became desperate, they were likely to have felt that they had already forfeited the appearance and the feeling of being 'normal'. Therefore they may have had to jettison the hope of counselling making their problems seem normal, which may well account for the fact that normalization was a very minor theme in respondents' vocabularies.

6 The counsellor: guidance and advice

To some extent respondents in our study distinguished between guidance and advice. Some said that counsellors should guide the counselling without necessarily telling people what they should be doing or aiming at. To some degree the difference is reflected in the distinction between Marriage *Guidance* counselling, done by trained voluntary lay persons, and marital therapy carried out in medical settings, which derives from a basis of specialized knowledge and practice. Mr Ascot made the following distinction in talking about his Marriage Guidance counsellor:

'I mean she guides, tries to guide in a broad sense the way she would like things to go, not too obviously but firmly . . . I don't think they give advice. I think it would be a mistake to do that.'

Those who indicated a preference for a 'guiding' approach were more likely to have been satisfied with their experience of Marriage Guidance than those who thought that counsellors should be in the business of giving advice. In our study certain respondents specifically mentioned that counsellors should advise, whilst others suggested that counsellors ought 'to solve their problems', or 'rectify the faults in the marriage', or 'tell people where they are going wrong and how to put things right again'. The following respondents, as their comments illustrate, approached Marriage Guidance (two of them in past help-seeking episodes) with the hope and expectation of a more directive approach than they in fact experienced.

Mr Rugby, aged 37, fitter:
'I didn't think much of them. The conversation was just negative . . . There wasn't a point . . . They seem to think there's humming and hahing about situations.'

Mrs Derby, aged 40, nurse, said:
'They were just there to listen, to chew the cud as it were and I felt it wasn't very helpful.'

Mr Flint (aged 44, clerical worker) whose wife left him just before the first appointment at the Marriage Guidance Council said:

'After the first two occasions I said I thought you [the counsellor] would do some talking and give me some advice . . . and she said: "All we're here to do is just to listen and occasionally make a comment." I was disappointed. But she was such a nice lady I continued to go . . . I talked to her about my week and how I got through . . . and she would listen but she had no advice to offer. I thought there would be someone there with experience of marital or sexual problems who would act like an ombudsman or an arbitrator and it wasn't like that at all.'

Mr Flint's critical remarks about Marriage Guidance might be interpreted within a 'counselling perspective' as evidence of his anger at the counsellor's impotence in bringing his wife back. Although this may well be true, we would also argue that Mr Flint's expectations and prescriptions for counselling are part of a more general set of attitudes, whereby he expected solutions to his problems once they had been identified. In relation to his marriage, he had overlooked his wife's first two affairs and had regarded them as 'unproblematic'. It was only after a third affair that he felt he ought to regard the matter as a serious threat to their marriage. Moreover, just as he himself had

taken positive and remedial action by approaching the Marriage
Guidance Council after his wife's latest affair, so did he consider that
the counsellor should take a highly directive part in the counselling
(and one largely in his own interests).

As we mentioned earlier, it was largely hubands, and not wives,
who preferred a directive counselling approach. We suggested that
these preferences reflect the goals of the public arena and men's
general expectations of power and control, expectations which are
based on a persisting and greater share of economic resources and
opportunities (compared with women's) in our society. The following
comments by a husband who went to Marriage Guidance again illustrate the predominantly male preference for the problem-solving
approach, and they also suggest the presence of a hidden agenda
which is connected with this respondent's wish to exert power and
control over his situation. Mr Mold had recently been served with
divorce papers by his wife, whom he had previously thrown out of the
house, and his response to the situation had been to approach the
Marriage Guidance Council.

> Mr Mold, aged 53, self-employed plumber:
> '*And what sort of things did you say to the counsellor?*'
> 'Well I told her what I thought had been wrong in my marriage.
> What she did basically was to let me talk . . . Well there was no real
> advice.'
> '*Is that what you expected?*'
> 'Well, to me . . . it's a really involved subject isn't it? [Laughs.] As I
> was saying, I thought that somewhere along the line I might get
> somebody who really would advise me or something.'
> '*Is that what you went there expecting?*'
> 'Not really, no. I went there expecting some sort of acknowledge-
> ment that I'd been there twice and that would go before the court.
> My wife is suing me for divorce . . . I have got to defend myself with
> every means possible . . . And when it came before the court, I
> could say "Well I have done my best, I've gone to the Marriage
> Guidance Council." So anything in my favour that I could put up in
> the court I did, I didn't really go there [Marriage Guidance] think-
> ing they were really going to help.'

In this chapter we have examined what respondents considered to
be the goals and assumptions underlying counselling, the approaches
adopted in the counselling situation, and the meanings of counselling
for clients. The first was the more difficult to explore; most people

seemed to have tacitly accepted that their own goals and assumptions and those of counsellors should and did coincide. It was taken for granted that the goal of both counsellors and clients alike was to preserve and repair marriages if at all possible. We have indicated a number of factors which tended to militate against both the counselling organizations and the individual counsellors fully looking at and articulating this assumption with their clients. We noted that the 'house style' of Marriage Guidance counsellors generally involved a non-directive, empathetic and 'listening' approach, with the emphasis on the client, whereas the approach of therapists in medical settings focused on practitioner-defined goals. We have argued that where the agency approach happened to coincide with respondents' *own* preferences and strategies for disclosing or dealing with their personal troubles, a bias that was both hidden and unchallenged was thereby very easily subsumed in the counsellor−client relationship.

We also explored the different nuances in respondents' perceptions and preferences for counselling approaches, which we conceptualized as lying along a continuum. At one end of the continuum respondents emphasized the role of the client and considered that the counselling relationship was simply a vehicle for the expression of their feelings, whilst, at the opposite end, respondents stressed the role of the counsellor and the importance of the counsellor in solving the clients' problems. However, in so far as it was the women rather than the men who sought help in the first place, and that women and men displayed distinctly different preferences for counselling approaches, we would argue that counselling has a distinctive meaning and impact for each of the genders. Thus it is one of our main contentions that the meanings and prescriptions respondents constructed about counselling are not simply determined by what went on in the counselling situation, but that they are shaped and structured by respondents' prior expectations and by gender-defined relationships within their families, their social networks, and the wider society. We would therefore argue that one of the most important factors which influences respondents' preferences for, and definitions of, counselling is gender.

Notes

1 In a very few cases (2/14), respondents had been in counselling for longer periods. However, since there were only two of them and they had taken the trouble to contact us, we decided to interview them. We found that these data, although sometimes difficult to disentangle, were reasonably

compatible with data obtained from the other interviews and we have therefore included them.

2 Personal observation in meeting and talking with a wide range of Marriage Guidance counsellors.

3 When respondents were asked to give their views on the permanence or otherwise of marriage, although there were several who considered that 'ideally' marriages should last, yet only three would totally oppose divorce in practice. However, when we probed their attitude to divorce in marriages where there were young children, a greater reluctance to countenance the possibility of divorce was revealed: 11/48 considered it would then be an acceptable solution to marital discord, and most of these expressed their approval of divorce in such situations only because they considered it would be less damaging for the children than if the marriages were to continue.

11

Perceptions of the ideal situations for disclosure

We began the examination of our data with an analysis of respondents' attitudes towards the disclosure of personal and marital problems, and it is perhaps fitting that in our penultimate chapter we should explore their perceptions of what they regarded as the *ideal* situation for disclosure. In reply to the question 'What would be the ideal situation for turning to others with personal problems?' the answers in many cases reflected the diversity of themes concerning both formal and informal help-seeking which we have examined in this book. In addition, a rather unexpected and surprising theme emerged, which concerned the role of the interviewer and the meaning of the interview for our study group. Undoubtedly, these responses were influenced by respondents' experiences of counselling and, since this question was placed in the latter part of the interview schedule, also by the interview itself.

When we consider the *categories* of persons to whom respondents said they would ideally turn, they were not always very explicit. They talked less in terms of the status of persons (professional, family member, friend) and more in terms of their personal characteristics. Moreover, even those respondents who seemed to imply that they preferred professionals often described as desirable characteristics more usually associated with friendship. Respondents frequently stressed the desirability of being able to trust the person turned to, the importance of their keeping confidences to themselves, and of being unbiased.

Mr Luton, aged 30, sales representative:
'Implicit trust in a person. That's the only condition I would make.'

Mrs Rugby, aged 40, school and play-group worker:
'You've got to tell the right sort of people. You've got to know your

friends. Otherwise, as I say, you can be in trouble really because they can add to it or just use it as sheer gossip or a bit of scandal. Perhaps they've got a dull life and it's terribly exciting. So by the time they've heard it all, it's "My God!" and you would expect to hear it at the Old Bailey!'

Mr Frome, aged 32, systems analyst:
'It would have to be someone that, the other persons was as impartial as possible. It would have to be someone outside the family . . . an outside friend. The only person I would talk to would be Ben, probably because I feel an affinity for him.'

Where people indicated a preference for one particular category of persons, the reasons for their choice were often described in terms of the perceived disadvantages of *other* categories.

Mr Ryde, aged 37, school teacher:
'I think I would generally rather turn to professionals rather than to friends or acquaintances, not because of their professionalism or because of being able to help a lot, but because they seem to be *impersonal*.'

Mrs Clare, aged 43, clerical worker:
'Well, a close friend. [Pause.] My parents — I haven't confided in my parents because I don't particularly want to worry them at this time . . . whether if they were both well, I don't know. I still think I wouldn't have done because it was my husband's problem. If it was mine, I would probably. They'd probably know by now.'

As we have shown, the theme of the inappropriateness of parents as repositories for marital problems in particular recurred throughout the interviews, and also figured in people's accounts of their ideal preferences. While most did not cite relatives, several respondents stipulated that disclosure ought to take place 'outside the family', and only three thought relatives ideal at all. Brief mention of those who would choose relatives is perhaps instructive. One woman who said she regarded parents as ideal had grown up in the Far East, and because of war-time evacuation was placed in an institution. Her parents had died before the family could be reunited. Eventually she and two surviving brothers came to England, and she had recently lost touch with one of them. She clearly mourned the recent and past losses of close kin, and said with considerable sadness:

'Ideally I would turn to my own parents or to a very close aunt . . . but I have none of these, not even my brother. I just felt it would be unfair to talk about one's marital problems to anyone outside the family.'

Another respondent, although he subscribed to the predominantly working-class notion of mutual instrumental help amongst kin, appears to have always been a non-discloser and saw almost nothing of his relatives. He ideally wished for a male member of his own family, though also someone who was worldly wise. Mr Flint (aged 44, clerical worker) said with some regret:

> 'Well, I would have liked to have had some close male relatives like uncles, a favourite uncle, a man of the world, someone who knows a bit about life and its problems. Someone there, that you'd got for advice which would still be within the family, but I haven't got uncles like that.'

The first respondent, having virtually always lacked parents, clearly had an idealized picture of what it would be like to have some. Mr Flint, on the other hand, believing only family members to be appropriate sources of help, justified his failure to turn to them in terms of their not being the 'right sort' of relatives. Thus, some respondents (especially men) who were basically opposed to disclosure in attitudinal terms, sometimes explained their failure to disclose as being due to limited or inappropriate resources.

A handful of male respondents did, however, suggest 'professionals' as being ideal but interestingly they made no mention of professional competence, training, or formal skills, so that professionals may simply have been the only people they could think of to mention. We believe it to be significant that these men were non-disclosers both in attitude and practice and, moreover, belonged to truncated networks. They had consulted informal others only rarely and they lacked confidants. Furthermore, those of them who had approached agencies appear to have done so under very extreme and adverse situations, and others among them had not turned to an agency at all.

In describing their ideals for disclosure, significantly it was usually women who had a preference for a *particular* friend.

Mrs Hythe, aged 25, telephonist:
'I prefer to talk to a friend, to someone like Betty you know. She's very good. I can talk to her about anything. I think with something like that, you do need somebody to talk to, rather than just Jim [her husband] that if you are feeling anything, or you're worried, you can talk to somebody else.'

The persons respondents mentioned were generally those who had been particularly helpful to them in their current predicaments. Mr and Mrs Neath both gave as their ideal the doctor's receptionist with whom his wife was in almost daily contact, and who in reality had had a marked influence upon the way in which his wife's problems had been dealt with in the past.

Mr Neath, aged 41, draughtsman:
'Well I think they'd have to know both parties very well and know their thoughts and strengths and be sympathetic. That is why Ann is so good. She knows us so well. She's virtually perfect almost, to cry on her shoulder as it were.'

Some respondents appear to have visualized specific concrete situations which, in the past, had been conducive to disclosure and which had since come to signify their ideal. One woman described the settings in which she had talked intimately with significant people in her life.

Mrs Poole, aged 29, dancer:
'Well just the quietness somewhere where there are just the two of you really. If I really used to want to talk to Sid [her husband] we always used to go to the beach and we would walk along the beach. And I had this specific place on the rocks where we would go and we would sit and talk there. Or when I used to talk to Robin and Sally then it was always in the apartment and always at night time. And I guess with my sister, well, just when we were on our own.'

Where respondents preferred to turn to 'somebody who is objective . . . and not involved like your friends are', they also suggested the importance of a 'caring' relationship. Thus, some respondents described their ideals in terms of certain characteristics of practitioners and professionals, whilst others tended to locate these characteristics in specific persons and friendships from their social networks. But on balance respondents seemed ideally to prefer trusting and caring relationships with significant and informal others, who were nevertheless able to maintain a degree of social and emotional distance from the troubled situations. Moreover, it has been one of our main contentions in this book that it is the *structure* of respondents' social networks which ultimately determines the form of these preferred relationships. For some people, therefore, a relationship with a practitioner or professional is the closest available approximation to this ideal.

It was significant, as well as totally unexpected, that a group of respondents mentioned the research interview as the ideal setting for the disclosure of personal problems. It seems to us that many of the reasons given for this particular preference fit with the optimal conditions for disclosure which respondents described. Although the format of our interview was semi-structured, and the key questions standardized, the instrument was deliberately designed to allow respondents to give accounts in their own terms, and to elaborate at some length whenever they wished. Respondents were seen in their own homes and appointments were made at times convenient to them. The interviews were conducted with a certain degree of informality, and respondents were assured they would remain anonymous and that their confidences would be dealt with in a responsible fashion. In short, we were accessible, uninvolved personally, and most important, we were trusted by them. Our respondents were confident that the information they had entrusted to us would not be given to people they knew, and this emerged as having considerable importance for them.

Mrs Crewe, aged 23, cashier:
'*What would be the best situation . . . for you to be able to talk to someone about problems?*'
'I think the way the situation we have got at the moment . . . I know the confidence isn't going to be broken and none of the people that I don't want to know are going to find out. It's all sort of − it's all under control, put it that way.'

Another theme which emerged from respondents' ideal preferences for disclosure concerns the 'right moment'.

Mrs Bath, aged 56, housewife:
'*What would be the ideal conditions for someone to be able to turn to somebody for help − what would be the setting?*'
'Well it would be impossible really, because I would want to ring them up and say "Can I come round now?" [laughs] there and then!'

Later in the interview she drew attention to the fact that the interviewer had come to her home, and she elaborated on why she had felt unable to approach an agency with her own problems.

'Last night . . . I was saying you were coming tomorrow and that I would probably be too upset and that I didn't particularly want to. So he [husband] said: "Well, cancel it," and he also said "Would

you discuss it [the problems] with you?" and I said "No". And yet
you see the opportunity arose and so I did. But if he'd said to me
"Would you go and see somebody in the morning?" and I'd got to
commit myself, I don't know whether I would have done. I don't
think I would.'

'You feel that it actually made a difference that I came to you?'
'Yes and that you were here. If it had been a couple of days time I
don't suppose I would have done . . . I wouldn't have thought I was
the sort of person that could talk about that kind of thing. I would
consider it my personal, too personal, between my husband and
myself, and this has always been one of the reasons why we haven't
done anything about it sooner, that I haven't been able to discuss it
with anybody, or thought I wouldn't be able to, which is why the
time and place are so important. Mm, I was staggered today.'

In a few instances respondents commented in a personal way about
the interviewers, saying they felt able to talk to us as people, but it was
also quite clear to us that the interview situation was of paramount
significance.

Mr Bath, aged 59, retired manager:
'I find I can speak very freely to you. Now it may be purely that and
this isn't soft soap, that you're approachable, because I am con-
vinced other people would come in and I would shut up like a clam.
But I think one is more likely to open up to a stranger than to an
acquaintance or friend.'

Mr Bath, like his wife, was particularly affected by the interview. The
couple had been married thirty-five years, and in spite of the
considerable long-term conflict between them they had not sought
help. The difficulties in their relationship had only emerged as a consequence of Mr Bath's visits to the doctor in connection with several
recent bouts of serious illness. Although they had a large family their
social networks approximated to the truncated type: their children
were growing up and leaving home, and as elderly dependent relatives
had died the couple had not established any new close relationships
outside the family's origin and procreation. This was additionally
exacerbated by Mr Bath's retirement and subsequent illness. It was
within the context of this type of social network, and at a time of
crisis, that the researchers were so favourably greeted by this couple.
It is probably significant that those who mentioned the characteristics
of professionals and agency practitioners, however obliquely, as being

ideal for disclosure, and those whose ideal consisted of the interview situation, were amongst those with truncated social networks. One explanation for this is that, in the absence of informal confiding relationships, they lacked a model of such relationships, and this may have been subsequently provided by their contact with agencies or in the interview itself.

One way or another, all respondents, when discussing the disclosure of very personal information, were concerned with issues of control. Those who preferred formal help noted the importance of confidentiality, whilst others selected particular informal others on the basis of their ability to be discreet. In some way the interview was able to provide some of the safeguards and confidentiality of the agency, but without the potential stigma involved in becoming a client. It also provided a degree of power for respondents which was more akin to relationships with confidants, since the interviewers were on a more informal and equal footing with respondents than practitioners or professionals would have been, and additionally, respondents were interviewed in their own homes.

The research interview may be regarded as providing some of 'the luxury of intimate disclosure to a stranger' (Eliot 1958: 29). Simmel has described with insight some of the qualities of this type of disclosure when he wrote:

'Certain external situations or moods may move us to make very personal statements and confessions, usually reserved for our closest friends only, to relatively strange people. But in such cases we nevertheless feel that this 'intimate' *content* does not yet make the relationship an intimate one. For in its basic significance, the whole relation to these people is based only on its general unindividual ingredients.' (Wolff 1950: 127)

Furthermore, especially since we saw respondents on only one or two occasions, the role of the interviewer in this study is to some extent elucidated by the anthropological use of the term 'stranger'. In face-to-face societies the stranger has been regarded as playing a key role in the avoidance and diminution of conflict between opposing groups (Frankenberg 1957). In our study the interviewers walked into people's lives at highly critical moments and, moreover, they did so *because* the couples were enmeshed in conflict with one another in that closest of relationships, marriage. Where two researchers interviewed the partners separately since each partner would have his or her own interviewer, each could regard him or her as being at once neutral and partisan. It is possible that the interview symbolized for respondents the crisis and distress which they were currently experiencing and for some even offered an opportunity for catharsis, which was at the same time legitimated for them since they were aware that they were giving *us* something of considerable value. There was an important element of reciprocity involved in the interviewer—respondent relationship, even though ultimately the interest of the research was paramount. It is our contention, therefore, that the interviewers in this study can be regarded as having had the *potentiality* of the role of the stranger as unwitting agents in the diffusion of conflict but, unlike 'the stranger' in a closed community, we the interviewers disappeared. On this last point, it was perhaps significant that the respondents themselves preferred to use the term 'outsider'.

It should not be assumed that everybody was able to envisage an ideal situation in which to turn to others. Predictably, some male non-disclosers were unable to do so (6/48). These husbands agreed, albeit reluctantly, to be interviewed by us probably because their wives had so readily agreed. Moreover, to have refused to do so might perhaps have exacerbated even more the crises through which their marriages were going and which, in some cases, had arisen as a consequence of their wives' help-seeking actions.

Mr Ripon, aged 53, entertainer:
'I don't think I want to discuss anything with anyone really. So I don't know what the right conditions would be. The only time I would discuss anything personal is if I wasn't married or I was living alone.'

Mr Ripon's attitude accurately reflected his behaviour and social situation; the only person in whom he confided anything at all was his wife, and both he and his wife had almost no close friends. Moreover, he regarded the exclusivity of marriage as both total and normal, so much so that, even given his problematic marriage, he was unable to imagine the desire to disclose outside marriage or a couple relationship.

Few people articulated their ideals for disclosure exclusively in terms of an agency or professional, despite the fact that many had recently had some satisfactory and positive contact with agencies. But, as people appeared to lack a firm basis on which to build their expectations of agencies, so they developed their ideals for disclosure by abstracting from their own experiences of interpersonal relationships and by idealizing their social and personal worlds. Finally, we think it significant that certain people mentioned the research interview as being amongst their ideals and as having been very helpful to them.[1] In many ways the kind of 'one-off' interview we conducted embraced elements of both formal and informal help-seeking. It provided some of the impersonality and neutrality which people expected of agencies without many of the inherent disadvantages, such as being labelled a client, and the hierarchical authority dimension of client–practitioner relationships. It also fulfilled some of the criteria of friendship and sociability, in particular the suspension of some status differences, together with the fact of being conducted in an informal setting. In effect, it epitomized many of respondents' own preferences and definitions concerning the conditions for help-seeking and disclosure on intimate matters by conferring an opportunity for full disclosure, on respondents' own terms and territory, and with minimal possibility of negative sanctions.

Notes

1 After the interviews were over many respondents said they felt that the interviews had been useful to them, and in particular had helped to provide them with a broad and sympathetic over-view of their own lives and situations which was something quite new to them. Many seemed to like the way the interview explored their lives systematically, and we were frequently able to observe respondents making new connections during the interview between past and current experiences, and past and present attitudes. At the same time, we did not set out with a therapeutic interview in mind, and we did not ask people directly to talk about their problems. Reference to their difficulties came up incidentally, though inevitably in the course of the interviews.

12

Postscript

In this our final chapter we shall first of all suggest some of the ways in which marital troubles and sexuality are part of public discourse in Britain today. We think it appropriate to do so since the ideas which prevail concerning marriage and its troubles constitute the context in which both the research project was undertaken and our research subjects defined their situations. Next, we turn to a discussion of issues surrounding the formulation and conceptualization of respondents' help-seeking careers and those factors which shaped them. Finally, we shall turn to the agencies with an interest in marital work and we shall examine some implications of particular types of practitioner–client relationship.

Marital problems as a social construction

According to Chester (1980) recent estimates of what widely passes in American society for the 'normal' family have suggested that currently only 44 per cent of families correspond to this model. In Britain the proportion of variant forms is likely to be smaller but 'it may well be large enough to challenge traditional assumptions about normal family structure' (Chester 1980: 9). Given that the proportion of variant forms is growing, it may not be unreasonable to conclude that what is usually conceptualized as constituting the norm is dependent upon ideas about what it *ought* to be and not what is statistically the case. Thus, in so far as 'normal' marriage consists of 'the permanent, monogamous cohabiting couple developing with their children through a structural series of family life cycle stages' (Chester 1980: 10) marital problems may be said to occur when the prerequisites of a normal marriage no longer pertain. Chester makes the further point that in abandoning assumptions about normal marriage there is no necessary agreement about whether a given situation is a marital problem or some other kind of problem. In understanding the sociological and political significance of the concept, the definitional issue of *what* is defined as a marital problem is important, but equally crucial is a second issue which concerns the groups and persons seeking to impose these definitions. It is this second issue which we shall discuss here.

At the present time marital problems can be seen to refer to a variety of phenomena ranging from, at one level, the macroscopic problems of contemporary society, as indicated by high rates of divorce, to the particular problems experienced by individual members of society in the course of their marital and cohabiting relationships (whether or not these break up). We propose to outline here three of the main discussions or debates surrounding the concept of marital problems and to note certain interest groups which have contributed to them. In so doing our aim is to illustrate some of the ways in which the concept of marital problems is *socially constructed* and is thereby subject to and a product of wider social and political processes.

The three discussions

The first discussion takes place amongst members of a number of interlinked power élites — the churches, politicians, and the law. In such circles the concept of marital problems frequently attains the status of an overtly political issue. From time to time, especially during periods of economic and social instability, members of such élites take on the guardianship of public morality, sometimes coming together in an *ad hoc* fashion and invoking consensus values concerning 'the common good'. Such concern sometimes results in the creation of bodies for the alleviation of individuals' difficulties, bodies which are not *overtly* political in nature. For example, after the war the Marriage Guidance service, which was originally set up in 1937 by influential persons and groups, began to expand; it received considerable encouragement from the Denning Report (1947) which was concerned with reducing divorce and with promoting reconciliation procedures (Wilson 1980). During the economic recession which has affected Britain in recent years, there have been a number of indications of increasing public concern, especially on the part of dominant groups, over the institutions of marriage and the family. It has been noted that in the 1970s 'There was an almost unseemly haste on the part of politicians to claim the family as their own' (Craven, Rimmer, and Wicks 1982: 2). In 1979 and 1980 two bodies with a focus on the family and family policy were set up. The Family Forum (1980) was set up under the chairmanship of the conservative Member of Parliament, Peter Bottomley, and the Study Commission on the Family (1979) is chaired by Sir Campbell Adamson, formerly Director of the Confederation of British Industry.

The generation of fears about the state of marriage and the family in our society has been facilitated by the collection and publication of divorce statistics, which are seen to constitute an index (albeit a crude one) of increasing marital breakdown. Significantly, the fact that the increase in divorce rates (following the changes in divorce law in 1971) may not reflect a 'true' increase in the break-up of marriages is rarely recognized explicitly, nor is it highlighted (Thornes and Collard 1979). If it is even *partly* true that divorce statistics exaggerate the break-up of marriages, which appears likely, then it would seem reasonable to suggest that it is not the objective social conditions that have changed so much as the visibility of the problem. In this sense the increase in public concern over marital problems and marital breakdown may be in part an indirect consequence of the fact of formally quantifying the phenomenon called divorce.

In recent years there has been a marked resurgence of interest in the family. Those who have a rather greater monopoly of 'say' at the present time are those committed to the *status quo*, persons who seek to preserve the institutions of marriage and the family in a somewhat idealized form. Such a concern was characteristically portrayed in a recent report by the Society of Conservative Lawyers entitled *The Future of Marriage* (1981). This report followed a considerable amount of recent lobbying (still continuing) by a variety of interest groups, most of whom (including the original proposer of the Divorce Law Reform Act 1969) are seeking ways of modifying the present divorce laws though in different ways and with a variety of aims. The report, which received headline coverage in the media, makes a clear and persuasive statement and invokes a consensus model of public opinion which was in turn reinforced by the treatment accorded to it by the media.

'The family is the foundation of our free democratic society. For the great majority of people in Britain today, the family is formed by the institution of marriage, which is a union for life and is the vital link which binds the family. A stable family life lived within the bonds of matrimony is still the popular ideal . . . If the marriages break down or are unstable, then the whole of society is weakened. The State is therefore vitally concerned in the preservation of marriages, and when there are children, vitally concerned to preserve a stable two parent family united in marriage.' (The Society of Conservative Lawyers 1981: 11)

Another recent example of this type of current political and moral concern is a paper commissioned by the Policy Studies Institute (Brayshaw 1980). This report sets out to investigate how public policy can reduce the incidence of marital breakdown. It is significant that the report is critical of a recent public document produced by a working party on marriage guidance (WPMG 1979) on the grounds that it fails explicitly to advocate the 'mending' of marriages. Moreover Brayshaw (who was at one time the chief officer of the National Marriage Guidance Council) goes on to criticize the NMGC: 'One would have expected a clearly expressed hope and preference that – when indeed it is possible – marriages would be mended rather than ended' (Brayshaw 1980: 61). This report, like the report of the Society for Conservative Lawyers, appeals to consensus values in suggesting that even 'the tax payer' expects bodies such as Marriage Guidance to engage in reconciliation work.[1]

There is a certain amount of ambivalence amongst proponents of this point of view as to how far (if at all) it is 'the proper function of the state' (Denning 1947) to intervene in family life. Patrick Jenkin, in a speech at a symposium on marriage, divorce, and the family in 1981, noted the contradictions, at an ideological level, for government: on the one hand an awareness of the family as a 'safeguard for the freedom of the individual to live life as he chooses', but on the other, a commitment to the family as 'the stable bedrock of society', 'the stable and lasting marriage of parents'.[2] He went on to say that in his view the family is the best means of the transmission of values and culture from one generation to another and that therefore society is concerned with the stability of marriage, a concern also felt (he said) by government. However, Jenkin's statement failed to draw attention to the contradiction between the rhetoric of the government's concern about marriage and the effects of its economic policies, which, in their labour market and housing market effects, have put a great deal of strain on families, and which have diminished the amount of help available to families in difficulty from the Welfare State. The contrast between an ideological commitment to the preservation of family life and, at the same time, a commitment to laissez-faire policies of market forces is a stark one.

The main point about the nature of the above discussion is its acceptance of (or rather its ideological commitment to) what are said to be existing norms and values. There are of course reformist as well as conservative elements who are concerned about the state of marriage and the family. However, the former have tended to focus on issues concerned with families, attempting to avoid the more emotive issues of marriage and divorce. For example, one of the major pressure groups concerned with family poverty (The Child Poverty Action Group) developed a concern in the 1970s with families in general (Craven, Rimmer, and Wicks 1982), especially at those stages in the family life cycle when the financial load on families is greatest, and to some extent with the increasingly large number of families whose structure does not conform to the orthodox nuclear model.

Reformists, like conservatives, accept the existing norms and values but tend to use them to criticize the social fabric when it is under attack. By contrast, revolutionary social movements *challenge* existing norms and values and attempt to reconstruct the entire social order (Blumer 1951). A major ideological alternative to the above positions, and one which seeks to define the issue differently, can be seen in some of the discussions that are being conducted within the women's movement. The women's movement has been the centre of a critical debate on marriage and family and views the institutions as themselves problematic: the principal sites and origin of gender socialization and patriarchy, which render women subordinate. Feminists have drawn attention to the many ways in which 'the personal is also political' and have therefore emphasized the necessity for changing consciousness within the private world of the family, as well as outside it. They have argued the importance of creating conditions for *constructive* change whereby the kind of social relationships (presently contained within the family) would become more successfully supportive and nurturant (Wilson 1977: 187). An important contribution of the women's movement to the discussion and construction of marital problems concerns marital violence, and especially male violence towards women. Refuges for the women who are victims of violence have been set up with the intention that they should be run and controlled by the women themselves. The contribution of the women's movement in this area has been succinctly summarized by Pahl:

'In the broadest sense this means that changing ideas about the

relative positions of men and women in society have led to changes
in what is seen as appropriate behaviour between the sexes in marriage . . . in a narrower sense many individuals who would describe
themselves as members of the women's movement have also been
active in setting up refuges and in campaigning for a greater public
understanding of the problems of battered women.'

(Pahl 1980: 27)

It is important to note that the women's refuges were not intended as
palliatives by those who were instrumental in setting them up.
Instead, the establishment of refuges constitutes part of a broad
strategy aimed at changing the consciousness and position of women
in general. The women's movement has also made a radical critique
over broader issues of sexuality, both inside and outside marriage. As
Wilson notes:

'The women's movement has concentrated on a rejection of the
"sexual objectification" of women while affirming women's rights
to sexual enjoyment. Feminists speak to women of the moral issues
of jealousy and possessiveness and of the economic functions of
marriage. They speak of sexuality within marriage as a system of
enslavement justifying violence and rape . . . To say that the
personal is political was to say that sexual relations were the site of
coercion and power relations.'

(Wilson 1980: 111)

The third site where a discussion concerning marital problems is
taking place is among groups of professionals and practitioners in the
'human service' industries (Stevenson 1976), a considerable number
of whom appear increasingly to see marital problems as part of their
constituency of practice. A few years ago a working party was set up to
investigate the provision of help for marital problems, constituting a
clear sign of greater interest and involvement in marital work on the
part of agencies in general. The report notes that historically the
agencies reflected the concern of dominant social groups and that
their concern has been 'with the provision of services designed in the
first place to keep marriages together and later to help couples to
resolve their problems' (WPMG 1979: 3). The working party, consisting of the heads and senior officers of a variety of agencies, published its report in 1979 (WPMG 1979) and a response to its
recommendations from the government of the day is still awaited.

There is a general trend among the professionals and practitioners (counsellors, therapists, social workers, clinical psychologists, and psychiatrists) to 'treat' their clients' marriages and families, rather than focusing exclusively on presenting or presented individuals. This kind of treatment, exemplified by family therapy, is seen by its practitioners as quicker and more effective than therapy for individuals. Yet in spite of the focus adopted by family therapists on groups rather than on individuals, marital problems are not seen by them in structural terms. Family therapy does not provide for a critique of power relationships: individuals' relationships are simply analysed as functional or dysfunctional for families in terms of patterns of verbal and non-verbal communication (Poster 1978). Nonetheless, family therapy and like approaches represent some movement away from medical models, largely dispensing with the necessity for the diagnosis of symptoms and the application of medical labels, and being more concerned with social interaction which is seen as generating the symptoms and problems of individuals in the first place.

Medicine has shown some interest in marital problems, the origin of which lies in its mandate to manage and treat individual sexuality and sexual practices. Medical practitioners and those in allied professions appear to make no clear-cut distinctions between marital and sexual problems. This situation originated in the legal prescriptions which have traditionally surrounded marriage and sexuality, for only within marriage have sexual acts historically been regarded in our society as positively legitimate. As Foucault (1981) has argued, in so far as sexuality came to be regarded as an area of public discourse so it also became designated as an area of individual pathology. Furthermore, the consequent solutions to pathology, in terms of treatment, were prescribed by experts as lying *within* marriage.

Foucault (1981) has analysed how madness and sexuality became the province of medicine; madness was transformed into a disease in the nineteenth century, with its origins being said by medical practitioners to lie in sexual excesses and perversions. According to Foucault: 'This was in fact a science made made up of evasions since, given its inability and refusal to speak of sex itself, it concerned itself primarily with aberrations, perversions, exceptional oddities, pathological abatements, morbid aggravations' (Foucault 1981: 53). Sexuality, like other areas of human experience, became subject to the discourse of science and to the management of doctors. By implication, *normal* sexuality also came to be defined by medicine: that is, the absence of sexual pathology.

The important theoretical contribution made by Foucault to our understanding of sexuality (and of other phenomena as well) is in terms of his analysis of sexuality as *knowledge*, which he argues is in itself a source of power and control. In Foucault's terms, power is not simply seen as prohibition and constraint; power penetrates through discourse 'right down to [individuals'] most private pleasure, using the negative methods of refusal and prohibition, but also, in a positive way, excitation and intensification' (Sheridan 1980: 170). According to Foucault, medicine eventually took over the management of sex, but first of all it had to overcome a fundamental theoretical problem whereby 'the science of the subject' could be constructed (Sheridan 1980: 178): that is, a science based on subjects' own introspections. Foucault perceived the traditional confessional mechanism as indispensable for this process:

> 'Yet the working of sex remained largely hidden, not only from the scientist or doctor, but also from the subject or patient himself. Its truth could only emerge, therefore, in two stages: first, in the form, blind in itself, in which the patient offered it and secondly, in the form of interpretation, given back to the patient by the specialist. The work of producing the truth could only take place within the dual relationship; only in this way would it be scientifically validated. Furthermore, this confession/interpretation had a therapeutic effect; spoken in time, to a qualified interpreter, or "analyst", the truth could heal.'

> (Sheridan 1980: 178)

Thus Foucault describes the process by which sexuality as a topic of discourse was constructed within medicine and thereby reveals how individuals' sexual problems came to be recognized and treated by experts. Moreover, an important link between the treatment of sexuality and marriage at the time was that whether sexual problems occurred inside or outside marriage, marriage was declared a solution to them.

In outlining some of what appear to be the current discussions concerning marital problems we have noted a number of different groups which hold very different views and stances concerning marriage and its problems. We have identified three main sites where these discussions are located: influential sections of the law, church, and state; the women's movement; and the human service industries. We are suggesting that such groups contribute to the construction of marital problems as knowledge and thus facilitate their status as a social problem. For, according to Blumer, social problems are the outcome of the pronouncement of social problem movements. 'Social problems are fundamentally products of a process of collective definitions instead of existing independently as a set of social arrangements with an intrinsic make-up' (Blumer 1971: 29).

Haines (1979) has suggested that definitions of reality concerning the nature of the social problem can be ranged along a continuum, at one end of which the social problem is 'open' and is designated an overt political issue. At the other end, the social problem becomes 'closed'; its overt political character is largely suppressed and replaced by a 'cognitive' perspective.

At the open end of the continuum a debate exists about the nature of the problem, which is conducted between competing groups with different normative and value positions. At the other end of the continuum, political 'closure' takes place around the problem, a process which, according to Haines (1979), involves 'depoliticization'. Here the search for social causation and the impetus for creating or resisting change become obsolescent activity since the phenomenon is removed from the public realm of ethical discussion to the province of experts concerned with the definition of 'cognitive problems' and appropriate modes of intervention and treatment. The phenomenon or problem becomes transposed to the category of the problems of individuals, which are viewed as objectively *pathological* behaviour and, in the process, the phenomenon becomes alienated from its original meaning and context. At the same time it tends to be subjected to the discourse of scientific and technical knowledge, and to the management of paid professionals and other experts.

It seems to us that, at the present time, marital problems occupy positions at *both* ends of this continuum. As we have indicated, there is political pressure of various kinds to keep alive issues surrounding marriage and its troubles. It is notable how, for example, the women's movement has endeavoured, with some success, to avoid focusing on the problems solely of 'battered wives', thus diminishing the risk of reducing battered wives to yet another social problem group to whom 'help' is delivered by outside experts and paid professionals. The approach of the women's movement differs radically from the individualistic explanations of much of the research on the subject in which marital violence is viewed primarily as a consequence of individual pathology or pathological patterns of interaction. Similarly, the women's movement has departed from traditional therapeutic models used by agencies since it places emphasis on women helping themselves both individually and collectively. As Pahl (1980) has argued, the women's movement has not only endeavoured to make marriage and violence political issues but it has also sought to redefine the problem in radical terms. According to Pahl (1980) this has occurred largely because of the deliberate strategy of involving helpers and helped alike in a movement, the aims of which are to draw attention to and to change the lot of women in general. Pahl identifies specific mechanisms adopted to achieve this goal, such as self-help, mutual support, and power-sharing in the women's refuges. Currently there are signs of pressure emanating from various sources to continue to keep marital problems in the public political arena. It is also evident as well that the human service industries are increasingly designating marriage as an appropriate area of intervention, though at present in fairly *ad hoc* ways. The growing interest in this area, which reflects a general trend towards greater intervention in people's lives, is likely to be hampered however by the current considerable economic constraints.

The principal *means* by which these debates and discussions have become part of public discourse are the various organs of the mass media which consistently treat marriage and divorce as topical issues. The marriages and divorces of the rich and famous are continually reconstituted in popular ideology through representation in the media. The media serve as a means by which the views and concerns of influential groups in society are disseminated but they are also a site in which the reproduction of ideologies takes place, especially in their way of 'classifying out the world within the discourse of the dominant ideologies' (Hall 1977: 346).

In addition to playing on people's curiosity about others' marriages, the media have provided some degree of opportunity for the participation of their audiences in projecting images of marriage and family life; two examples of this are the growth of the agony column industry and radio phone-in programmes (especially in the London area). The popularization of the 'talking therapies' has largely been a media achievement and the personal and interpersonal problems of 'ordinary' individuals have, to some extent, acquired a public voice. However, the emphasis in the media's treatment of people's personal lives has undoubtedly been concerned with the *specificity* of their problems rather than with their structural implications. Nonetheless, given the invisibility of marriage and people's dependence upon those images of marriage projected by the mass media, such coverage is likely to heighten public awareness of the typical and widespread nature of marital and personal problems in our society and may bring about some change in attitudes to disclosure. (The extent to which this media phenomenon can be seen as an extension of self-help, which is a movement away from conventional therapeutic help provided by professionals and practitioners, is presently unclear.)

In considering marital problems as a social construction, we have proposed that they are a product of an ideological debate to which a number of groups and movements have contributed and much of which has been conducted through the media. We went on to suggest that the ideological aspect of marital problems tends to be suppressed once they are transformed into the problems of individuals, which then become subject to treatment from formal agencies providing technical expertise.

Moreover, the ways in which the extent and nature of marital discord in our society is defined, and the ways in which it is articulated by various interest groups and becomes part of general public discourse, provided the macro-context in which we undertook this research project. Our research attempted to avoid the value perspectives and models used by these various interest groups by focusing specifically on the ways in which *clients* and their spouses understood their own situations. Nonetheless, we would also wish to argue that the ways in which marital problems have become public issues are likely to have influenced our respondents' definitions of their private troubles. Certainly our respondents thought that marital agencies were in the business of repairing marriages and this seemed to concur with their own wishes. However, they were not necessarily opposed to divorce in itself unless young children were involved.

Becoming a client: an interpretative approach

We took as our starting point the perspectives and situations of clients and their spouses who sought or came to be offered formal help with marital problems. We adopted an interpretative approach; help-seeking behaviour was seen as grounded in action, meaning, and intention. In seeking to understand and explain what had led up to a person becoming a client in this study we had to work backwards, and we envisaged the help-seeking process *retrospectively* as a series of stages forming a career, conceptualized primarily as a sequence of meanings and actions. There was therefore no single pathway to help but rather a variety of trajectories which branched out in different directions at each stage in the help-seeking career.

Some of the characteristic stages which emerged in our data were: the perception of something being wrong; the interpreting and labelling of a problem as of a particular kind; disclosing or turning to a significant other over that problem; the decision to seek help from a particular agency; and finally the approach to the agency itself. At any stage in the process an individual could change his or her view of the situation and short-circuit the process. At the first stage it was characteristically wives who first appear to have felt that there was something wrong in their marriages, and characteristically husbands who denied or chose to ignore their wives' complaints, sometimes by diverting attention on to individual health problems which were located in their wives. Thus the help-seeking careers of husbands and wives appear from their very beginnings to have diverged.

Movement on to the next stages in the career involved interpreting the problem. This sometimes occurred as a consequence of the advent of a critical event, where, for example, one partner said he or she was about to leave the marriage or consult a solicitor about divorce. Such an event would remove any previous ambiguity that might have existed over the way in which each partner had viewed the marital relationship. Instances of this constituted the most clear-cut cases where problems were defined as marital. However, as we have shown, not all critical events invoked reinterpretations of marriage. The death of a parent, a fairly common event amongst our study group, did not directly provoke the definition of a marital problem, although such events may well have added considerably to the stress that respondents were already under.

According to the *kind* of problem that was defined, the person selected a particular agency which he or she thought most appropriate to consult. However, as we discovered, it was women and not men who were more likely to consult agencies, no matter what type of problem was defined. Where men did approach agencies on their own, it appeared that frequently they had been prevailed upon by their wives to do so. Moreover, even though all the marriages in our study had come to the attention of one kind of agency or another, there was no necessary association between marital discord or dissatisfaction and help-seeking for marital problems. One group of clients in the study would not have received help for marital problems at all had it not been for the redefinition of the problem by an agency. Such marriages came to the notice of agencies through the action of one partner, usually the wife, who sought help for an individual health problem.

We have analysed help-seeking behaviour in terms of the meanings

actors placed upon it and the beliefs they brought to bear in particular situations and contexts, and, most importantly, in their interaction with significant others — spouses, family, relatives, friends —
whoever constituted their social networks. Although we have sought
to understand the movement of individuals through their help-
seeking careers in terms of their definitions and actions, we have
provided explanations which were rarely at the forefront of actors'
own accounts.[3] Respondents only occasionally gave accounts of themselves and their situations which directly corresponded with those
structural explanations which we, as sociologists, applied. Actors'
accounts are necessarily fragmentary; memories of events are partial
and actors can only have access to a limited number of accounts at any
particular moment in time. We, as sociologists, endeavoured to elicit
and provide the concepts and structural explanations. Sociologists
can never attain complete expositions from their subjects but they can
counterbalance this disadvantage by having more cases than
individual actors and by systematic strategies of 'sampling' them. By
means of theoretical concepts and methodology it is possible to construct typical explanations in relation to particular categories of
experience. The kinds of explanations and constructs we drew upon
to explain our respondents' help-seeking behaviour included a range
of factors — gender, social networks, critical life events, and the
impact of agencies — and we have sought to apply these as part of an
overall interpretative approach.

Social network is perhaps a good example of a construct which
bridges a gap between actors' subjective accounts and structural
concepts of sociological analysis. As Morgan has suggested: 'Work in
these directions would fruitfully involve a two-way process between
concepts analysts use to construct reality and the concepts actually
used by actors in their daily business of living in families' (Morgan
1975: 210). It was therefore pertinent to examine the kinds of social
relationships and social structures in which marriage troubles arose,
in order to explore questions as to why in some marriages conflict
came to a head whilst in others it did not. Such questions are at the
heart of understanding why some people seek help for their marital
difficulties and others do not. (These issues were explored in Chapters
4 and 6.)

We also applied the concept of social network to the examination of
another issue, namely the significance of seeking help from agencies,
looked at in the context of traditional sources of help — family,
relatives, and friends. According to previous research in this field,

the availability of traditional sources of social and emotional support is highly related to whether or not people seek help from agencies. In this project, however, we did not pose our hypotheses in such narrow terms, since we sought to explore how much importance respondents placed upon disclosing to others very personal information concerning themselves and their marriages, as well as how far in practice they turned to them. This stance was reinforced by our recognition that marriage and its problems was a highly charged topic and an extremely privatized area.

When we considered respondents' attitudes to disclosure, they emerged as displaying a remarkable stability and as having considerable salience for respondents' core identities. Women respondents were more disposed towards disclosure than men although they stressed the risks and consequent need for safeguards. Respondents' accounts suggested that their attitudes were shaped by sanctions which appeared to match or 'fit' with gender-defined positions and experience. Men seemed to fear losing their self-esteem most of all whilst women were more afraid that their disclosures might adversely affect others and their relationships with them; characteristically, wives more than husbands were concerned about being disloyal to their spouses if they disclosed what they regarded as discrediting information about their marriages.

In order to examine the extent to which respondents in practice disclosed and turned to significant others in adversity, we systematically explored the range of critical events and problems (and not simply the marital issues) which had occurred in respondents' lives in a defined period. This enabled us to explore respondents' informal help-seeking and disclosure in some depth and to a considerable extent. We found that particular types of social network appeared either to generate or to reinforce particular kinds of support. (These findings have been described in considerable detail in Chapters 7 and 8.)

A second structural concept, namely gender, was elucidative in this study, and emerged as a critical factor in distinguishing between help-seeking careers. Wives rather than husbands were more likely to perceive their marriages as problematic and to take some action about them, even if this meant accepting their husbands' definitions of the situation and seeking help for health problems in the first instance. The fact that wives tended to utilize their social networks as sources of help and support to a greater extent than did husbands, testifies to their need for such support. In other kinds of unequal relationships, the observation can be made that it is almost always subordinates and not superordinates who tend to complain first and most of all. Thus, if it is accepted that men's and women's experiences are distinctively different in our society and that this is underpinned by an unequal distribution of power, both in marriage and in other key areas of human activity, it is not unreasonable to hypothesize that their careers as clients will also be different. In our study gender did indeed emerge as a key factor in the understanding of respondents' action and interaction.

We do not intend to reiterate here all our arguments concerning how each of the factors we have identified has influenced respondents' help-seeking careers. Our main point so far in this section has been to suggest that such sociological explanations as we had recourse to are not only theoretical constructs but are also grounded in respondents' actions and accounts.

We turn now to the final section of this concluding chapter in which we shall discuss some of the implications of particular types of agency and practitioner involvement in marital work.

Some implications of practitioner involvement in the 'treatment' of marital problems

Haines (1979) has argued that the debate about the basic orientations to the solution of social problems tends to become limited to the terms of a dominant paradigm. So far this does not appear to have happened in the case of marital problems, nor have they been appropriated by any one practitioner group. In this study we have been concerned with clients of Marriage Guidance counsellors and also with clients referred within a medical context. There are, however, other groups of practitioners amongst whom it is becoming fashionable to make interventions from marital and family perspectives.

At the present time medicine, particularly psychiatry, is concerned in the treatment of sexual rather than marital problems. It remains to be seen how far, and in what ways, medicine will in the future increase its interest in marriage as a suitable case for treatment. Nonetheless, it can be observed that certain other groups of practitioners, such as clinical psychologists and hospital social workers with an interest and involvement in marital work, are tied into organizational hierarchies where medicine is dominant. Thus, in so far as medicine, especially psychiatry, is making bids to intervene at the levels of marriage and family, it operates from a relatively stronger power base than these other contenders. Moreover, the dominance of 'straight' medicine among practitioners (both medical and non-medical) with an involvement in marital work is likely to make it difficult for them to operate from different perspectives, such as that which would be required by a family therapy approach. This situation is likely to be especially difficult where such approaches are equally accessible to, and involve an equal participation of, practitioners who are not equal in the formal hierarchies of the settings in which they work. For example, hospital social workers and clinical psychologists frequently perform similar work to psychiatrists, especially when acting as family or marital therapists. However, as Goldie (1976) has observed, activities carried out by non-medical personnel in medical settings are in actuality *supplementary* to the treatment given by such medical personnel as psychiatrists, being subordinated to medical judgement and responsibility. Thus Goldie suggests that even though psychiatrists may allow, and even encourage, their patients to be treated by non-medical staff, this is conditional upon the acceptance by these practitioners of 'those tenets of psychiatric practice that make up the medical mandate' (Goldie 1976: 193). Interestingly, *within* the medical profession itself there are hierarchical divisions. In cases where the referral of patients takes place *between* medical practitioners, the status of the family or marital therapist (even though he or she is a qualified doctor) is likely to be low in the medical pecking order and, as we ourselves found in this study, such therapists were frequently used as a final resort — the last port of call in a chain of medical referrals.

Earlier we noted medicine's involvement in the treatment of *sexual* problems. Certainly this is one obvious route by which medicine may increase its involvement in the treatment of marital problems and there is a definite and growing emphasis within sex therapy to treat sexual problems within the context of couple relationships and not deal only with their sexual aspects. In a recent critique of sex therapy Szasz (1981) has examined the ways in which therapists have sought to make their work widely acceptable and hence respectable. Szasz suggests that one of the principal ways they have done this has been by promoting their methods of treatment and intervention as scientific. Citing the work of Masters and Johnson as the apotheosis of sex therapy, Szasz notes their 'obsession' with treating marriages and couples as units and suggests that this is especially questionable where the individuals seeking help do not have any sexual partner. Szasz emphasizes that even in these cases treatment was (at one time at least) always given by surrogates. He suggests that the scientific nature of Masters and Johnson's work was in practice based on specific notions of the norm of adjustment within legal, monogamous, and heterosexual relationships.

A consequence of the practice of treating marriages and couples as units is that it serves to perpetuate the lack of visibility and privatization of marital and couple relationships in our society and thus significantly fails to take note of and to reveal the different gender experiences of those who compose them. Moreover, it is notable that the failure on the part of the majority of practitioner groups explicitly to take account of gender inequality and difference in their therapies has occurred *in spite of* the increased public consciousness of gender issues, a situation which is perhaps indicative of the distinction made earlier between open and closed social problems.

It is significant that questions whether or not agencies should intervene, or intervene more than they do already, are rarely raised in our society, either by the agencies themselves or in wider public debate, nor are discussions about the appropriateness of particular modes of treatment and intervention made easily accessible and intelligible. These questions are contained by and are subject to the exigencies of scientific knowledge and practitioner expertise. In this way clients' definitions of their problems and their views concerning the possible solutions to them tend to be overlooked and ignored.

One consequence of the division which exists between helpers and helped (practitioners and clients) is the fragmentation of people's problems. Problems almost never come singly, and where they have a structural basis they are almost always interlinked with other problems. Even where people bring their problems to the attention of agencies, they have to negotiate separately with each relevant specialist agency. Since each agency operates from a particular base of knowledge and practice, it would not be surprising to find clients caught between different and competing definitions and remedies. Clients are frequently depicted (and criticized) by agencies in terms of contrasting stereotypes, either for being too passive in the receipt of services or for being mischievous manipulators playing one agency off against another (see e.g. Mattinson and Sinclair 1979: 14.) It is our contention that such stereotypes are a reflection of certain types of therapeutic encounter, which vary according to the amount of power vested in the particular type of practitioner.

Stacey (1981) has argued that men tend to predominate in occupations in the human service industries where work is done *to* people, whereas women predominate in services where work is done *for* people. Significantly, the former activity incurs relatively more prestige and correspondingly greater financial rewards than the latter. Thus, in relation to marital problems, where psychiatrists and other medical practitioners (mainly men) become involved, it is significant that they perform work *to* or *on* patients' marriages and relationships, an idea which the medical terminology of 'treatment' itself suggests. On the other hand, Marriage Guidance counsellors more typically perform activities *for* clients (or more probably *with* them) by listening to their troubles and by counselling them. Up to now such workers have been more commonly women. As far as economic rewards and prestige are concerned, it is clear that such activities are not equally prized: in the case of Marriage Guidance counsellors the majority are unpaid voluntary workers, women who freely donate their time and energy. By contrast, marital therapists in medical settings are generally specialists in their particular professional groups who have undergone 'higher' or 'additional' training. Psychiatrists have relatively high status and economic rewards, noticeably more so than non-medical therapists (clinical psychologists and hospital social workers) in medical settings.

Stacey has highlighted the similarity of the kind of work which involves work for or with people (as distinct from work to or on people) to the caring and servicing activity women perform in the domestic arena as housewives, wives and mothers. She argues that a considerable portion of people-work activities were 'formerly dealt with in the domestic arena and have been transferred into the public arena, as the latter has become increasingly evasive and dominant' (Stacey 1981: 186). Stacey is critical of applying to practitioner–client relationships in the human service industries concepts originally developed to analyse relationships between employers and employees in industry. Moreover, she goes on to suggest that in order to appreciate fully the significance of this kind of activity, exemplified here by counselling, it is necessary to take account of the gender order, and in particular the social and economic division of labour within the family. It seems to us that counselling represents the epitome of a kind of activity which is in the process of being transferred from the domestic to the public arena. Moreover, Stacey goes on to argue that this analysis needs a total reconceptualization of what constitutes work in our society.

Our study provided an opportunity to contrast two types of practitioner involvement (practitioners in medical settings and Marriage Guidance counsellors), though only in terms of how this was perceived by the client. In Chapters 9 and 10 we explored the ways in which men and women clients perceived and evaluated their experiences of different agencies, and also what they thought such agencies should be doing. Overall, doctors were seen by clients as offering highly specialist knowledge and competence, which clients perceived as largely unintelligible and inaccessible to themselves and as being generally inappropriate to understanding problems in personal relationships. Nonetheless, respondents as patients appear to have behaved towards their doctors with deference: they seem rarely to have questioned their pronouncements or even to have criticized the absence of information given to them (as when, for example, they were referred elsewhere for their marital problems). Women patients especially seemed to fear a dismissive reaction from doctors (of being thought 'silly').

By contrast, clients of Marriage Guidance, and women clients in particular, were more likely to expect counsellors to perform a generalist role, expectations which we would argue are fostered within their social networks and are reinforced by their experience of counsellors as unpaid female volunteers. Women clients described counsellors as unbiased friends and even as allies and, if the counsellors did not act thus, the desire was expressed that they should do so. There was a tendency amongst men clients to expect and to desire a directive approach from marriage counsellors, an expectation and wish broadly similar to the perception of the doctor who tells his patients 'what's wrong' and 'what you should do'. Allied to this was men's disappointment with, and their denigration of, the Marriage Guidance counsellor—client relationship as another example of 'women talking'. In Chapter 10 we displayed clients' prescriptions for the counselling of marital problems along a continuum: at one end counselling was designated as counsellor-centred, whilst at the other end the emphasis was on the role of the client in the counselling process.It seems therefore probable that clients' perceptions of and prescriptions for client—practitioner relationships are related to models of power which derive from both public and private domains.

We detected some characteristic tendencies by which the different agencies (medical practitioners and Marriage Guidance counsellors) responded to their clients. The 'house style' of the Marriage Guidance Councils places considerable emphasis in counselling on the practice of getting the clients talking; by contrast, medical practitioners are concerned with priorities such as diagnosis and identifying the appropriate method of 'treatment'. These differing types of agency practice have implications for the power of the client in the practitioner–client relationship. In the counsellor–client relationship (exemplified in Marriage Guidance) the client is likely to be a fairly active participant since the emphasis is on working *with* the client, while in the therapist–patient relationship (within a medical setting) the patient is likely to be somewhat passive since he or she becomes the *object* of the practitioner's work.

We suggested earlier that non-medical therapists in medical settings are in practice likely to be subordinated to medical dominance although it is important to notice that they do not necessarily view their situations thus (Goldie 1976). Like medical practitioners, clinical psychologists and hospital social workers tend in general to subscribe to models of professional expertise and to curative models of care (work *on* people). Moreover, unlike in medicine as a whole, a fairly high proportion of such non-medical practitioners are women. However, as Gamarnikow (1978) and Evers (1981) have argued in relation to nursing, the low status currently accorded to *care* work (work with or for people) and the correspondingly high status of *curative* work (on or to people) arises not only from domination by professional élite groups, such as medicine, but also from a *sexual* division of labour 'in which male-dominated, technological interventionist, curative work takes precedence over female-dominated care work' (Evers 1981: 112). Thus, it seems likely that, if Marriage Guidance counselling becomes paid and professionalized, counsellors may espouse the curative model in the same way that non-medical therapists have already done.

It is significant also that counselling and therapeutic services operating in medical settings rarely provide for clients to make their approaches to them directly. Entry to such services is through discretionary referral by other professional agencies (usually medical) and clients' approaches are thereby managed for them. In contrast Marriage Guidance, together with self-help groups such as women's refuges, are directly accessible to people who can approach them on their own initiative. As we have shown, entrée to treatment is more highly controlled by those operating within a curative model compared with those working within a care model.

The division between the Marriage Guidance counselling model (work *with* clients) and the professional therapeutic model (work *on* clients) is at present maintained by the separateness and voluntary nature of Marriage Guidance Councils, which are dependent for recruitment on a pool of predominantly middle-class women who can afford to work without pay and who are prepared to do so. However, as such women begin to demand access to equal economic rewards with men and increasingly find it economically necessary to engage in paid employment, they are likely to seek and press for professionalization and payment. Indeed, such pressure is already considerable within the organizations and schemes for paying counsellors are in existence within some Councils.[4] If and when such changes take place within Marriage Guidance, it will undoubtedly lead to a reduction in their separateness and to greater contact with and influence from professional practitioner groups involved in marital work. Although there are advantages to be gained by counsellors from such changes, the costs are likely to involve a greater mystification of counselling. Such changes may also lead to an 'objectification' of clients and to a corresponding reduction in clients' access to and power in counsellor–client relationships.

In future research in this field it may be fruitful to pursue an investigation of counsellor–client relationships along the lines proposed by Stacey (1981). Such research would involve asking the following kinds of questions: How far do particular kinds of practitioners make their knowledge accessible to lay persons and clients? To what extent is the model of help which is offered congruent with a traditional model of help in the domestic arena? How far is the work of practitioners concerned with work on or with clients? In what ways are the goals of practice defined and by whom? A theoretical approach which would take account of the ways in which the gender order and the domestic and public arenas structure and permeate different areas of human service practice might prove fruitful in extending our theoretical understanding in this area.

The notion of the impersonal agency providing resources and 'help' is peculiar to advanced industrial society and might be contrasted with more traditional sources of help and help-seeking. Whether a 'Brave New World' situation, with impersonal agencies being the major provider of such help, will arise in the future cannot be predicted. However, in the current 'transition' period, both formal and informal sources of help persist and coexist and it seems likely that people will continue to seek help in both these spheres. Moreover, it also appears to be the case that divisions of power and status within the human service industries and amongst their clients are underpinned by gender inequality which derives from the domestic sphere. Given such tendencies, it is our contention that patterns of practitioner–client relationships are likely to reflect this state of affairs.

Marital troubles and sexuality are now widely established topics in public discourse. Dominant groups in our society have tended to declare marital problems pathological, out of a concern either for the well-being of society or for individuals and their marriages. Concomitant with the entry of marital problems into public discourse, there has been a growth in the body of experts and agencies concerned with marital work; moreover, the historical development of some of these (in particular, medicine) has tended to reflect the priorities of dominant groups. How far the practice of agencies is likely to continue to be informed in this way by dominant ideological models of individual and societal pathology, will depend upon the relative power and influence of other groups in society to cast the debate differently. Furthermore, the fact that agencies tend to aspire to professional status and to the appropriation and monopolistic possession of bodies of knowledge and expertise (which operate as buffers against intrusion by outsiders) acts as a barrier to opening up the debate on marriage and its troubles. There is a danger that the provision of help for people with marital problems may therefore become encapsulated within the discourses of the scientific and technical, which are largely conducted by professionals. Such a situation would serve to alienate people even further from their marital troubles and from taking charge of their own lives. An understanding of the structural origins of marital difficulties and the constraints operating both upon the agencies and upon their clients is essential if more effective help is to be provided.

Notes

1 The reference to the taxpayer is to the fact that the Home Office gives grant aid to the Marriage Guidance Councils.

2 Patrick Jenkin, at that time the Secretary of State at the Department of Health and Social Security, spoke at a conference on 'Marriage, Divorce and the Family', organized by Dr Jack Dominian and held at the Royal College of Physicians in March 1981. These remarks were made by him in a speech: 'Government Policy towards the Family'.

3 It is recognized that what respondents said in their interviews does not constitute a complete elucidation or account of their situations since interviews are collaborative enterprises in which the interviewer takes a directive role in the information that is elicited.

4 There has been some considerable discussion within the NMGC concerning professionalization and recently NMGC produced a consultative document concerning professionalism and payment for counsellors.

References

Acheson, H. W. K. and Fitten, F. (1979) *Doctor/Patient Relationship: A Study in General Practice.* London: HMSO. (A Department of Health and Social Security Report.)

Arber, S. and Sawyer, L. (1979) *Changes in the Structure of General Practice: The Patients' Viewpoint.* Report submitted to the Department of Health and Social Security by the University of Surrey.

Babchuk, N. and Bates, A. P. (1963) The Primary Relations of Middle-Class Couples: A Study in Male Dominance. *American Sociological Review* 21: 377–84.

Balint, M. (1968) *The Doctor, His Patient and the Illness.* London: Pitman Medical.

Barrett, M. and Roberts, H. (1978) Doctors and Their Patients: The Social Control of Women in General Practice. In C. Smart and B. Smart (eds) *Women, Sexuality and Social Control.* London: Routledge and Kegan Paul.

Bates, A. P. and Babchuk, N. (1961) The Primary Group: A Reappraisal. *Sociological Quarterly* 2: 181–91.

Becker, H. S. (1963) *Outsiders: Studies in the Sociology of Deviance.* New York: Free Press.

Becker, H. S. and Geer, B. (1960) Participant Observation: The Analysis of Qualitative Field Data. In R. N. Adams and J. J. Preiss (eds) *Human Organization Research.* Homewood Illinois: Dorsey Press.

Bell, C. and Newby, H. (1976) Husbands and Wives: The Dynamics of the Deferential Dialectic. In D. Leonard Barker and S. Allen (eds) *Dependence and Exploitation in Work and Marriage.* London: Longman.

Bernard, Jessie (1973) *The Future of Marriage.* London: Souvenir Press.

Bevan, J. M. and Draper, G. J. (1967) *Appointment Systems in General Practice*. London: Oxford University Press for Nuffield Provincial Hospital Trust.

Bloor, M. J. and Horobin, G. W. (1975) Conflict and Conflict Resolution in Doctor/Patient Interactions. In A. Cox and A. Mead (eds) *A Sociology of Medical Practice*. London: Collier Macmillan.

Blumer, H. (1951) Social Movements. In A. M. Lee (ed.) *New Outline of the Principles of Sociology*. New York: Barnes and Noble.

—— (1971) Social Problems as Collective Behaviour. *Social Problems* 18 (3): 298–306.

Bott, E. (1968) *Family and Social Network*. London: Tavistock Publications.

Brannen, J. M. (1980) Seeking Help for Marital Problems: A Conceptual Approach. *British Journal of Social Work* 10: 457–70.

Brayshaw, A. J. (1980) *Public Policy and Family Life*. Discussion Paper No. 3. London: Policy Studies Institute.

British Medical Association (1970) *Report of the Working Party on Primary Medical Care*. Planning Unit Report No. 4. London: British Medical Association.

Brophy, J. and Smart, C. (1981) From Disregard to Disrepute: The Position of Women in Family Law. *Feminist Review* 9: 3–16.

Brown, G. W. and Harris, T. (1978) *Social Origins of Depression*. London: Tavistock Publications.

Burgess, E. W. and Wallin, P. (1953) *Engagement and Marriage*. Chicago: Lippincott.

Burgess, E. W., Locke, H. J., and 'Thomes, M. M. (1963) *The Family*. New York: Van Nostrand Reinhold.

Burgoyne, J. and Clark, D. (1980) Why Get Married Again? *New Society* 52 (913): 12–14.

Byrne, P. S. and Long, B. E. (1976) *Doctors Talking to Patients: A Study of the Verbal Behaviour of General Practitioners Consulting in Their Surgeries*. London: HMSO.

Campbell, B. (1980) Feminist Sexual Politics. *Feminist Review* 5: 1–18.

Caplan, G. (1974) *Support Systems and Community Mental Health*. New York: Behavioural Publications.

Cartwright, A. (1967) *Patients and Their Doctors: A Study of General Practice*. London: Routledge and Kegan Paul.

Cartwright, A. and Anderson, R. (1979) *Patients and Their Doctors 1977*. Occasional Paper No. 8. London: Royal College of General Practitioners.

Cartwright, A. and O'Brien, M. (1976) Social Class Variables in Health Care and in the Nature of General Practitioners' Consultations. In M. Stacey (ed.) *The Sociology of the National Health Service*. Sociological Review Monograph No. 22. University of Keele.

Census of England and Wales (1971). London: HMSO.

Central Policy Review Staff and Central Statistical Office (1980) *People and Their Families*. London: HMSO.

Central Statistical Office (1981) *Social Trends 11*. London: HMSO.

—— (1982) *Social Trends 12*. London: HMSO.

Chester, R. (1971) Health and Marriage Breakdown: Experience of a Sample of Divorced Women. *British Journal of Preventive and Social Medicine* 25: 231–35.

—— (1980) A Survey of Recent U.K. Literature on Marital Problems: A Report for the Home Office Research Unit (typescript version).

Cooper, D. (1972) *The Death of the Family*. Harmondsworth: Penguin Books.

Cozby, P.C. (1973) Self-disclosure: Literature Review. *Psychological Bulletin* 79 (2): 73–91.

Craven, T., Rimmer, L., and Wicks, M. (1982) *Family Policy*. Forthcoming Occasional Paper. London: Study Commission on the Family.

Davis, F. (1963) Passage Through Crisis: *Polio Victims and Their Families*. Indianapolis: Bobbs Merrill.

Delphy, C. (1976) Continuities and Discontinuities in Marriage and Divorce. In D. L. Barker and S. Allen (eds) *Sexual Divisions and Society: Process and Change*. London: Tavistock Publications.

Denning, A. T. (Chairman) (1947) *Committee on Procedure in Matrimonial Cases*. (Final report.) London: HMSO.

Dobash, R. Emerson, and Dobash, R. (1980) *Violence Against Wives*. London: Open Books.

Dominian, J. (1980a) *Marriage in Britain 1945–80*. Occasional Paper No. 1. London: Study Commission on the Family.

—— (1980b) *Marital Pathology*. London: Darton, Longman and Todd and the British Medical Association.

Edgell, S. (1980) *Middle-Class Couples: A Study of Segregation, Domination and Inequality in Marriage*. London: George Allen and Unwin.

Ehrenreich, B. and English, D. (1979) *For Her Own Good: 150 Years of the Experts' Advice to Women*. London: Pluto Press.

Eliot, T. S. (1958) *The Cocktail Party*. London: Faber.

Evers, H. (1981) Care or Custody? The Experiences of Women Patients in Long-Stay Geriatric Wards. In B. Hutter and G. Williams (eds) *Controlling Women: The Normal and the Deviant*. London: Croom Helm in association with the Oxford University Women's Studies Committee.

Finlayson, A. and McEwen, J. (1977) *Coronary Heart Disease and Patterns of Living*. London: Croom Helm; New York: PRODIST.

Foucault, M. (1981) *The History of Sexuality*. vol. 1. *An Introduction*. Harmondsworth: Penguin.

Frankenberg, R. (1957) *Village on the Border: A Social Study of Religion, Politics and Football in a North Wales Community*. London: Cohen and West.

Friedson, E. (1961) *Patients' Views of Medical Practice*. New York: Russell Sage Foundation.

—— (1970) *Professional Dominance: The Social Structure of Medical Care*. New York: Atherton Press.

Fry, J. (ed.) (1979) *Trends in General Practice*. London: Royal College of General Practitioners and the British Medical Association.

Gamarnikow, E. (1978) Sexual Division of Labour: The Case of Nursing. In A. Kuhn and A. Wolpe (eds) *Feminism and Materialism*. London: Routledge and Kegan Paul.

Goffman, E. (1968) *Stigma: Notes on the Management of Spoiled Identity*. Harmondsworth: Penguin Books.

Goldie, N. (1976) Psychiatry and the Medical Mandate. In M. Wadsworth and D. Robinson (eds) *Studies in Everyday Medical Life*. London: Martin Robertson.

Gorer, G. (1970) Report on Sex and Marriage, *The Sunday Times*, 22 March.

Gove, W. R. (1972) The Relationship between Sex Roles, Marital Status and Mental Illness. *Social Forces* 51 (September): 34.

Gove, W. R. and Tudor, J. F. (1973) Adult Sex Roles and Mental Illness. *American Journal of Sociology* 78: 812–35.

Greenley, J. R. and Mechanic, D. (1976) Social Selection in Seeking Help for Psychological Problems. *Journal of Health and Social Behaviour* 17 (September): 249–62.

Griffiths, T. (1976) *The Comedians*. London: Faber and Faber.

Gurin, G., Veroff, J., and Feld, S. (1960) *Americans View Their Mental Health: A Nationwide Survey*. New York: Basic Books.

Haines, H. H. (1979) Cognitive Claims-Making. Enclosure and the

Depoliticization of Social Problems. *The Sociological Quarterly* **20**: 119–30.

Hakim, C. (1979) *Occupational Segregation: A Comparative Study of the Degree and Pattern of the Differentiation between Men and Women's Work in Britain, the United States and Other Countries.* Research Paper No. 9. London: Department of Employment.

Hall, S. (1977) Culture, the Media and the 'Ideological Effect'. In J. Curran, M. Gurevitch, and J. Wollacott (eds) *Mass Communication and Society.* London: Edward Arnold in association with the Open University Press.

Hart, N. (1976) *When Marriage Ends: A Study in Status Passage.* London: Tavistock Publications.

Heisler, J. (1975) *The National Marriage Guidance Client.* Rugby: NMGC.

——(1977) Aspects of the Selection Process. *Marriage Guidance* **17** (6): 414–21.

—— (1980) The Client Writes. *Marriage Guidance* **19** (3): 115–25.

Heisler, J. and Whitehouse, A. (1976) The NMGC Client 1975. *Marriage Guidance* **16** (6): 188–93.

Henderson, S., Byrne, D. G., Duncan-Jones, P., Adcock, S., Scott, R., and Steele, G. P. (1978) Social Bonds in the Epidemiology of Neurosis: A Preliminary Communication. *British Journal of Psychiatry* **132**: 463–66.

Henderson, S., Byrne, D. G., Duncan-Jones, P., Scott, R., Adcock, S. (1980) Social Relationships, Adversity and Neurosis: A Study of Associations in a General Population Sample. *British Journal of Psychiatry* **136**: 574–83.

Horwitz, A. (1977) The Pathways into Psychiatric Treatment: Some Differences between Men and Women. *Journal of Health and Social Behaviour* **18**: 169–78.

—— (1978) Family, Kin and Friend Networks in Psychiatric Help-Seeking. *Social Science and Medicine* **12**: 297–304.

Hutter, B. and Williams, G. (1981) (eds) *Controlling Women: The Normal and the Deviant.* London: Croom Helm in association with the Oxford University Women's Studies Committee.

Illich, I. (1975) *Medical Nemesis: The Expropriation of Health.* London: Calder and Boyars.

Jourard, S. M. and Lasakow, P. (1958) Some Factors in Self-Disclosure. *Journal of Abnormal and Social Psychology* **56**: 91–8.

Kadushin, C. (1958/59) Individual decisions to undertake psychotherapy. *Administrative Science Quarterly* 3 (December): 379–411.

Keithley, J. (1977) Marriage Guidance Research: A Preview. *Marriage Guidance* 17 (5): 368–407.

Komarovsky, M. (1967) *Blue Collar Marriage*. New York: Vintage Books, Random House.

Koos, E. (1954) *The Health of Regionville: What the People Felt and Did about It*. New York: Columbia University Press.

Kuhn, A. and Wolpe, A. (1978) (eds) *Feminism and Materialism*. London: Routledge and Kegan Paul.

Lee, G. (1979) Effects of Social Networks on the Family. In W. R. Burr, R. Hill, F. Ivan Nye, and Ira L. Reiss (eds) *Contemporary Theories About the Family*. vol. 1 *Research-Based Theories*. New York: Free Press.

Lee, N. H. (1969) *The Search for an Abortionist*. Chicago: University of Chicago Press.

Leete, R. (1979) Changing Patterns of Family Formation and Dissolution in England and Wales 1964–76. *Studies on Medical and Population Subjects*, No. 39. London: HMSO.

Leonard, D. (1980) *Sex and Generation: A Study of Courtship and Weddings*. London: Tavistock Publications.

Levinger, G. and Senn, D. J. (1967) Disclosure of Feelings in Marriage. *Merrill Palmer Quarterly* 13: 237–49.

Lieberman, S. and Hyde, K. *Interactions between Predisposition to Marital Conflict, Marital Dissatisfaction and Neurotic Symptoms*: A Survey of 30 Couples Referred for Marital/Family Therapy. Unpublished.

Locker, D. (1981) *Symptoms and Illness: The Cognitive Organization of Disorder*. London: Tavistock Publications.

Mace, D. R. (1948) *Marriage Counselling: The first Full Account of the Remedial Work of the Marriage Guidance Councils*. London: Churchill.

McKinlay, J. B. (1973) Social Networks, Lay Consultations and Help-Seeking Behavior. *Social Forces* 51: 275–91.

Marris, P. (1974) *Loss and Change*. London: Routledge and Kegan Paul.

Marsden, D. (1973) *Mothers Alone* (revised edition). Harmondsworth: Penguin Books.

Marsh, G. and Kaim-Caudle, P. (1976) *Team Care in General Practice*. London: Croom Helm.

Mattinson, J. and Sinclair, I. (1979) *Mate and Stalemate*. Oxford: Basil Blackwell.

Mayer, J. E. (1967) Disclosing Marital Problems. *Social Casework* **48**: 342–51.

Mayer, J. E. and Timms, N. (1970) *The Client Speaks: Working Class Impressions of Casework.* London: Routledge and Kegan Paul.

Mechanic, D. (1975) Practice Orientations among General Practitioners in England and Wales. In C. Cox and A. Mead (eds) *A Sociology of Medical Practice.* London: Collier Macmillan.

—— (1978) Sex, Illness Behaviour and the Use of Health Services. *Social Science and Medicine*, **12B**: 207–14.

Meyerowitz, J. H. and Feldman, H. (1968) Transition to Parenthood. *Psychiatric Research Reports* **20**: 78–94.

Miller, P. McC. and Ingham, J. C. (1976) Friends, Confidants and Symptoms. *Social Psychiatry* **11**: 51–8.

Mitchell, A. K. (1981) *Someone to Turn to: Experiences of Help Before Divorce.* Aberdeen: Aberdeen University Press.

Mitchell, J. C. (ed.) (1969) *Social Networks in Urban Situations.* Manchester University Press for the Institute for African Studies, University of Zambia.

Morell, O. G., Gage, H. G., and Robinson, N. A. (1971) Referrals to Hospital by General Practitioners. *Journal of The Royal College of General Practitioners* **21**: 77–85.

Morgan, D. H. J. (1975) *Social Theory and the Family.* London: Routledge and Kegan Paul.

NMGC (1947–1961, 1969) *Annual Reports.* Rugby: NMGC.

—— (1975) *Notes for Prospective Counsellors.* Rugby: NMGC.

Nathanson, C. A. (1975) Illness and the Feminine Role: A Theoretical Review. *Social Science and Medicine* **9**: 57–62.

Oakley, A. (1974) *The Sociology of Housework.* London: Martin Robertson.

—— (1980) *Women Confined: Towards a Sociology of Childbirth.* London: Martin Robertson.

—— (1981) Interviewing Women: A Contradiction in Terms. In Helen Roberts (ed.) *Doing Feminist Research.* London: Routledge and Kegan Paul.

Office of Health Economics (1974) *The Work of Primary Medical Care.* Studies in Current Health Problems No. 49. London.

—— (1975) *The Health Care Dilemma.* Studies in Current Health Problems No. 53. London.

OPCS (1974) *Morbidity Statistics from the General Practitioner Second National Study (1970–71).* Studies on Medical and Population Subjects No. 26. London: HMSO.

Pahl, J. (1980) Refuges for Battered Women: Social Provision or Social Movement? *Journal of Voluntary Action Research* **8**: 25–35.

Pahl, J. I and Pahl, R. E. (1972) *Managers and Their Wives.* Harmondsworth: Penguin Books.

Parkes, C. M. (1971) Psycho-Social Transitions: A Field for Study. *Social Science and Medicine* **5**: 101–15.

Poster, M. (1978) *Critical Theory of the Family.* London: Pluto Press.

Rainwater, L., Coleman, R. P., and Handel, G. (1959) *Workingman's Wife: Her Personality, World and Life-Style.* New York: Oceana Press.

Rapoport, R. and Rapoport, R. (1976) *Dual Career Families Re-examined*: New Integrations of Work and Family. London: Martin Robertson.

Rex, J. (1974) *Sociology and the Demystification of the Modern World.* London: Routledge and Kegan Paul.

Richardson, S. A., Dohrenwend, B. S., and Klein, D. (1965) *Interviewing: Its Forms and Functions.* New York: Basic Books.

Roberts, H. (1981) (ed.) *Doing Feminist Research.* London: Routledge and Kegan Paul.

Robertson, F. (1975) *Work and the Conjugal Family: A Study of the Inter-relationship between Work and Family in the Life Interests of Hospital Doctors and General Dental Practitioners.* Unpublished PhD thesis, University of Edinburgh.

Rollins, B. C. and Cannon, K. L. (1974) Marital Satisfaction over the Family Life Cycle: A Re-evaluation. *Journal of Marriage and the Family* **36** (2): 271–82.

Rollins, B. C. and Feldman, H. (1970) Marital Satisfaction over the Family Life Cycle. *Journal of Marriage and the Family* **32** (1): 20–8.

Sanctuary, G. (1968) *Marriage under Stress.* George Allen and Unwin.

Sawyer, L. (1979) *The Inarticulate Patient: A Study of Some of the Factors Associated with Patients' 'Muted' Behaviour during Consultation with Their General Practitioners.* Unpublished MSc thesis, University of Surrey.

Shapiro, A. and Swensen, C. (1969) Patterns of Self-Disclosure among Married Couples. *Journal of Counseling Psychology* **16** (2): 179–80.

Shepherd, M., Cooper, B., Brown, A. C., and Kalton, G. (1966) *Psychiatric Illness in General Practice.* Oxford University Press.

Sheridan, A. (1980) *Michel Foucault: The Will to Truth*. London: Tavistock Publications.

Simmel, G. *The Sociology of Georg Simmel*. Translated, edited, and with an introduction by Kurt H. Wolff. New York: Free Press.

Smart, C. and Smart, B. (eds) (1978) *Women, Sexuality and Social Control*. London: Routledge and Kegan Paul.

Society of Conservative Lawyers (1981) *The Future of Marriage. A Report by a Research Sub-Committee of the Society of Conservative Lawyers*. London: Conservative Political Centre.

Stacey, M. (1981) The Division of Labour Revisited or Overcoming the Two Adams, 1981. In P. Abrams, R. Deem, J. Finch, and P. Rock (eds) *Practice and Progress: British Sociology 1950–1980*. London: George Allen and Unwin.

Stacey, M. and Price, M. (1981) *Women, Power, and Politics*. London: Tavistock Publications.

Stark, E. (1981) *Psychiatric Perspectives on the Abuse of Women. A Critical Approach*. In A. Lurie and E. Quitkin (eds) *Spouse Abuse Identification and Treatment*. L.I. Jewish-Hillside Medical Centre.

Stevenson, G. (1976) Social Relations of Production and Consumption in the Human Service Occupations. *Monthly Review* **28** (3): 78–87.

Stimson, G. (1976) General Practitioners, 'Trouble' and Types of Patients. In M. Stacey (ed.) *The Sociology of the N.H.S.* Sociological Review Monograph 22. University of Keele.

Suchman, E. A. (1965) Stages of Illness and Medical Care. *Journal of Health and Human Behaviour* **6** (1): 114–28.

Szasz, T. (1981) *Sex: Facts, Frauds and Follies*. Oxford: Basil Blackwell.

Thornes, B. and Collard, J. (1979) *Who Divorces?* London: Routledge and Kegan Paul.

Timms, N. and Blampied, A. (1980) *Formal Friendship: An Exploratory Study of Marriage Counselling, Clients and Their Counsellors*. Report to the Catholic Marriage Advisory Council. London.

Tyndall, N. (1972) *The Work of Marriage Guidance Councils*. Rugby: NMGC.

Wadsworth, M. and Robinson, D. (eds) (1976) *Studies in Everyday Medical Life*. London: Martin Robertson.

Walker, C. and Chester, R. (1977) Marital Satisfaction amongst British Wives. *Marriage Guidance* **17** (1): 219–27.

Weiss, R. S. (1969) The Fund of Sociability. *Transaction* **6**: 36–43.

Wilson, E. (1977) *Women and the Welfare State*. London: Tavistock Publications.

—— (1980) *Only Halfway to Paradise: Women in Post-War Britain 1945–1968*. London: Tavistock Publications.

Wolff, Kurt H. (1950) *The Sociology of Georg Simmel*. Translated, edited, and with an introduction by Kurt H. Wolff. New York: Free Press.

Working Party on Marriage Guidance (1979) *Marriage Matters* (a consultative document). London: HMSO.

Wright, Mills C. (1959) *The Sociological Imagination*. Oxford: Oxford University Press.

Wynne, C. C., Rickoff, I. M., Day, J., and Hirsch, S. I. (1967) Pseudo-Mutuality in the Family Relations of Schizophrenics. In G. Handel (ed.) *The Psychosocial Interior of the Family*. London: George Allen and Unwin.

Zelditch Jr, M. (1960) Role Differentiation in the Nuclear Family: A Comparative Study. In N. W. Bell and E. F. Vogel (eds) *A Modern Introduction to the Family*. New York: Free Press.

Zola, I. K. (1973) Pathways to the Doctor: From Person to Patient. *Social Science and Medicine* 7: 677–89.

Index of couples

These names and occupations are fictional. The page numbers concern quotations and references made to respondents in the text. Names of spouses who were not interviewed are in brackets.

Name index

Subject index